P9-APY-899

Interventions

Interventions

ACTIVISTS AND ACADEMICS RESPOND TO VIOLENCE

Edited by
Elizabeth A. Castelli and Janet R. Jakobsen

INTERVENTIONS: ACTIVISTS AND ACADEMICS RESPOND TO VIOLENCE

Copyright © Elizabeth A. Castelli and Janet R. Jakobsen, 2004.
All rights reserved. No part of this book may be used or reproduced in any manner whatsoever without written permission except in the case of brief quotations embodied in critical articles or reviews.

First published 2004 by PALGRAVE MACMILLAN™
175 Fifth Avenue, New York, N.Y. 10010 and
Houndmills, Basingstoke, Hampshire, England RG21 6XS.
Companies and representatives throughout the world.

PALGRAVE MACMILLAN is the global academic imprint of the Palgrave Macmillan division of St. Martin's Press, LLC and of Palgrave Macmillan Ltd. Macmillan® is a registered trademark in the United States, United Kingdom and other countries. Palgrave is a registered trademark in the European Union and other countries.

ISBN 1–4039-6581–1 hardback
ISBN 1–4039-6582-X paperback

Library of Congress Cataloging-in-Publication Data

Interventions : activists and academics respond to violence /
    edited by Elizabeth A. Castelli and Janet R. Jakobsen.
        p. cm.
    Includes bibliographical references and index.
    ISBN 1-4039-6581-1—ISBN 1-4039-6582-X (pbk.)
        1. Violence—Congresses. 2. Violence—Prevention—Congresses. 3. Feminist theory—Congresses. I. Castelli, Elizabeth A. (Elizabeth Anne), 1958-
II. Jakobsen, Janet R., 1960-

HM1116.I67 2004
303.6'082—dc22

                                                                    2004048369

A catalogue record for this book is available from the British Library.

Design by Autobookcomp.

First edition: November 2004
10 9 8 7 6 5 4 3 2 1

Printed in the United States of America.

Contents

Acknowledgments

Interventions is based on a colloquium held in October 2002 at Barnard College. This colloquium could not have taken place without the generous support of the College's Gildersleeve Lecture Series, the Wings of Change Foundation, and the Barnard Center for Research on Women. The center's staff also contributed enormously to the success of the colloquium. Special thanks go to Associate Director David Hopson and Administrative Assistant Hope Dector.

Two essays in this volume have appeared previously in other publications:

"Domestic Terror" by Catherine Lutz and Jon Elliston is reprinted with permission from the October 14, 2002 issue of *The Nation*. For subscription information, call 1–800-333–8536. Portions of each week's *Nation* magazine can be accessed at http://www.thenation.com.

"The Best Defense? The Problem with Bush's 'Preemptive' War Strategy" by Neta C. Crawford is adapted from *Boston Review* 28(1) (February/ March 2003), and included here with permission of the author. *Boston Review* can be accessed at http://www.bostonreview.net.

Elizabeth Castelli did her editorial work on this volume while enjoying the generous intellectual hospitality and material support of the Center for Religion and Media at New York University, where she was Senior Research Scholar during the 2003–2004 academic year. She wishes to thank codirectors Angela Zito and Faye Ginsburg; Associate Director Barbara Abrash; working group leader Meg McLagan; post-doctoral fellows Jeremy Stolow and Mazyar Loftalian; center staff members Kristen Meinzer and Omri Elisha; along with Leshu Torchin, Danielle Filion, and Melissa Cefkin; and the members of the Religion, Human Rights, and Media working group as well as the members of the center's yearlong bridging seminar. The center has been an exceptionally engaging and rigorous place to work and think, and a very hospitable place to complete the editorial work on *Interventions*. Elizabeth is also grateful to Jen Simington of CopyRight for her expert copyediting of the penultimate version of this manuscript. Finally, she owes a debt of thanks to Rosamond C. Rodman, who lent her professionalism, wit, and excellent eye for detail to the final preparation of this book for publication, and to Jill Pasquarella for her attentive proofreading.

Janet Jakobsen wishes first and foremost to thank Elizabeth Castelli, who took over our joint editorial duties for *Interventions* in a moment of crisis. Janet is also deeply grateful to Christina Crosby for the courage and dedication she has shown in the months since her serious bicycling accident. Finally, Janet would like to thank Jody Williams, whose creative responses to violence inspired our project and whose good spirits made it more enjoyable.

Introduction

Feminists Responding to Violence

Theories, Vocabularies, and Strategies

Elizabeth A. Castelli

This Book Is Not about September 11

HV6432. This is the Library of Congress call number assigned to a recently created Subject heading: "September 11 Terrorist Attacks, 2001." By early 2004, over 250 titles appeared under this heading in a brief search of a research university library's database. For me, the creation of such a call number suggests a disturbing or at least ambivalent routinization of knowledge production around violence. I recall thinking, in the days and weeks after September 11, in the midst of all the rescue and recovery efforts and the many vigils and the countless and overwhelming rituals of mourning here in New York City, that within a couple of years (a generous publishing cycle), the shelves of bookstores and libraries would be populated by the books about "the events of September 11." These and so many other attempts to capture the day and its aftermaths would shape the vocabularies, conceptual frameworks, and idioms for describing the world around us. The semiotics and symbolisms of spectacularized violence, the radical and violent disruption of the everyday through terrorist intervention, the rationalizations of violent response and reaction (the bombing of Afghanistan, the detentions of "enemy combatants," the invasion of Iraq, the abrogation of civil rights through legislative mandate) through recourse to theological categories ("evil") and the mobilization of apocalyptic affect—all of these post–September 11 effects magnified the degree to which coercion, constraint, and wounding inexorably shape human life in the current moment.

This book is not about September 11, 2001. Nevertheless, the specter of September 11 extends over many of the essays in this book. This should not be surprising since the contents of this volume comprise the contributions of activists and academics to a conference, "Responding to Violence," held in October 2002 at Barnard College in New York City, cosponsored by the Center for Research on Women and the Department of Religion (see Castelli 2004 and also the colloquium's website at http://www.barnard.edu/bcrw/respondingtoviolence). The participants in the conference responded, in the first instance, to an invitation and set of questions formulated during the previous spring by Janet R. Jakobsen (the center's director) and myself. September 11 was not our focal point, in spite of the fact that this spectacular occasion of violence had obviously transformed both the skyline of New York City and many global political, economic, and military alignments in its wake. Indeed, it was the position of many participants in the conference that September 11 had *not* represented a radical change in the dynamics of the global situation, but rather suggested an intensification of existing tensions and conflicts or a spectacular and flaring symptom inviting a cautious diagnosis of underlying causes and pre-existing conditions. That said, what the assumed singularity of "September 11" has inspired by way of policies and purported self-evidencies served in many respects as a spring-board for many participants' contributions to the conference.

The colloquium grew out of our shared understanding that, irrespective of the debated significance of September 11, violence constitutes one of the most profound threats to human well-being around the world. We invited academic specialists in international relations, literary and cultural studies, anthropology, human rights, religion, and women's studies along with longtime peace activists, cultural workers, lawyers, and development profes-sionals to explore international efforts toward disarmament and peace and to theorize feminist responses to war and other forms of violence. As a broadly construed feminist project, the colloquium's conversations focused on the intersections between the global structures of violence—militarism, most obviously, but also systems of incarceration and punishment—and more localized and intimate forms of violence—police brutality, hate crimes, domestic violence, among others. We sought to keep in view the myriad structures of domination and exchange that sustain frameworks of violence: global and local economic inequalities, patterns of (forced and voluntary) migration, transnational trafficking in small arms, institutional and ideo-logical structures that continuously legitimate violence as the default re-sponse to a situation of conflict or hostility. It was our hope that the colloquium would contribute to the development of new and more compre-hensive vocabularies for analyzing violence and revitalized strategies for antiviolence activism.

Analyzing Violence: Protocols and Problems

The analysis of violence in the abstract can result in a kind of intellectual vertigo, just as the activist impulse to develop antiviolence protocols requires carefully specified objects on which to focus if it is to succeed in creating meaningful change. Moreover, theorizing always takes place in time and space, situated in history and in particular places of enunciation. Hence, the contributions in this volume tend to analyze and theorize from concrete examples—whether specific texts (the National Security Strategy of the United States, for example, or politically engaged theatrical performances at different places around the globe), particular geopolitical locations (Palestine/Israel, East Timor, the Philippines, the U.S./Mexico border, Fort Bragg in North Carolina, the Indian province of Gujarat), or communities of struggle (the Cherokee nation, the Filipino Ecumenical Women's Forum, national and international movements for peace and justice). If the urgency of the present moment drives many of the contributors to this volume, their work is nevertheless nuanced by historical examples, precursors, and traces. Thus, while engaging their particular examples, the writers whose work appears here also interrogate the charged character of many of the signifiers that circulate in the semiotics of violence: home, nation, security, protection, and borders, among others.

Violence is less a thing than a characteristic of relationality, a coercive mode by which one (individual or collective) body acts upon another (individual or collective). Scholars have long debated over the scope and conditions of violence. Charles Tilly, for example, defines violence in a relatively focused fashion, as immediate physical injury. Violence, he writes, "immediately inflicts physical damage on persons and/or objects . . . includ[ing] forcible seizure of persons or objects over restraint and resistance" (Tilly 2003, 3). In this definition, he rejects more capacious portraits of violence that emphasize the corrosive (and sometimes fatal) impacts of social, political, and economic exploitation and oppression (e.g., Weigert 1999; Farmer 2003). Meanwhile, theorists and theologians both have a long history of contestation over the limits of legitimate violence, from notions of "just war" (which have recently enjoyed a renewed interest in the present climate) to countercultural programs of radical nonviolence/pacifism. Moreover, the reach of what purportedly counts as justifiable and legitimate violence broadens perilously and disproportionately into the realms of "justifiable torture," "preemptive war," and the general collapse of judicial restraint of law enforcement and military over-exuberance. The line has so successfully been moved that, even in a recent article that criticizes the Bush administration's duplicity in its representations of the rationale for the war in Iraq, one journalist closes his essay with this extraordinary claim, clothed in a twin-set of self-evident Realpolitik and reasonableness: "Congress and the public will most likely have to grant to this and future administrations vast and unprecedented latitude to take pre-emptive paramilitary and military measures—measures that may even appear to be in violation of international law. The public may well have to accept a large degree of ignorance regarding such actions and the reasons behind them" (Schwarz 2004, 31). The inexorability reflected in the rhetoric of "will most likely have to" and "may well have to" performs its own forms of violence, coercion, and constraint. Meanwhile, the anxiety over violence's legitimacy may be recognized in the special role played by euphemism on the political stage and at the rhetor's podium. "Collateral damage" is perhaps the most cynical of these abstractions, a term standing in, coolly and dispassionately, for so many dead women, men, and children (see Collins and Glover 2002).

The question of violence raises numerous other questions. What arguments, stories (whether narratives or histories), and emotions are mobilized

in situations where coercive force is put in the service of competing ideologies and regimes of truth? How do different acts or programs of violence
map bodies and spaces? What are the technologies of violence? By what
physical, institutional, cognitive, ideological, and affective instruments is
violence staged and enacted? And, since the metaphors that frame this last
question imply both the performative and the specular/spectacular, how is
violence constituted through the practice of looking, through the gaze?
What are, in other words, the optics of violence? How do we account for
violence's visibilities and invisibilities, and how do we answer the ethical
demand that these in/visibilities articulate? (See, for example, Boltanski
1999; Cohen 2001; Feldman 1997, 2002; Wexler 2000.)

How is the story of time told in relation to violence? This last question
concerns the claims people often make about the historical roots and
embeddedness of violence: How often, when discussing a particular scene of
violent conflict, does the conceptualization of "time immemorial" or "from
the beginning of history" become the obstacle standing in the way of
imagining some alternative mode of relationship besides the coercive? In a
related way, how often are the adjectives "medieval" or "tribal" used to
describe acts of violence that take place in a modern frame—thereby
constructing another "time" for violence and an "other" who is nonmodern,
unaffiliated with post-Enlightenment categories of civil society, distanced
from "ourselves"?

Beyond bodies and spaces, narratives and time, the question of violence
also raises the question of alternatives. Liberal political theory has often
enshrined the state as the prime institution charged with the containment of
violence (see Vogler and Markell 2003), and often as the only legitimate
deployer of violence (Warner 2003, 44–45). Yet analyses of the state's
violent excesses—in the policing and militarization of everyday life, most
notably—inspire a salutary wariness of state-sponsored solutions, which are
themselves cloaked in the authorizing garb of force. This recognition causes
us to turn to critiques and responses emerging out of other institutions and
political locations—primarily, feminisms.

Feminisms and Responses to Violence

The colloquium upon which this collection is based grew up around the
premise that feminist analyses could bring distinctive insights to the question
of violence. This is not to say that the colloquium in any way embraced the
view that women are somehow the embodiment of an essentialized femininity (linked, for example, to motherhood), a femininity that is naturally
opposed to violence or war (cf., for example, Ruddick 1989). Nevertheless,
the important history of women's antiviolence organizing grounded in
feminist politics is a history too often neglected or forgotten (Alonso 1993,
1997; Berkman 1990; Early 1997; Evans 1987; Foster 1989; Gioseffi 2003;
Melman 1998; Schott 1997; Swerdlow 1993) even as gender-specific forms

of violence (e.g., rape as a weapon of war [see Allen 1996; Askin 1997; Copelon 2000; Stiglmayer 1994]) display no signs of disappearing from the arsenals of conflict—and even as the protection of women from violence has become a cynically convenient rationale for other acts of violence. Feminist work on militarism and militarization (Cohn 1987; Enloe 1983, 1990, 1993, 2000; Lorentzen and Turpin 1998; Lutz 2001; Waller and Rycenga 2000), feminist analyses of international relations and the politics of global conflict (Brown 1988; Crawford 1991, 2000; Grant and Newland 1991; Hoffman 2001; Peterson 1992; Steans 1992; Sylvester 1994, 2000; *SAIS Review* 2000; Tickner 1992; Zalewski and Parpart 1998), and feminist ethical interventions that draw our attention to the specificities of gendered experiences of violence (Matthews 2003; Puechguirbal 2003; Turshen and Twagiramariya 1998) and that disrupt the self-evidency of violence as a default response to conflict—all of this feminist work supplements the narrow set of discourses and practices that have taken center stage in debates over the character, scope, and inevitability of violence in the contemporary world situation. Moreover, transnational feminist alliances that organize against violence offer a unique opportunity for solidarity across myriad differences and occasions for critically engaging the material and ideological conditions and effects of violence on the lives of women around the globe. Such solidarity and engagement serve to challenge the cynical cooptation of women's struggles for liberation and self-determination by militarist agendas, cooptation all too common in post–September 11 U.S. rhetorics (Bacchetta et al. 2001).

Interventions seeks to bring to the table this body of work, generated dialogically and collaboratively, in the hopes of intervening in contemporary discussions, whether discussions aimed primarily at theory-building or those addressing practical activist concerns. No single volume can possibly address every issue circulating around the hydra-headed concept of "violence" or its multiply embodied, experiential articulations. *Interventions* captures a moment of conversation and analysis. It archives portions of a conversation, and we hope it also inaugurates further discussion.

The book is divided into four parts. Part One brings together seven essays that explore in different ways some of the central concepts that animate the conversation preserved in this book as a whole: time and trauma, injury and the gaze, home and protection, the secular and the religious. Part Two acknowledges the influential role of U.S. state-sponsored violence at the current political moment, analyzing its theological and ideological underpinnings, its morally questionable presuppositions, and its deleterious effects on democracy itself. Part Three focuses on specific sites of violence, conflict, and resistance to violence—geopolitically, ideologically, and practically. Part Four highlights several examples of alternatives and initiatives that seek to disrupt the culture of violence—through strategic transnational religious and feminist alliances, through the affecting interventions of theatrical arts, through ethical reimagining and pragmatic reordering of the structures of blame.

Interventions represents but one set of exchanges in many different, ongoing conversations. The work begun at the "Responding to Violence" colloquium at Barnard in October 2002 continued at a second colloquium, "Feminist Responses/Alternatives to Violence in a Transnational Context," held in November 2003 at San Francisco State University and organized by Minoo Moallem of the Women Studies Department of SFSU and Janet R. Jakobsen of the Center for Research on Women at Barnard. The collaborations that these ongoing conversations represent constitute important intellectual, institutional, and political alliances across disciplines and fields of activism. By preserving a partial archive of the "Responding to Violence" colloquium, we hope to contribute to the development and elaboration of critically engaged responses and alternatives to the violence that overshadows the lives of so many around the world today.

On a practical level, we are pleased to have assigned the royalties from *Interventions* to Madre, an international women's human rights organization based in New York City. Madre was founded in 1983 and is a "women-led, women-run organization, dedicated to informing people in the U.S. about the effects of U.S. policies on communities around the world." As an international organization devoted to solidarity, Madre is committed to building "real alternatives to war and violence by supporting the priorities of [its] sister organizations and linking them to the needs of women and families in the U.S. through a people-to-people exchange of direct relief and understanding" (http://www.madre.org/mission.html). In assigning the (albeit modest) royalties of this book to Madre, we seek to connect our intellectual work and activist writing to the everyday struggles to which the women of Madre devote themselves and to support their work in a practical and concrete fashion.

Works Cited

Allen, Beverly. 1996. *Rape Warfare: The Hidden Genocide in Bosnia-Herzegovina and Croatia.* Minneapolis: University of Minnesota Press.

Alonso, Harriet Hyman. 1993. *Peace as a Women's Issue: A History of the U.S. Movement for World Peace and Women's Rights.* Syracuse: Syracuse University Press.

Alonso, Harriet Hyman. 1997. *The Women's Peace Union and the Outlawry of War, 1921–1942.* Syracuse: Syracuse University Press.

Askin, Kelly. 1997. *War Crimes against Women: Prosecution in International War Crimes Tribunals.* The Hague: Martinus Nijhoff.

Bacchetta, Paola, Tina Campt, Inderpal Grewal, Caren Kaplan, Minoo Moallem, and Jennifer Terry. 2001. "Transnational Feminist Practices against War." Available at: http://www.geocities.com/carenkaplan03/transnationalstatement. html. Reprinted in 2002: *Meridians: Feminism, Race, Transnationalism* 2(2): 302–8.

Berkman, Joyce. 1990. "Feminism, War, and Peace Politics: The Case of World War I." In *Women, Militarism, and War: Essays in History, Politics, and Social Theory*, ed. Jean Bethke Elshtain and Sheila Tobias, 141–60. Savage, MD: Rowman and Littlefield.

Boltanski, Luc. 1999. *Distant Suffering: Morality, Media and Politics*. Trans. Graham Burchell. New York: Cambridge University Press.

Brown, Sarah. 1988. "Feminism, International Theory, and International Relations of Gender Inequality." *Millennium: Journal of International Relations* 17: 461–75.

Castelli, Elizabeth A., ed. 2004. *Reverberations: On Violence*. Special issue of *Scholar and Feminist Online* at www.barnard.edu/sfonline/reverb/.

Cohen, Stanley. 2001. *States of Denial: Knowing about Atrocities and Suffering*. London: Polity Press.

Cohn, Carol. 1987. "Sex and Death in the Rational World of Defense Intellectuals." *Signs: Journal of Women in Culture and Society* 12: 687–718.

Collins, John, and Ross Glover, eds. 2002. *Collateral Language: A User's Guide to America's New War*. New York: New York University Press.

Copelon, Rhonda. 2000. "Gender Crimes as War Crimes: Integrating Crimes against Women in to International Criminal Law." *McGill Law Journal* 46: 217–40.

Crawford, Neta C. 1991. "Once and Future Security Studies." *Security Studies* 1: 283–316.

Crawford, Neta C. 2000. "The Passion of World Politics: Propositions on Emotion and Emotional Relationships." *International Security* 24(4) (spring): 116–56.

Early, Frances H. 1997. *World Without War: How U.S. Feminists and Pacificists Resisted World War I*. Syracuse: Syracuse University Press.

Elshtain, Jean Bethke, and Sheila Tobias, eds. 1990. *Women, Militarism, and War: Essays in History, Politics, and Social Theory*. Savage, MD: Rowman and Littlefield.

Enloe, Cynthia. 1983. *Does Khaki Become You? The Militarization of Women's Lives*. London: Pandora.

Enloe, Cynthia. 1990. *Bananas, Beaches, and Bases: Making Feminist Sense of International Politics*. Berkeley: University of California Press.

Enloe, Cynthia. 1993. *The Morning After: Sexual Politics at the End of the Cold War*. Berkeley: University of California Press.

Enloe, Cynthia. 2000. *Maneuvers: The International Politics of Militarizing Women's Lives*. Berkeley: University of California Press.

Evans, Richard J. 1987. *Comrades and Sisters: Feminism, Socialism, and Pacifism in Europe, 1870–1945*. New York: St. Martin's Press.

Farmer, Paul. 2003. *Pathologies of Power: Health, Human Rights, and the New War on the Poor*. Berkeley and Los Angeles: University of California Press.

Feldman, Allen. 1997. "Violence and Vision: The Prosthetics and Aesthetics of Terror." *Public Culture* 10(1): 24–60.

Feldman, Allen. 2002. "Ground Zero Point One: On the Cinematics of History." *Social Analysis* 46(1): 110–17.

Foster, Catherine. 1989. *Women for All Seasons: The Story of the Women's International League for Peace and Freedom*. Athens: University of Georgia Press.

Gioseffi, Daniela, ed. 2003. *Women on War: An International Anthology of Women's Writings from Antiquity to the Present*. 2nd. ed. New York: Feminist Press.

Grant, Rebecca, and Kathleen Newland, eds. 1991. *Gender and International Relations*. Bloomington: Indiana University Press.

Hoffman, John. 2001. *Gender and Sovereignty: Feminism, the State, and International Relations*. London: Palgrave.

Lorentzen, Lois Ann, and Jennifer Turpin, eds. 1998. *The Women and War Reader*. New York: New York University Press.

Lutz, Catherine. 2001. *Homefront: A Military City and the American Twentieth Century*. Boston: Beacon Press.

Matthews, Jenny. 2003. *Women and War*. Ann Arbor: University of Michigan Press.

Melman, Billie, ed. 1998. *Borderlines: Genders and Identities in War and Peace, 1870–1930*. New York: Routledge.

Peterson, V. Spike, ed. 1992. *Gendered States: Feminist (Re)Visions of International Relations Theory*. Boulder: Lynne Rienner.

Puechguirbal, Nadine. 2003. "Women and War in the Democratic Republic of the Congo." *Signs: Journal of Women in Culture and Society* 28: 1271–81.

Ruddick, Sara. 1989. *Maternal Thinking: Towards a Politics of Peace*. Boston: Beacon Press.

SAIS Review. 2000. 20(2): Special Sections on "Gender in Gender in International Relations" and "From Theory to Practice: Women Policy Makers."

Schott, Linda K. 1997. *Reconstructing Women's Thoughts: The Women's International League for Peace and Freedom before World War II*. Stanford: Stanford University Press.

Schwarz, Benjamin. 2004. "Clearer than the Truth: Duplicity in foreign affairs has sometimes served the national interest. But the case of Iraq is different." *Atlantic Monthly* 293(3) (April): 27–31.

Steans, Jill. 1998. *Gender and International Relations*. New Brunswick: Rutgers University Press.

Stiglmayer, Alexandra, ed. 1994. *Mass Rape: The War against Women in Bosnia-Herzegovina*. Lincoln: University of Nebraska Press.

Swerdlow, Amy. 1993. *Women Strike for Peace: Traditional Motherhood and Radical Politics in the 1960s*. Chicago: University of Chicago Press.

Sylvester, Christine. 1994. *Feminist Theory and International Relations in a Postmodern Era*. Cambridge: Cambridge University Press.

Sylvester, Christine. 2002. *Feminist International Relations: An Unfinished Journey*. Cambridge: Cambridge University Press.

Tickner, J. Ann. 1992. *Gender in International Relations: Feminist Perspectives on Achieving International Security*. New York: Columbia University Press.

Tilly, Charles. 2003. *The Politics of Collective Violence*. New York: Cambridge University Press.

Turshen, Meredeth, and Clotilde Twagiramariya, eds. 1998. *What Women Do in Wartime: Gender and Conflict in Africa*. London: Zed Books.

Vogler, Candace, and Patchen Markell. 2003. "Introduction: Violence, Redemption, and the Liberal Imagination." *Public Culture* 15(1): 1–10.

Waller, Marguerite R., and Jennifer Rycenga, eds. 2000. *Frontline Feminisms: Women, War, and Resistance*. New York: Garland.

Warner, Michael. 2003. "What Like a Bullet Can Undeceive?" *Public Culture* 15(1): 41–54.

Weigert, Kathleen Maas. 1999. "Structural Violence." In *Encyclopedia of Violence, Peace, and Conflict*, ed. Lester Kurtz, 3: 431–46. San Diego: Academic Press.

Wexler, Laura. 2000. *Tender Violence: Domestic Visions in an Age of U.S. Imperialism*. Chapel Hill: University of North Carolina Press.

Zalewski, Marysia, and Jane Parpart, eds. 1998. *The "Man" Question in International Relations.* Boulder: Westview Press.

Part I

Terms of Engagement

Chapter 1

Feminism in the Time of Violence

Karen Beckman

How should feminism respond to the violence that has erupted in the wake of September 11? First, it needs to challenge the impulse to treat September 11 as a point of origin for the waves of violence that have followed in its wake. Although the singularization of this date functions as an act of memorialization, its isolation also posits this day as one that is simultaneously without history and the beginning of history. Temporally as well as spatially, the attacks on the Twin Towers are now thought through the concept of zero, and to begin one's story before that date, that is, to think historically, suddenly seems unpatriotic or irreverent to the dead.[1] Consequently, as time begins again, questions surrounding the legitimacy of Bush's election are hushed because they precede "our time," and the dissenting voices trying to speak outside of the new temporality are quickly denounced. Pretending that history did not exist prior to September 11, George W. Bush stated on September 14, 2001, the ironically entitled National Day of Prayer and Remembrance: "Americans do not yet have the distance of history. But our responsibility to history is already clear: to answer these attacks and rid the world of evil" (G. Bush 2001, 6). By setting the clock back to zero, we allow history to be something that is always to come, the future story of American "answers" to acts of violence that can only ever be understood outside of time, which means that they can never be understood at all. A few days later, in his "Address to a Joint Session of Congress and the American People" (September 20), Bush once again betrayed his anxiety about time as he urged the nation to take control of it: "This country will define our times, not be defined by them. . . . We have found our mission and our moment" (G. Bush 2001, 16).

If the terrorist attacks served to clarify the "mission" and the "moment" of the Right in the United States, did they do the same for feminists? Does this date mark a new era of clarity for all political groups, including feminism, creating a renewed sense of solidarity in the wake of our longstanding internal doubts and divisions? Well, yes and no. One could argue that feminism, or at least the language of women's liberation, attracted more public attention, even support, than it had for some time as a result of Laura Bush's address to the nation about the plight of Afghan women. A couple of my self-proclaimed feminist colleagues felt proud to see feminists putting aside partisan politics in order finally to *do* something concrete for real women (this was especially true of the person who helped draft Laura Bush's speech). Yet I, like many others, was, and still am, angered by both the speech and its impact. I am angry that feminist discourse was appropriated by the Bush administration to justify its militarism, its Christian, right-wing social agenda, and its dismantling of hard-won civil liberties. I am angry that the endlessly repeated film footage depicting violence against Afghan women contained no historical information that would have enabled audiences to understand the role the U.S. played in allowing the political situation in Afghanistan to reach such disastrous levels in the first place. The Bush administration used Laura Bush's "speaking for" Afghan women to create the impression that Afghan women had no voices of their own. This allowed the United States systematically to disregard the appeals of the Revolutionary Association of the Women of Afghanistan (RAWA) to desist from military invasion of Afghanistan and later of Iraq. This administration has since shown remarkable indifference to the U.S.-backed warlords' treatment of the very women whose dignity it promised to restore, confirming that abating Afghan women's suffering was never seriously on the agenda. Reporting on life in post-Taliban Afghanistan, freelance reporter Shauna Curphey writes: "Even more disheartening is the situation of women in Afghan's warlord-ruled provinces. According to a U.N. report on women . . . there have also been arson attacks on girls' schools in several provinces. The report also indicates that forced marriages, domestic violence, kidnapping of young girls, harassment and intimidation of women continue unabated" (Curphey 2003).

As public support for Laura Bush's white, middle-class, militaristic women's movement grew, feminist peace activists and academic or "elite" feminists began to be repeatedly ridiculed and misrepresented for their resistance to Bush's domestic and global violence. Most commonly, these attacks, written almost exclusively by female journalists, accuse antiwar feminists of indifference to the real plight of women under threat. Self-described individualist feminist Wendy McElroy, for example, recently published an article/fantasy for Fox News entitled, "Iraq War May Kill Feminism as We Know It," in which she appropriates the voices and subject positions of Islamic feminists in order to advance a right-wing, Christian, antifeminist political agenda.[2] The argument begins by claiming that, "Western feminists . . . are hostile to religion, and especially to Christianity," a sentiment that McElroy suggests "places Western feminism on a collision course with its Muslim counterpart. . . . Islamic feminism tends to be pro-family and not inherently anti-male." She goes on to draw a correlation between American feminism's purported indifference to Islamic feminists and its long-standing disrespect of "women who are stay-at-home moms, pro-life, home-schoolers, or who disagree with them on virtually anything." "It has discounted the majority of American women," she declares. "Why would it treat foreigners with more respect?" (McElroy 2003).

Similarly, columnist Cathy Young, in a *Boston Globe* article entitled "Feminism and Iraq" (March 24, 2003), accuses feminists and antiwar protesters of tending to "lapse into moral equivalency" and quotes Tammy Bruce, former head of the Los Angeles chapter of NOW, as stating that NOW put "political concerns . . . over the good of women." Young continues, "Bruce believes that the American feminist elite is doing it again in its opposition to the war in Iraq." Perhaps most disturbingly, Young quotes Bruce's message to NOW president Kim Gandy, Alice Walker, and other feminist war protesters: "There are thousands of dead Iraqi women who know how you betray them, in the name of politics, in the name of hating George W. Bush, in the name of your own cynical political hypocrisy." Like Laura Bush, who told the nation what "Afghan women know" in her radio address of November 17, 2001, Bruce shamelessly transforms dead Iraqi women into ventriloquist puppets who know only what she knows, and who are too dead to protest.[3]

These attacks on feminism can be simply annoying, but they can also confuse us at what is, by any standards, a particularly difficult time for feminism, potentially leaving us as silent subjects. Theorist Judith Butler has recently described this as "a sad time for feminism, even a defeated time," and suggests that feminist theory may "have no other work than in responding to the places where feminism is under challenge" (Butler 2001, 418). But when faced with the urgent need for effective political resistance to Bush's acts of death and destruction, the time we spend on these discussions can come to seem indulgent. Feminist literary scholar Ranjana Khanna comments that, while conflict within feminism has become "part of the agenda to be addressed," it can also result in "paralysis, or a rather self-satisfied navel gazing on the part of some who agonize about how to be ethical when it comes to dealing with gender politics outside of one's own context" (Khanna 2001, 101). Political paralysis is something we surely cannot afford at the moment, but patient, deliberate, and historical thinking, I would argue, is not the same as paralysis. It may well be that academic feminism, like poetry, "makes nothing happen," but we should remember that poetry for W. H. Auden still "survived" as "A way of happening, a mouth" (Auden 1977, 242). In these times when the need to "make things happen" becomes a reason to give up on thought, diplomacy, human rights, international law, and the U.N., feminism's insistence on retaining internal complexity and difference in the face of violent events may constitute its most valuable contribution, allowing it to emerge as an indispensable "mouth," one that has as much to say to the newly-invigorated Left-in-formation as it does to Bush.

What We Do Now

As we face the challenge of removing Bush from office, the rhetoric of the Left is necessarily, though sometimes problematically, action oriented. Peace Studies scholar David Cortright, for example, ends his recent *Nation* article, "What We Do Now," with the rallying cry, "We have no time to mourn. A lifetime of organizing and education lies ahead" (Cortright 2003). This call to dismiss mourning assumes that mourning and activism are in fact separable, but it also inadvertently mirrors Bush's suppression of history, whether private or public, through the rhetoric of the urgent moment. The language of political action tells us that we have no time for times past. Does this mean that there is also no time to consider the potentially devastating political consequences of this clean-slate mentality?

Writing about the place of mourning in AIDS activism in 1989, Douglas Crimp questions the utility of slogans like "Don't mourn, organize!" or "Turn your grief to anger" precisely because they rely on the same underlying assumption that mourning can simply be converted into something more useful. To pay attention to mourning, however, is not to focus exclusively on the emotional lives of individuals at the expense of activist goals; rather, it is, according to Crimp, to recognize that the unconscious plays significant roles in political movements, and that understanding these roles can lead to more effective organization: "It is because our impatience with mourning is burdensome for the movement that I am seeking to understand it. I have no interest in proposing a 'psychogenesis' of AIDS activism. The social and political barbarism we daily encounter requires no explanation whatsoever for our militancy. . . . On the contrary, what may require explanation . . . is the quietism" (Crimp 2002b, 139). More recently, political theorist Wendy Brown has made a similar point in relation to "Left Melancholia": "My emphasis on the melancholic logic of certain contemporary Left tendencies is not meant to recommend therapy as the route to answering these questions. It does, however, suggest that the feelings and sentiments—including those of sorrow, rage, and anxiety about broken promises and lost compasses— that sustain our attachments to Left analyses and Left projects ought to be examined for what they create in the way of potentially conservative and even self-destructive undersides of putatively progressive political aims" (Brown 2003, 464).

While mourning can occur in response to the death of a friend or loved one, as the AIDS activist community, which has sustained such devastating losses, well knows, it can also be triggered, according to Freud, by the loss of an ideal, such as the fatherland, or liberty (Freud 1963, 164). If we accept this formulation, then feminism, currently burdened by an overwhelming sense of lost ideals, has to consider how it will mourn, rather than cut, its losses so that it can avoid falling into a melancholia that will prevent it from developing much-needed radical political visions for the future.

What We Have Lost

Laura Bush's speeches made clear that we have, at the very least, lost control of the slogans and catch phrases that have come to be associated with women's liberation and radical feminist politics. When we hear of the right of women to "laugh out loud" or of the freedom to fly kites, we may like to think of Hélène Cixous's Medusa (Cixous 1976) or Monique Wittig's singing, kite-flying *guérillères* (Wittig 1985, 84); but now, sadly, we must also think of Laura Bush, who has absorbed these metaphors into speeches that define the nation as an "us" made up solely of Americans who will "hold our families even closer . . . and who will be thankful for all the blessings of American life." She even goes so far as to invite all Americans "to join our [the Bush] family in working to insure that dignity will be secured for all the women and children of Afghanistan."[4] This appropriation misuses the suffering of Afghan women, but it also actively works to reduce feminism, now stripped of its radical sexual and anticapitalist agendas, of its struggle to imagine kinship relations differently, to the philanthropic gestures of the Bush family.

One interesting, if uncomfortable, question in all of this is how feminist language could so easily be appropriated in this way. A few days before I began to write this essay, I attended the National Women's Studies Association conference, where many women complained that "our" metaphors and slogans had been robbed. We have been robbed, but do we necessarily want our slogans back? While the radical spirit of the sixties and seventies still produces nostalgia for a time when feminism seemed less tame, less institutionally acceptable, do we not also feel a twinge of shame when we recognize how close some of the language of second-wave feminism can seem to the "us and them" context in which it now appears? But what shall we do with our shame, and how can we prevent it from turning into a form of melancholia that will render us politically ineffective?[5]

We have lost more than our slogans. Like the Left, we have lost the belief that adherence to "the cause" will provide us with what Brown has called "a clear and certain path toward the good, the right and the true" (Brown 2003, 460). In the wake of what feels like the failure of revolutionary politics, many of us also feel that we have lost our communities, but it may be that community happens precisely in the space of what is lost. Philosopher Jean-Luc Nancy reminds us, "At bottom, it is impossible for us to lose community. . . . Community is given to us—or we are given and abandoned to the community: a gift to be renewed and communicated, it is not a work to be done or produced" (Nancy 1991, 35).[6] "Community," according to Nancy, is "far from being what society has crushed or lost"; rather, it is "*what happens to us*—question, waiting, event, imperative—*in the wake of society*" (Nancy 1991, 11). As we feel and mourn our losses, as we lack clear or collectively agreed-upon paths or responses, uncertainty becomes our new foundation and is perhaps the precondition for us to be able to do what Nancy calls the task of "thinking community, that is, of thinking its insistent and possibly still *unheard* demand, beyond communitarian models or remodelings" (Nancy 1991, 22).

Freedom Dreams

If the future of feminism is intimately bound up with our ability to mourn our losses, we may have to look backward in order to move forward, and

Robin D. G. Kelley's *Freedom Dreams: The Black Radical Imagination* offers an inspiring model of how this can be done. Kelley recognizes the "awful things" that have been done in the name of black liberation without falling into the trap of "merely chronicl[ing] the crimes of radical movements," which "doesn't seem very useful" (Kelley 2002, xi). This decision to de-emphasize black activists' violence seems right here, especially given the fact that, on the rare occasions when the mass media does represent black social movements, it tends to select images of armed resistance, vastly overemphasizing this strategy at the expense of other less sensational, highly successful, and nonviolent forms of protest. But I can't help thinking that a comparable feminist project would need to treat the question of violence differently. Looking back at the feminist peace movement, I am struck less by the need to downplay the "awful things" done in its name than to challenge the movement's tendency to equate violence with men and peace with women (and with mothers in particular), a tendency that continues to haunt the language of some feminist peace activists today. In the current climate of moral binarism, where political rhetoric is dominated by phrases like "the axis of evil" and "us and them," feminism must continue to challenge its reliance on intransigent gender binaries so that it can model the persistence of complex thinking in the midst of political crisis. Indeed, I would suggest that the feminist nonviolence movement's reliance on fixed gender categories, as well as its subordination of questions of radical sexual freedom, class, race, and religion to a more abstract idea of peace, have contributed to a heteronormative idealization of white, middle-class, and often maternal femininity within feminist movement and have inadvertently made our language particularly vulnerable to appropriation by the Right. As human rights activist Mallika Dutt argues,

> For women of color/immigrant women/Third World women, the issue of culture is further complicated in the context of women's organizing. The tendency of many white women who are part of the dominant culture and/or religion not to recognize the patterns of oppression fostered within their own culture makes it difficult for women of color/immigrant women/Third World women to work in solidarity with them. This difficulty is exacerbated when white women perceive the oppression of women in minority communities as an inevitable aspect of those minority cultures or religions, which are then labeled as inferior to their own Western/Christian context (Dutt 1998, 232–3).

But how can feminists work toward peace without adopting this model of white, Western/Christian supremacy? If the best thing feminists have to offer in response to violence is our fundamental commitment to complexity, as I think is the case, then we might begin to resist the current climate of moral simplicity by acknowledging, rather than repressing, our own ambiguous and complicit relationship with violence.[7] This work of ambiguity is by no means new to feminism, and we might usefully glance backward into our own history as we try to envision a better future.

"They say, let those who call for a new language first learn violence" (Wittig 1985, 85)

If feminist nonviolence movements have sometimes confused the violence of patriarchy with the violence of men, these movements have also often challenged the rigid gendering of violence through their own reliance on violent metaphors and fantasies. At a San Francisco antinuclear rally in March 1982, for example, Alice Walker began her speech by quoting a curse-prayer that Zora Neale Hurston collected in the 1920s. Her comments on this curse are worth quoting at length:

> I have often marveled at it. At the precision of its anger, the absoluteness of its bitterness. Its utter hatred of the enemies it condemns. It is a curse-prayer by a person who would readily, almost happily, commit suicide, if it meant her enemies would die. Horribly.
>
> I am sure it was a woman who first prayed this curse. . . . And I think, with astonishment, that the curse-prayer of this colored woman—starved, enslaved, humiliated and carelessly trampled to death—over centuries, is coming to pass. . . . And it is this hope for revenge, finally, I think, that is at the heart of People of Color's resistance to any anti-nuclear movement.
>
> In any case, this has been my own problem.
>
> When I consider the enormity of the white man's crimes against humanity. Against women. Against every living person of color. Against the poor. Against my mother and my father. Against me. . . . When I consider that he is, they are, a real and present threat to my life and the life of my daughter, my people, I think—in perfect harmony with my sister of long ago: *Let the earth marinate in poisons. Let the bombs cover the ground like rain. For nothing short of total destruction will ever teach them anything* (Walker 1982, 264).

After September 11, Jean Baudrillard described the "new terrorists" as people who turn "the violence mobilized by the system" against it, and who "do not play fair, since they put their own deaths into play" (Baudrillard 2002, 18–19). Walker here seems to share these traits, the traits of a terrorist imagination. As she repeats the curse of the woman who "would readily . . . commit suicide, if it meant her enemies would die," what distinguishes her from Baudrillard's new terrorists? On one level, it seems important to say something like, "Not much," to acknowledge that feminist activists have repeatedly spoken threats of violent destruction and have occasionally acted upon them.[8] From this, we can learn that, for feminism, social justice begins with the acceptance of, and commitment to wrestle with, the extremes of violence that exist within ourselves. Refusing to inhabit a position of uncontaminated purity, Walker places herself inside a long history of feminist-terrorist imaginings and, as a result, she cannot be assimilated to the "us" of "us and them." Yet nor is she simply one of "them," for Walker's feminist-terrorist thinking is marked by her unwillingness to idealize the banality of death: "Life is better than death," she asserts, "if only because it is less boring, and because it has fresh peaches in it" (Walker 1982, 265). This statement does not cancel out Walker's recognition of the appeal, even the pleasure, of violent language and action; it simply shows her stepping back from enacting Hurston's curse, at least for now, because the world still has "fresh peaches" in it. These peaches come in varied forms, they are often hard to find, and they grow in strange places—sometimes even in our classrooms. As feminists, we must cultivate their growth wherever we happen to be and fiercely protect and expand the spaces where they thrive. Then, as our peaches ripen, we must dare to eat and share them, for their sweetness holds both our melancholia and our violence at bay.

Notes

1. Shortly after the attacks, Judith Butler commented on this temporal prohibition: "It is that date . . . that propels the narrative. If someone tries to start the story earlier, there are only a few narrative options" (Butler 2002, 58).
2. McElroy is the editor of ifeminists.com.
3. Caryl Rivers (2003) has recently noted, "As the war dominates the headlines, journalists, scholars and others interested in public policy have noticed a growing silence: the absence of women's voices in the nation's elite media. . . . The situation is dire for women scholars and journalists who wish to influence the public agenda of the nation," she complains. "I haven't seen it so bad since the pre-women's movement days when women were completely invisible in the media."
4. I am, of course, referring to Hélène Cixous's 1976 essay, "The Laugh of the Medusa." Early in her November 17, 2001 radio address to the nation, Laura Bush states: "Children aren't allowed to fly kites; their mothers face beatings for laughing out loud."
5. The political utility of the affect of shame has been central to recent discussions in queer theory, and feminism might usefully benefit from this work as it continues to address the problem of internal oppression. For further reading on shame, see Crimp 2002a, Sedgwick 1993, and Warner 1999.
6. Nancy distinguishes community from a "communion that fuses the *egos* into an *Ego* or a higher *We*" (Nancy 1991, 15), a communion that effectively describes the oppressive and potentially fascistic consequences of the Bush administration's mobilization of the language of "us" and "them." For a helpful discussion of this language, see Michael 2003.
7. On feminist coalition politics and complexity, see Jakobsen 1998.
8. Radical feminist manifestos often actively embrace this terrorist mindset. See Crow 2000 and Stansill and Mairowitz 1999 for a sample of these, including the SCUM (Society for Cutting Up Men) Manifesto, the Redstockings Manifesto, the Bitch Manifesto, and the WITCH (Women's International Terrorist Conspiracy from Hell) Manifesto. It is also important to note that there have also been feminist terrorist organizations that have acted on these fantasies of violent destruction, such as the Wimmin's Fire Brigade and the still-active German feminist group, Rota Zora, which first appeared in 1973. See Dark Star 2002.

Works Cited

Auden, W. H. 1977. "In Memory of W. B.Yeats" (1939). In *The English Auden: Poems, Essays and Dramatic Writings 1927–1939,* ed. Edward Mendelson, 241–243. London: Faber and Faber.

Baudrillard, Jean. 2002. *The Spirit of Terrorism.* London: Verso.

Brown, Wendy. 2003. "Resisting Left Melancholia." In *Loss,* ed. David L. Eng and David Kazanjian, 458–65. Berkeley and Los Angeles: University of California Press.

Bush, George W. 2001. *United We Stand: A Message for All Americans.* Ann Arbor, MI: Mundus.

Bush, Laura. 2001. "Radio Address by Laura Bush to the Nation." November 17. http://www.whitehouse.gov/news/releases/2001/11/20011117.html.

Butler, Judith. 2002. "Explanation and Exoneration, or What We Can Hear." *Grey Room* 7 (spring): 57–67.

Butler, Judith. 2001. "The End of Sexual Difference?" In *Feminist Consequences: Theory for the New Century,* ed. Elisabeth Bronfen and Misha Kavka, 414–34. New York: Columbia University Press.

Cixous, Hélène. 1976. "The Laugh of the Medusa." *Signs* 1 (summer): 875–99.

Cortright, David. 2003. "What We Do Now." *The Nation.* April 21. http://www.thenation.com/docprint.mhtml?i=20030421&s+cortright.

Crimp, Douglas. 2002a. "Mario Montez, For Shame." In *Regarding Sedgwick: Essays on Queer Culture and Critical Theory,* ed. Stephen M. Barber and David L. Clark, 57–70. New York: Routledge.

Crimp, Douglas. 2002b. "Mourning and Militancy." In *Melancholia and Moralism: Essays on AIDS and Queer Politics,* 129–50. Cambridge, Mass.: MIT Press.

Crow, Barbara A. 2000. *Radical Feminism. A Documentary Reader.* New York: New York University Press.

Curphey, Shauna. 2003. "Women in Afghanistan Fear New Taliban-Like Rule." May 15. http://rawa.fancymarketing.net/womensenews.htm.

Dark Star. 2002. *Quiet Rumours: An Anarcha-Feminist Reader.* San Francisco: AK Press USA.

Dutt, Mallika. 1998. "Reclaiming a Human Rights Culture: Feminism of Difference and Alliance." In *Talking Visions: Multicultural Feminism in a Transnational Age,* ed. Ella Shohat, 225–46. Cambridge: MIT Press.

Freud, Sigmund. 1963. "Mourning and Melancholia." *General Psychological Theory: Papers on Metapsychology,* ed. Philip Rieff, 164–79. New York: MacMillan.

Jakobsen, Janet R. 1998. *Working Alliances and the Politics of Difference: Diversity and Feminist Ethics.* Bloomington: Indiana University Press.

Kelley, Robin D.G. 2002. *Freedom Dreams: The Black Radical Imagination.* Boston: Beacon Press.

Khanna, Ranjana. 2001. "Ethical Ambiguities and Specters of Colonialism: Futures of Transnational Feminism." In *Feminist Consequences: Theory for the New Century,* ed. Elisabeth Bronfen and Misha Kavka, 101–25. New York: Columbia University Press.

McElroy, Wendy. 2003. "Iraq War May Kill Feminism as We Know It." March 18. http://www.foxnews.com.

Michael, John. 2003. "Beyond Us and Them: Identity and Terror from an Arab-American's Perspective." *South Atlantic Quarterly* 102: 701–28.

Nancy, Jean-Luc. 1991. *The Inoperative Community,* ed. Peter Connor. Minneapolis: University of Minnesota Press.

Rivers, Caryl. 2003. "Where Have All the Women Gone?" April 17. http://www.alternet.org/story.html?StoryID=15677.

Sedgwick, Eve Kosofsky. 1993. "Queer Performativity: Henry James's *The Art of the Novel." GLQ* 1(1): 1–16.

Stansill, Peter, and David Zane Mairowitz, eds. 1999. *BAMN (By Any Means Necessary): Outlaw Manifestos and Ephemera, 1965–70.* Brooklyn: Autonomedia.

Walker, Alice. 1982. "Only Justice Can Stop a Curse." In *Reweaving the Web of Life: Feminism and Nonviolence,* ed. Pam McAllister, 262–65. Philadelphia: New Society.

Warner, Michael. 1999. *The Trouble with Normal: Sex, Politics, and the Ethics of Queer Life.* New York: Free Press.

Wittig, Monique. 1985. *Les Guérillères.* Boston: Beacon Press.

Chapter 2

The Wrong Victims

Terrorism, Trauma, and Symbolic Violence

Sally Bachner

In mainstream journalism, public discourse, and some of the most impassioned interdisciplinary discussions about violence in the humanities, there is a constant and insidious misidentification of the primary victims of violence. This misidentification operates under the aegis of two disparate but surprisingly symbiotic terms: trauma and terrorism. These terms provide emotionally compelling but politically distressing justifications for preferring the victims of symbolic violence to those who suffer from direct physical harm and routine privation. While we should resist what historian Peter Novick has called the "sordid game" of trying to claim superior victimization for one group or another on the basis of specific historical horrors, we should—indeed we must—make a distinction between symbolic violence and physical violence, particularly when these differences are indices of the very structures of inequity that violence maintains (Novick 1999, 9–10). As Edward Said suggests at the close of his classic essay, "The Essential Terrorist," which applies to our investment in trauma as well, our preoccupation with terrorism "is dangerous because it consolidates the immense, unrestrained, pseudopatriotic narcissism we are nourishing" (Said 1988, 158). Our involvement in the drama of our terror and trauma, so often established through forms of proxy and identification, blinds us to violence suffered across the globe.

Terrorism

I should say at the outset that I use the term "terrorism" out of necessity, not because I am convinced of its conceptual coherence. I should also say that by speaking of terrorism's symbolic victims I am *not* referring to those who have lost their lives, or of their immediate families. Indeed, I would like to suggest that those who lost their lives were not victims of terrorism but of violence. This may seem a mere semantic game, but the discourse of terrorism increasingly names for us not a set of political practices, such as the targeting of civilians through violence, but the production in civilians of a sense of vulnerability.[1] For, although policy makers and terrorism "experts" have found it difficult to establish a coherent definition of terrorism, it is generally said to be something more than violence perpetrated against civilians. The majority of the latter, after all, is committed by governments. Even if we narrow the definition to acts of political violence carried out against civilians by nongovernmental organizations, we are still left with a quandary: How did the affective question of terror come to name only one form of violence against civilians, when all forms are presumably frightening to potential victims? None of the answers to this question, on the rare occasion that they are proffered, are particularly convincing, but the question does help reveal why it might be useful to speak of terrorism apart from the violence that accompanies it. For while terrorism is said to be motivated by the perpetrator's desire to cause fear, this effect can hardly be realized in what we would conventionally think of as its primary victims, that is, those who are killed. It is those who "survive"—a group that encompasses not just those who were materially effected by the act but were not killed, but the larger identifying community—who are deemed terrorism's truest victims.

In this sense, "terrorism" as a term works to evacuate the violence from the events it describes, shifting our attention and our sympathy instead to the fear that violence is assumed to provoke. Terrorism discourse does not suggest that fear is the worst thing a person can suffer, but it does install that fear as the primary sign of fully realized personhood. The terrified victim of violence stands in stark contrast not only to the cruel terrorist, but to those who are victims of sanctioned governmental aggression and whose suffering is part of the undifferentiated landscape of the international section of American newspapers. Terrorism thus enables a further victimization of those for who live under the threat of routine violence, for while routine violence may very well induce fear, it may also be transmuted through repetition into despair or anger. Yet most importantly, routine violence wreaks material devastation that must be coped with above and beyond the emotions it provokes.

The process by which we become "terrorized" is not innocent of economics or politics, that is, it is not a matter of mere cognitive mechanics in the face of a horrific spectacle. It is a commonplace that terrorism seeks to achieve political effects by generating fear, but this truism fails to provide an adequate analysis of whose fear counts or to identify the mechanisms that are required to authenticate and reproduce that fear. Terrorism discourse is sustained by the identifications and affiliation we make with other victims of violence, whose lives and whose fears must be recognized as somehow like our own. These habits of recognition, identification, and dis-identification sustain the focus of many Americans on the Israeli who cannot go to a nightclub or a café because there *might* be a suicide bombing rather than on the Palestinian who cannot leave her camp to get medical attention because there *are* men with automatic weapons positioned to stop her. The problem of course goes beyond our habits of empathy, the objects of which need to be authenticated by the media. And here more powerful nations are in a position to reinforce and reproduce their status as primary victims. The mechanics of this were visible during the U.S bombing campaign in Afghanistan that followed the attacks on the World Trade Center. Access to sites of violence against civilians was limited, and as a result, footage of such violence rarely appeared on news outlets. In order for a group to be recognized as the victim of terrorism, its plight must be represented as such in the media through by now conventional visual signals that include the devastated site of otherwise normal civilian congress.

Terrorism discourse invites us to forget the enormous U.S. power across the globe, or rather, it asks us to transvalue that power into vulnerability. As literary scholar Robert Merrill has noted, "the United States is more often imagined as severely disadvantaged by its democratic ideals and the deep benevolence of the American people when confronting towering 'madmen' like Saddam Hussein" (Merrill 1993, 28). In a stunning inversion of the realities of power and suffering, those for whom fear is most deeply aberrant in their lives become the world's most pressing victims. For while many Americans suffer daily abuse as victims of racial and sexual oppression, and many experience the structural violence of poverty, the United States is still a rare target for violence from outside.

Trauma

Trauma Studies—and by this I mean the largely nonclinical body of writing on trauma that has emerged as an interdisciplinary subfield among historians, cultural critics, philosophers, and literary theorists—has provided some of the most influential modes of thinking about violence in the academy.[2] Arguably born in the wake of revelations about Paul de Man's collaborationist wartime writings, Trauma Studies emerged as his former students and followers sought to confront the urgent, but sometimes elusive, historical questions associated with the scandal. While this origin story is too serpentine to outline here, it does suggest some of what is at stake in the turn to trauma, a concept with a rich if sometimes discontinuous clinical history.[3] Throughout that history, trauma as a concept has refused to distinguish between the survivors of violence and those who perpetrate it: Both perpetrator and victim suffer from the same psychic ailment. Within this logic, violence itself is the agent, one that victimizes anyone within its proximity. Post-Traumatic Stress Disorder (PTSD), after all, gained entry into the Diagnostic and Statistical Manual of Mental Disorders of 1980 through the efforts of professionals and activists advocating on behalf of Vietnam War veterans (Leys 2000, 5). While this may make for a sound clinical theory and therapeutic practice, the conflation of perpetrators and victims is far more troubling in the domain of cultural analysis.

This systematic extension of the category of victim does not enmesh just perpetrators, but those born after the traumatic events in question. It has been crucial to the establishment of an adequately broad theoretical field for cultural theorists to suggest that trauma reproduces itself well beyond the scene of violence that is its ostensible origin. Most notably, in the work of Shoshana Felman the term *witness* has served to collapse the distinction between survivors of horrific events and those who read their testimonies or view a film. In an influential chapter from her seminal book on the subject, Felman tells the story of the graduate students in her indisciplinary seminar on trauma who, after viewing videotapes from Yale's Video Archive for Holocaust Testimonies, suffer a "crisis" in which a "shattering" "loss of language" akin to that of the Holocaust survivors themselves is said to have taken place (Felman and Laub 1992, 47, 49, 50). And while Felman is perhaps the most unembarrassed in her effort to describe trauma as a generalized cultural experience, her claim has been widely repeated. Thus it has become commonplace for critics to claim, to offer just one example, that the postmodern imagination is a "traumatic imagination," one that has been scarred by the successive "experiences" of the Holocaust, the bombing of Japan, the wars in Korea and Vietnam, the civil rights movement, the women's movement, and Watergate, to name just a few (Elias 2001, 49, 50). Trauma Studies has diffused the concept of the victim to the point that merely living after the Holocaust places one within the purview of the post-traumatic. Not only does such a diffuse conception of trauma—as cultural and collective—appropriate history and convert it into a spurious collective memory, it obfuscates the radical discrepancies between survivors of trauma and consumers of their story.[4]

While some see this as an unfortunate but correctable excess, Trauma Studies' investment in the symbolic victim is not merely mistaken, but internally productive.[5] In its attachment to the Holocaust as the ultimate, unparalleled, event of the modern age—one through which every contemporary claim to traumatic response is traced and authenticated—Trauma Studies establishes a historical frame that discourages the confrontation of new horrors and new violence. The aura of prohibition that surrounds the traumatic memory of this genocide perpetuates a new generation of victims that are necessarily symbolic, while it forbids attention to victims and forms of violence that fail to reify its historical status. For the enshrinement of the Holocaust as *the* central trauma of history (and not just of twentieth-century history, or European history) has occurred in tandem with an insistence that any attempt to heal this trauma—and thus to stop its perpetuation in later generations—would itself be a form of trauma-inducing violence.[6] The special status of the Holocaust within Trauma Studies aids and abets a process through which a largely symbolic sense of vulnerability and injury prohibits acknowledgment of those most in need of allies in their resistance to systemic violence. Yet beyond the fate of this particular historical event in popular memory and myth, it points to a risk that has been realized in the aftermath of the World Trade Center attacks and can be repeated ad infinitum: that we become so engrossed in the drama of our psychic harm that we fail to respond to, or even notice, the violence suffered by those in our midst and far away.

Beyond Victims?

Why must we be so parsimonious with the label of victim? Surely empathy is not a zero-sum game? Or better yet, might we not more profitably turn away from such adjudication among victim-claimants and instead assess the structural inequalities that at once depend upon and perpetuate violence? Yes, and I want to suggest that taking physical violence seriously, above and beyond diffuse forms of psychic distress, is a necessary beginning. The delimitation of violence in ways that renders invisible the systematic violence suffered by people of color, the poor, gays and lesbians, and women, needs to be exposed. But insofar as some of the efforts to combat this delimitation have focused on converting symbolic violence into physical violence—in proposed hate speech legislation, for example—we concede too much, and render the physical violence that is suffered invisible as such. Until we distinguish between those who suffer from largely symbolic wounds and those threatened with routine physical violence and deprivation, the politics of identification and empathy will misdirect our strategies of resistance. The diffuse application of trauma, like the preoccupation with a terrorist threat, occurs at the expense of attention to those at risk of imminent and wholly predictable harm. They allow for a kind of forgetting that, in its effects if not its intentions, is profoundly cruel.

Notes

1. For a stunning analysis of terrorism as a cultural narrative, and for an extended discussion of this issue, see Zulaika and Douglass 1996.
2. I am thinking of works such as Felman and Laub 1992; Caruth 1995; Caruth 1996; Friedlander 1993; LaCapra 2001.
3. My understanding of this clinical history is deeply indebted to Ruth Leys' recent genealogical study (Leys 2000), which is also a trenchant critique that touches on some of what I address here.
4. Walter Benn Michaels offers a particularly incisive analysis of how we have come to think of history as "memory." See his essay on Felman and Toni Morrison's *Beloved* (Michaels 1996).
5. Dominick LaCapra in particular has criticized these excesses while maintaining the usefulness of trauma as a tool of historical reckoning. See LaCapra 2001.
6. This idea circulates throughout the literature on trauma, but an especially vivid example is apparent in Santner 1992.

Works Cited

Caruth, Cathy, ed. 1995. *Trauma: Explorations in Memory*. Baltimore: Johns Hopkins University Press.

Caruth, Cathy. 1996. *Unclaimed Experience: Trauma, Narrative and History.* Baltimore: Johns Hopkins University Press.

Elias, Amy. 2001. *Sublime Desire: History and Post-1960s Fiction.* Baltimore: Johns Hopkins University Press.

Felman, Shoshana and Dori Laub. 1992. *Testimony: Crises of Witnessing in Literature, Psychoanalysis, and History.* New York: Routledge.

Friedlander, Saul. 1993. *Memory, History and the Extermination of the Jews of Europe.* Bloomington: Indiana University Press.

LaCapra, Dominick. 2001. *Writing History, Writing Trauma.* Baltimore: Johns Hopkins University Press.

Leys, Ruth. 2000. *Trauma: A Genealogy.* Chicago: University of Chicago Press.

Merrill, Robert. 1993. "Simulations and Terrors of Our Time." In *Violent Persuasions: The Politics and Imagery of Terrorism,* ed. David. J Brown and Robert Merrill, 27–46. Seattle: Bay Press.

Michaels, Walter Benn. 1996. "'You who never was there': Slavery and the New Historicism, Deconstruction and the Holocaust." *Narrative* 4(1): 1–16.

Novick, Peter. 1999. *The Holocaust in American Life.* New York: Mariner Books.

Said, Edward. 1988. "The Essential Terrorist." In *Blaming the Victims: Spurious Scholarship and the Palestinian Question,* ed. Edward Said and Christopher Hitchens, 149–58. London: Verso.

Santner, Eric. 1992. "Beyond the Pleasure Principle: Some Thoughts on the Representation of Trauma." In *Probing the Limits of Representation: Nazism and the "Final Solution,"* ed. Saul Friedlander, 143–54. Cambridge: Harvard University Press.

Zulaika, Joseba, and William A. Douglass. 1996. *Terror and Taboo: The Follies, Fables, and Faces of Terrorism.* New York: Routledge.

Chapter 3

Definitions and Injuries of Violence

Meredeth Turshen

Definitions of violence and the kinds of injury named as violence are related issues. One general definition of violence is "the intentional use of physical force or power, threatened or actual, against oneself, another person, or against a group or community, that either results in or has a high likelihood of resulting in injury, death, psychological harm, maldevelopment or deprivation" (WHO 2002, 5). This definition divides violence into three forms: self-inflicted, interpersonal, and collective violence. Although they are distinct, clearly all of these forms are found in situations of war and armed conflict. The WHO definition seems to be broad, but I will argue for an extension of the concept of violence in order to portray a more complete picture of how armed conflict disrupts women's lives.

Armed conflict is the focus of this essay, and the aim is to tie kinds of injury named as violence more specifically to types of violence. Although some of the effects of conflict-related violence apply equally to men and women, I am especially interested in the impact on women.

Definitions of Collective Violence

The World Health Organization (WHO) defines collective violence as "the instrumental use of violence by people who identify themselves as members of a group—whether this group is transitory or has a more permanent identity—against another group or set of individuals, in order to achieve political, economic or social objectives" (WHO 2002, 215). The definition is self-referential in that the violence described is "physical force or power," cited in WHO's general definition of violence. WHO subdivides collective violence into social, political, and economic violence, each described in terms of motivation and manifestation: social violence is used to advance a social agenda; political violence means war and conflict; and economic violence is carried out for economic gain, for example "attacks carried out with the purpose of disrupting economic activity, denying access to essential services, or creating economic division and fragmentation" (WHO 2002, 6).

Other than issues of rape, WHO makes no effort to differentiate the effects of collective violence on women from those on men. Because my interest is in developing a broader understanding of outcomes of collective violence and women's experience in the aftermath of war, I explore broader, gendered definitions of the subdivisions of social, political, and economic violence.

Social or interpersonal violence is the most common of the three (and the only category in which WHO differentiates the experiences of women and men). In the context of war and armed conflict, social violence includes torture (which should be expanded to show how torture is gendered and how those forced to witness torture are also abused); sexual mutilation and sexual abuse; food deprivation; sexually transmitted infections; trauma; and rape (both individual rape and militarized rape, which is systematic rape by armed forces as a war strategy, to increase or reduce the "enemy" population, or as payment and reward).

Political violence is less well studied and less well accepted, for example by WHO, which defines political violence as armed conflict. For women the salient political outcomes of armed conflict are slavery, kidnapping, and conscription; forced eviction leading to homelessness, landlessness, statelessness, and loss of citizenship; witch hunts, arbitrary detention, and imprisonment; loss of social standing in family and community as a result of rape (including repudiation, loss of marital status, and ineligibility for marriage after rape); widowhood and childlessness leading to loss of social standing in family and community; denial of a role for women in peace negotiations, conflict resolution sessions, and plans for post-conflict reconstruction; and forced adoption of new identities with material consequences for identity-based entitlements. These outcomes are political, not personal, and should not be considered individual causes or effects of psychological stress, as WHO maintains (2002, 224).

The third category is economic violence, which some women say is the worst of all. I accept WHO's general description of "attacks carried out with the purpose of disrupting economic activity, denying access to essential services, or creating economic division and fragmentation" (WHO 2002, 6). Armed conflict redirects economic production of goods and services for civilians to war production. Inflated military budgets reduce health and education budgets. The cessation of economic activity means collapsed economies and markets. The sowing of land mines hinders cultivation, and military operations displace women and children, forcing them into camps for displaced persons and refugees.

It is also important to document the concrete ways in which this economic violence affects women. In the context of armed conflict in which there is massive transfer of economic assets, economic violence against women includes theft; looting of material possessions and personal property (jewelry, cash, cooking pots, clothes); seizing control of women's productive and reproductive labor resulting in forced labor (cooking, cleaning, washing clothes, sewing, gardening/food production, and porterage) and forced sex work (prostitution and sex trafficking); loss of marital assets (house, land, animals); and loss of children (potential breadwinners, providers of old-age security). As with political violence, expanding the concept of economic violence in this way and working toward acceptance of this broadened definition in domestic and international agencies can help improve post-conflict planning.

Injuries

The kinds of injury named as "violence" are usually the mortality and morbidity associated with war, namely a much higher incidence of injuries from weapons, mutilation, land mines, burns, and poisoning. The life impact of injuries that result in disability is greater on women and girls than boys and men in countries with a low level of technological development (few mechanical aids and environmental adaptations) and a high degree of patriarchal social organization (emphasis on marriage and childbearing and few career opportunities for women). To capture a more complex, gendered picture it is necessary to use a wider lens to reveal physical and psychological injury in the context of specific types of conflict. I review briefly what is known about mortality and morbidity in war-torn African societies to establish the magnitude of the consequences of violent conflict, to describe the visible and invisible injuries of war, and to put terrorism in perspective.

Contemporary African conflicts stretch from Algeria to KwaZulu Natal and from Casamance to Mogadishu, touching nearly half of all African countries. Between 1945 and 1992 an estimated 6.5 million Africans died in wars, 70 percent of them civilians (Holdstock 2002, 189). Some current conflicts are more deadly than past ones: the International Rescue Committee conducted a mortality survey in 2002 in the Democratic Republic of the Congo and found that between August 1998 and August 2002 approximately 3.3 million people died from the ongoing conflict (www.theirc.org, accessed August 10, 2003). Some conflicts have lasted thirty or forty years (Angola, Chad, Sudan); most have displaced millions of people (half the country's population in Liberia, Rwanda, Somalia). Almost all conflicts in Africa today are internal, though they spill over into neighboring states, and some places, like the Congo, receive troops from many nations, sent in aid of one side or the other.

We know that population movements in war-torn societies create complex humanitarian crises of internally displaced persons and refugees, as well as public health problems ranging from environmental hazards to disease epidemics. And we know that women and children account for as much as 80 percent of the refugee populations. Unfortunately, we lack details on many problems apart from the AIDS epidemic, a focus that was only recently widened to include tuberculosis and malaria. In Africa AIDS affects more women than men. We suspect that war-torn societies experience dramatic demographic changes in both the size and structure of populations, especially when deaths exceed births. But there are few assessments of these consequences of war beyond the enumeration of internally displaced persons and refugees. Conflicting estimates of mortality and morbidity are part of the propaganda of warring sides, and health and population data are usually not collected in wartime.

The now-familiar line is that mortality and morbidity shifted from 90 percent of casualties occurring among soldiers at the beginning of the twentieth century to 90 percent occurring among civilians by the century's end. This generalization needs to be deconstructed. In groundbreaking work, Garfield and Drucker (2002) estimated deaths for four types of collective violence: genocide, international wars, internal wars, and terrorism (ranked in descending order of lethality).

Death rates are highest in genocidal wars: in Rwanda, an estimated 800,000 died during the 1994 genocide, an annual death rate of 44 percent; put another way, approximately 11 percent of the population died, raising the crude death rate to 4,266 per 10,000 per year (in 1994) from 172 per 10,000 per year (before 1994). Garfield and Drucker (2002) break down deaths in international wars into two categories: troops (the percent killed has fallen dramatically since World War II) and civilians (the highest recorded figure is 5 percent of Korean civilians in 1951–1953). About three times more soldiers than civilians die in international wars. It is not known whether more civilians die in international wars than in internal wars because it is difficult to distinguish soldier and civilian deaths in internal wars; it appears that civilians' risk of dying in international wars is half again as high as the risk of dying in internal wars. In three internal wars in Africa for which there are data—Burundi (1993–98), Sudan (1982–96), and Sierra Leone (1997–99)—the crude death rate was lower than the baseline rate. Terrorism appears to have a greater psychological than demographic impact. In the decade of Islamist terror in Algeria (1992–99) an estimated 60,000 people were killed, but the crude death rate remained far below the baseline.

Population surveys in Somalia determined that from 4 to 11 percent of deaths in ten months during 1992–1993 were caused by war-related trauma (Toole 2000, 207). As might be expected, war-related mortality is sex- and age-selective/specific, with higher deaths rates in three groups—adult men and young boys who are fighting, the elderly, and children. A 1999 study of the health consequences of the war in Congo-Brazzaville on the displaced population and residents found that 35 percent of the deaths occurred in children younger than 5 years and that the principal cause of death was malnutrition (Salignon et al., 2000). Stewart and Humphreys (1997) estimated the additional infant mortality incurred in conflict countries in 1994. Ethiopia bore the largest costs: 174,000 more infants died than would have had Ethiopian improvement followed the regional average. More than one million estimated total additional deaths cumulated in Ethiopia from 1965 to 1994, or nearly 5 percent of the 1994 Ethiopian and Eritrean population.

One obvious consequence of the higher mortality among adult men is more widows and more female-headed households. The percent of women who are widows is far higher in Africa than in industrial countries even when there is no conflict because of polygamy, age differences between spouses, and shorter life expectancy for men than women. War accelerates this trend. The available data are given below. (The figure of 42 percent for southern African household heads who are women is the highest in the world.)

The very high rates of widowhood and women-headed households raise urgent questions about discriminatory customary law regarding the inheritance of property, which affects women's access to housing and land. For women in Rwanda and Uganda, acute problems of dispossession led women's nongovernmental organizations to demand statutory legal reforms, but women still face patriarchal attitudes in their families and communities as well as the courts (Turshen 2000a).

Agreement is lacking on how to define and assess deaths related indirectly to war. What of the rise in criminality, homicide, and suicide? More adult men than women die in war, but a wider lens observes that women are acutely affected by the lack or inaccessibility of care during pregnancy and childbirth. Pregnancies may be unattended because of dangers in travel to clinics, because health personnel evacuated the area, or because rebel forces deliberately destroyed the clinics and killed or captured the health workers, a characteristic of civil war.

Causes of death are related to wartime interruption of medical services and public health activities: 65 percent of infectious disease epidemics occur in unstable countries (Zwi and Ramos-Jimenez 2002). As a result of war, malaria and tuberculosis epidemics are likely to spread. WHO estimates that up to 30 percent of the 960,000 annual deaths due to malaria in Africa occur in countries affected by complex emergencies (Whyte 2000). The spread of the ebola virus in central Africa is linked to military movements (Zwi and Ramos-Jimenez 2002). It is troubling that WHO and others make no attempt to disaggregate this data by sex.

The extent of mental trauma is even more difficult to estimate than physical injury and disease. First, baseline data on the mental health of Africans is lacking; for women, almost no studies have been carried out (Turshen 2000b). Second, the field of trauma studies is split between those researchers who believe war has traumatized whole populations, causing them to suffer from Post-Traumatic Stress Disorder, and those who consider most distress normal, maintaining that people are able to adapt to violent situations (Bracken 1998; Summerfield 1996). It follows that the need for specialized therapeutic services is as disputed as the diagnosis. Here the advantage of linking injury to the type of conflict is clear: In some cases, such as liberation struggles, people are protected by their belief in the cause they

Widowhood (1985/97)

	45-59	60+
Northern Africa	19%	59%
Sub-Saharan Africa	16%	44%
USA (55+ 1991/97)		34%

Household heads who are women (1985/97)

	All ages
Northern Africa	12%
Southern Africa	42%
Rest of Sub-Saharan Africa	21%

Source: UN 2000

are defending; in long, low-intensity wars, people are continually subjected to trauma—there is no *post*-traumatic stress, only ongoing insecurity and terror; and in civil wars, today's rapists and murderers were yesterday's next-door neighbors or worse, the neighbors' children.

The Aftermath

Rare are the states that emerge from armed conflict intact or with liberating practices honed in the trenches that give women new skills, new stature, and new opportunities. Few are the instances of state health and education services transformed to cater to women's needs. Too many conflicts are resolved without women's participation in peace talks and post-conflict planning. The result is that women have little influence on the definitions of violence and the kinds of injury named as "violence" that become the basis for post-war services. Of special concern is the failure of planners to recognize women's ongoing need for security and safety: Daily violence is often endemic after the truce and contributes to pervasive fear and insecurity in people's lives (McIlwaine and Moser 2003, 118). This paper argues for new definitions that will enable post-war planners to take account of the interrelationships among violence, security, and women's struggle for livelihood in war-torn societies.

Works Cited

Bracken, Patrick J. 1998. "Hidden Agendas: Deconstructing Post Traumatic Stress Disorder." In *Rethinking the Trauma of War*, ed. Patrick J. Bracken and Celia Petty, 38–59. London: Free Association Books.

Garfield, Richard and Ernest Drucker. 2002. "Counting the Dead: Epidemiologic Analysis of Civil Conflict, Warfare, and Genocide." Unpublished manuscript. Forthcoming in *Emerging Themes in Epidemiology* (http://www.lshtm.ac.uk/ideu/ete/).

Holdstock, Douglas. 2002. "Morbidity and Mortality among Soldiers and Civilians." In *War or Health? A Reader*, ed. Ilkka Taipale. London: Zed Books.

McIlwaine, Cathy and Caroline Moser. 2003. "Poverty, Violence and Livelihood Security in Urban Colombia and Guatemala." *Progress in Development Studies* 3(2): 113–30.

Salignon, P. et al. 2000. "Health and War in Congo-Brazzaville." *Lancet* Nov 18, 356 (9243): 1762.

Stewart, Frances and F. P. Humphreys.1997. "Civil Conflict in Developing Countries over the Last Quarter of a Century: An Empirical Overview of Economic and Social Consequences." *Oxford Development Studies,* Feb, 25(1): 11–42.

Summerfield, Derek. 1996. "The Impact of War and Atrocity on Civilian Populations: Basic Principles for NGO Interventions and a Critique of Psychosocial Trauma Projects." Relief and Rehabilitation Network Paper 14. London: Overseas Development Institute.

Toole, Michael J. 2000. "Displaced Persons and War." *War and Public Health*, ed. Barry S. Levy and Victor W. Sidel, 197–212. Washington, DC: APHA.

Turshen, Meredeth. 2000a. "The Political Economy of Rape: An Analysis of Systematic Rape and Sexual Abuse of Women during Armed Conflict in Africa." In *Victors, Perpetrators or Actors: Gender, Armed Conflict and Political Violence,* ed. Caroline Moser and Fiona Clarke, 30–51. London: Zed Books.

Turshen, Meredeth. 2000b. "Women's Mental Health." In *African Women's Health,* ed. Meredeth Turshen, 83–106. Trenton: Africa World Press.

UN [United Nations]. 2000. *The World's Women 2000: Trends and Statistics.* NY: United Nations.

WHO [World Health Organization]. 2002. *World Report on Violence and Health.* Geneva: World Health Organization.

Whyte, B. 2000. "Up to one third of malaria deaths in Africa occur in countries affected by complex emergencies." *Bulletin of the World Health Organization* 78(8): 1062.

Zwi, Anthony and Pilar Ramos-Jimenez. 2002. "Conflict, Crisis and Infectious Disease." *TDR News* no. 68, June, 8–10. Available at http://www.who.int/tdr/publications/tdrnews/pdf/news68.pdf.

Chapter 4

Filling the Sight by Force

A Meditation on the Violence of the Vernacular

Laura Wexler

If many kinds of violence are naturalized, and therefore invisible, and if everyday life for many people is itself a form of brutalization, then how do we render that violence visible without creating states of numbness and denial?

From my own disciplinary perspective as a feminist historian of photography, these two questions capture the drift of what needs to be considered about responding to violence in the current juncture. My scholarship concerns the relationship between photography and force. Is photography a kind of violence? Is seeing a kind of force? Do photographs of violent events simply make images of the violence, or are they in themselves violence magnified and repeated? What do we mean by all this talk about "the gaze"? And perhaps most important, what does it mean not to look but not to see—to turn toward the world what I have elsewhere called the "averted gaze" of the "innocent eye" of domestic sentiment (Wexler 2000)?

We already know that feminist theory and practice over the past two decades have contributed significantly to public discussion of visual culture. Feminist debates about pornography, the male gaze, race and body politics, and the spread of militarization all take images as central texts. Feminist filmmakers and photographers—for example, Donna Ferrato—have produced superb bodies of work on domestic violence. And female, if not always outright feminist, photojournalists—such as Jenny Matthews and Susan Meiselas, for instance—have "brought the war home" from many different places and in eye-opening ways (Ferrato 1991; Matthews 2003; Meiselas 1981). What I have to contribute here is the suggestion that as feminists ponder the multiple relations between photography and violence, both critical and constitutive, in the current moment, we ought not to focus solely on what we already understand to be images of violence. Instead, I want to propose that even domestic images, the most quotidian, most innocuous-seeming pictures—portraits of mothers, fathers, children—may be implements of terror depending upon how they are used. And, further, I suggest that such domestic images are currently a major conduit though which the militarization of U.S. society is being accomplished.

What makes an image violent is not necessarily only the palpable harm captured within its frame, but how that image is set into circulation and employed. That is to say, the violence of images is on the reception end as well as in production. During the nineteenth century slaveholders used the family portrait genre to circulate images that purported to show that slavery brought no harm to those they owned. After emancipation, domestic photographs arranged the image of both white and black families in an attempt to erase the fissures and fatalities of the racial order. During the Spanish-American War the U.S. government used domestic photographs taken by women photographers to indicate the purportedly higher level of "civilization" of the actively imperial nation, and thereby to rationalize conquest and colonization. And there are many more examples.

What this means in essence is that the various brutalities of everyday life that many people experience are not reserved for victims alone. Photography also produces a perpetrator's gaze that stages complicity in these violent arrangements. The visual imprint of this violence is different from the victim's receipt of it, but it is no less naturalized nor is it less toxic for being couched in domestic terms. Indeed, domestic imagery is a good example of how violence is linked and interwoven at the different scales of the intimate, the community, the national and the international. In family photographs we are repeatedly invited to see horrible conundrums of everyday life as if they were domestic peace.

Currently, we are also asked to support a foreign war to preserve exactly these images of domesticity. And at home, American family photographs have also been deployed in a variety of efforts to convince us to hand over more and more of our rights and freedoms to the government, which proposes to protect them.

It is clear, for instance, how images of the women and girls of Afghanistan were recently circulated as justification for a bombing campaign. But such use of images of women did not end with that phase of the war in Afghanistan. In the United States in the summer of 2002 the media circulated scores of photographs of beautiful little girls who had been abducted, violently abused, raped, and murdered. As the media frenzy about these horrific events reached its peak we were offered the "Amber Alert" as a reasonable redress. The "Amber Alert" was originally a California initiative that allows police to activate a statewide surveillance system, including lighted highway signs, hot lines, and requests to drivers to report all suspicious individuals. The Amber Alert is a materialization and naturalization of the security state that can easily slip from the honorable, even urgent, imperative to try to save these children to other realms of profiling and policing. Advocates have now suggested that the Amber Alert be extended to all fifty states. The family of the kidnapped (and miraculously recovered) Elizabeth Smart has been enlisted as a collective spokesman for this effort. The argument is not wrong that such an apparatus could be very useful for the protection of children. The problem is that the family tragedies of such abductions are being used as a screen against the perception of the potential abuses of such a system (Smart and Smart 2003).

Again that summer, after many hours of foregrounding Linda Franklin's photograph as the "face" of a victim who was shot going about her normal daily life putting purchases from Home Depot into the trunk of her car in Washington, D.C., Defense Secretary Donald Rumsfeld authorized the Pentagon to work with domestic law enforcement to help catch the "sniper" who was terrorizing the greater D.C. area. Law enforcement was to deploy secret surveillance planes to patrol the skies over the Washington area. Apparently, however, these arrangements—which may or may not be against the law—were hammered out some days before the Linda Franklin murder. It was the image of the female victim—in a family portrait—that paved the way for public acceptance of this coordination and intensification of the domestic police state and the need to erect a less permeable shield of defense over a wartime Washington.

Roland Barthes has written in *Camera Lucida* that a photograph is violent "not because it shows violent things, but because on each occasion it *fills the sight by force,* and because in it nothing can be refused or transformed (that we can sometimes call it mild does not contradict its violence: many say that sugar is mild, but to me sugar is violent, and I call it so)" (Barthes 1981, 91). I want to suggest that we can contest violence when we look to the force, and the forces behind, the domestic family photographs that so sugar our eyes. In the spirit of the Not In Our Name initiative, we must watch not only how our names—but how our images—are used.

Works Cited

Barthes, Roland. 1981. *Camera Lucida: Reflections on Photography.* New York: Hill and Wang.

Ferrato, Donna. 1991. *Living with the Enemy.* New York: Aperture Foundation.

Matthews, Jenny. 2003. *Women and War.* Ann Arbor: University of Michigan Press.

Meiselas, Susan. 1981. *Nicaragua: June, 1978–July, 1979.* New York: Pantheon.

Smart, Ed, and Lois Smart. 2003. *Bringing Elizabeth Home: A Journey of Faith and Hope.* New York: Doubleday.

Wexler, Laura. 2000. *Tender Violence: Domestic Visions in an Age of U.S. Imperialism.* Chapel Hill: University of North Carolina Press.

Chapter 5

Rethinking Responses to Violence, Rethinking the Safety of "Home"

Andrea Smith

Many mainstream feminist organizations, particularly antiviolence organizations, have applauded the United States attacks on Afghanistan to "liberate" Arab women from the repressive policies of the Taliban. This essay will discuss how this support for the war coincides with these same organizations' uncritical support of the criminal justice system as the primary tool to stop domestic and sexual violence. The mainstream antiviolence movement often supports the apparatus of state violence to eradicate gender violence. In this essay, I will argue that centering the histories and experiences of women of color within the antiviolence movement could prove to be a helpful corrective in the strategies the mainstream movement currently employs.

What was disturbing to so many United States citizens about the attacks on the World Trade Center is that these attacks disrupted their sense of safety at "home." Terrorism is something that happens in other countries; our "home," the United States is supposed to be a place of safety. The antiviolence movement, however, has always contested this notion of safety at home, as the majority of violence women suffer happens at home. Furthermore, the notion that violence happens "out there," inflicted by the stranger in the dark alley, makes it difficult to recognize that the home is in fact the place of greatest danger for women. Similarly, the notion that terrorism happens in other countries makes it difficult to grasp that the United States is in fact built on a history of genocide, slavery, and racism. Our "home" has never been a safe place for people of color.

At the same time that the antiviolence movement has contributed this important piece of analysis, ironically its strategies to defeat violence are all based on the premise that violence happens "out there" rather than at home. For instance, the antiviolence movement has relied on the criminal legal system as its primary tool to address violence. The use of the criminal legal system to address gender violence is based on the false notion that the perpetrators of violence are a few crazed men whom we need to lock up. When one-half of women will be battered in their lifetimes and nearly one-half of women will be sexually assaulted in their lifetimes, it is clear that we live in a rape culture that prisons, themselves a site of violence and control, cannot change. Alternative approaches to provide true safety and security for women must be developed.

Similarly, military responses to terrorism are premised on the false notion that "terrorism" is limited to a few countries run by seeming lunatics. But given that the U.S military has been the single greatest perpetrator of violence and terrorism in recent history, it obviously cannot provide true safety and security when it supports a society based on terrorism against people of color.

Because many mainstream feminist organizations are white-dominated, they often do not see themselves as potential victims in Bush's war in the United States and abroad. It is important, however, to consider how the definition of the "alien" in the United States, a category of people purportedly deserving of repressive policies and overt attack, is not limited to people of color. Since September 11, many organizations have reported sharp increases in attacks in LGBT communities, testimony to the extent to which gays and lesbians are often seen as "aliens" whose sexuality threatens the white nuclear family thought to be the building blocks of United States society. Furthermore, supporting these policies under the rationale that Afghanistan will now be freed of sexism and homophobia allows the Bush administration to remain unaccountable for its sexist and homophobic policies and its support of the Christian Right. Thus, support for Bush's policies will ultimately undermine feminist and LGBT struggles in the United States.

Beyond Inclusion: Centering Women of Color in the Antiviolence Movement

As the antiviolence movement has attempted to become more "inclusive," these attempts at multicultural interventions have unwittingly strengthened the white supremacy within the antiviolence movement. That is, inclusivity has come to mean: *take a domestic violence model that was developed largely with the interests of white, middle-class women in mind, and simply add a multicultural component to it*. But if we look at the histories of women of color in the United States, as I have done in other work (see Smith 1995, 1999, 2001), it is clear that gender violence functions as a tool for racism and colonialism for women of color in general, and hence suggests an alternative approach that goes beyond inclusion to centering women of color in the organizing and analysis. That is, what if we do not make any assumptions about what a domestic violence program should look like, but instead asked: What would it take to end violence against women of color? What would this movement look like? What if we did not presume that this movement would necessarily have anything we take for granted in the current domestic violence movement? Criminal Justice and Women's Studies Professor Beth Richie suggests that we go beyond just centering women of color, asking:

What if we centered those most marginalized within the category of "women of color"? She writes:

> We have to understand that the goal of our antiviolence work is not for diversity, and not inclusion. It is for liberation. For if we're truly committed to ending violence against women, then we must start in the hardest places, the places like jails and prisons and other correctional facilities. The places where our work has not had an impact yet. I think we have to stop looking for the easy clients, and we have to stop being the friendly colored girls as some of our antiviolence programs require us to be. We must not deny the part of ourselves and the part of our work that is least acceptable to the mainstream public. Just because we're a lesbian. Or maybe because a survivor is addicted and relapsing, or because she may be young and pregnant, again. Or because she's a sex worker or because she does not have legal status in this country. We must not let those who really object to all of us and our work, co-opt some of us and the work we're trying to do. As if this antiviolence movement could ever really be legitimate in a patriarchal, racist society. . . . Ultimately [the antiviolence movement] needs to be accountable not to those in power, but to the powerless (Richie 2000).

When we center women of color in the analysis, it becomes clear that we must develop approaches that address interpersonal and state violence simultaneously. In addition, we find that, by centering women of color in the analysis, we may actually build a movement that more effectively ends violence not just for women of color, but for all peoples.

Community Accountability and Political Education

I have already argued that if we grasp the extent to which we live in a society structured by rape and gender violence, it becomes clear that strategies relying on the criminal justice system will not effectively stop violence against women. Increasingly, many antiviolence advocates are recognizing some of the harms resulting from our reliance on the criminal justice system, such as the growing number of battered women being arrested under mandatory arrest laws. The harms, however, are much broader than those suffered by women directly affected by domestic violence legislation. The state is not simply flawed in its ability to redress violence, but it is a primary perpetrator of violence against women in its own right. In addition, the co-optation of the antiviolence movement by the criminal justice system has far-reaching effects beyond the effects on the immediate victims of domestic violence. For example, the Right has been very successful in using antiviolence rhetoric to mobilize support for a repressive anticrime agenda that includes three strikes legislation and antidrug bills. These anticrime measures then make abused women more likely to find themselves in prison if they are coerced by partners to engage in illegal activity, for instance. In addition, when men of color are disproportionately incarcerated because of these laws, laws that have been passed in part through the co-optation of antiviolence rhetoric, the entire community, particularly women, who are often the community caretakers, are equally affected.

Critical of the prison system, many activists now call for restorative justice models as appropriate intervention strategies. Restorative justice is an umbrella term used to describe a wide variety of programs and interventions (i.e., family conferencing, circle sentencing, victim-offender mediation, and so on), practices that involve an entire community holding perpetrators accountable. These programs have been widely criticized by antiviolence advocates for depending on a romanticized notion of "community" that will actually hold perpetrators of violence accountable; critics do not believe the programs provide sufficient measures to ensure safety for survivors. Just as problematic, however, is the extent to which restorative justice programs are usually tied to the criminal justice systems. Thus, if restorative justice programs are always tied to the state, they may actually serve to extend the power of the criminal justice system over more people rather than fundamentally challenge the system.

Therefore it might be helpful to think of what a model based on political organizing might look like. What if survivors were the organizers rather than clients? Such an approach could both (1) challenge state violence *and* (2) build communities that would actually provide safety for survivors by challenging the sexism, homophobia, and other forms of oppression that exist within communities. Such an approach is becoming increasingly popular in the United States as communities of color in particular are developing strategies that do not rely on the state, whether in the form of the traditional criminal justice system or of restorative justice programs that are increasingly co-opted by the state.

Beyond the Nation-State

Just as we have to think beyond the state in addressing violence, we need to think beyond the nation-state as the appropriate form of governance for the world. In particular, we must call into question the notion that the United States can ever be the guarantor of peace and freedom, and recognize the United States for the colonial, settler nation that it is. Much of the current antiwar movement never calls into question the legitimacy of the United States with its slogans like, "Peace is patriotic." The United States could not exist, however, without the genocide of indigenous peoples. To assume that the United States should or will always continue to exist is to sanction the genocide of Native peoples. It is incumbent upon all peoples who benefit from living on Native lands to consider how they can engage in social justice struggles without constantly selling out Native peoples in the interest of political expediency.

In questioning the United States, it necessarily follows that we question the nation-state as the appropriate form of governance for the world. Doing so allows us to free our political imagination to begin thinking of how we can begin to build a world in which we would actually want to live. Helpful in this project of imagination is the work of Native women activists who have begun articulating notions of nation and sovereignty that are separate from nation-states. Whereas nation-states are governed through domination and coercion, indigenous sovereignty and nationhood is predicated on interrelatedness and responsibility. As Crystal Ecohawk (Pawnee) puts it: "Sovereignty is an active, living process within this knot of human, material and spiritual relationships bound together by mutual responsibilities and obligations. From that knot of relationships are born our histories, our identity, the traditional ways in which we govern ourselves, our beliefs, our relationship to the land, and how we feed, clothe, house and take care of our families, communities and Nations" (Ecohawk 1999). In a similar vein, Ingrid Washinawatok (Menominee) argues, "While sovereignty is alive and invested in the reality of every living thing for Native folks, Europeans relegated sovereignty to only one realm of life and existence: authority, supremacy and dominion. In the Indigenous realm, sovereignty encompasses responsibility, reciprocity, the land, life and much more" (Washinawatok 1999). This interconnectedness exists not only among the nation's members but of all creation—human and nonhuman:

> Our spirituality and our responsibilities define our duties. We understand the concept of sovereignty as woven through a fabric that encompasses our spirituality and responsibility. This is a cyclical view of sovereignty, incorporating it into our traditional philosophy and view of our responsibilities. There it differs greatly from the concept of western sovereignty which is based upon absolute power. For us absolute power is in the Creator and the natural order of all living things; not only in human beings. . . . Our sovereignty is related to our connections to the earth and is inherent.
>
> The idea of a nation did not simply apply to human beings. We call the buffalo or the wolves, the fish, the trees, and all are nations. Each is sovereign, and equal part of the creation, interdependent, interwoven, and all related (Venne 1999).

This project does not depend on a political metanarrative that guarantees a utopic society for all. From our position of growing up in a patriarchal, colonial, and white supremacist world, we cannot even fully imagine how a world not based on this structures of oppression could operate. Nevertheless, we can be part of a collective, creative process that can bring us closer to a society not based on domination. To quote Jean Ziegler from the 2003 World Social Forum held in Porto Alegre, Brazil: "We know what we don't want, but the new world belongs to the liberated freedom of human beings. 'There is no way; you make the way as you go' [quoting from Antonia Machado during the Spanish Civil War]. History doesn't fall from heaven; we make history" (Ziegler 2003).

Works Cited

Ecohawk, Crystal. 1999. "Reflections on Sovereignty." *Indigenous Woman* 3(1): 21–22.

Richie, Beth. 2000. "Plenary Address." Color of Violence: Violence Against Women of Color Conference, Santa Cruz, Calif. April.

Smith, Andrea. 1995. "Christian Conquest and the Sexual Colonization of Native Women." In *Violence against Women and Children: A Christian Theological Sourcebook*, ed. Carol J. Adams and Marie M. Fortune, 377–403. New York: Continuum.

Smith, Andrea. 1999. "Sexual Violence and American Indian Genocide." *Journal of Religion and Abuse* 1(2): 31–52.

Smith, Andrea. 2001. "The Color of Violence: Violence Against Women of Color." *Meridians: Feminism, Race, Transnationalism* 1(2): 65–72.

Venne, Sharon. "The Meaning of Sovereignty." *Indigenous Woman* 2(6): 27–30.

Washinawatok, Ingrid. 1999. "Sovereignty is More than Just Power." *Indigenous Woman* 2(6): 23–24.

Ziegler, Jean. 2003. Presentation in "International Process on Developing Guidelines for the Implementation of the Right to Food (EED/Social Watch Movement)" Workshop. World Social Forum, Porto Alegre, Brazil. 24 January.

Chapter 6

Violence of Protection

Minoo Moallem

What does it mean for a word not only to name, but also in some sense to perform and, in particular, to perform what it names?

—Judith Butler (1997a: 43)

Thousands of watchful eyes there are doubtless estimating the number of vessels. Who will pass on the number? Who will write of it? Which of all these silent spectators will live to tell the tale when the encounter is over? Amable Matterer is at his post in the first squadron, which glides slowly westward; he gazes at the city, which returns his gaze. The same day he writes of the confrontation, dispassionately, objectively.

—Assia Djebar (1993: 7)

What does it mean for violence, as a signifier circulated transnationally, to perform violence? What is the relationship between what is codified as violence and what is constituted as nonviolence? What happens when violence is defined only in relation to what happens to the victims of violence? What if violence is intrinsic to the fixation of the gaze? How does protection against violence itself become a site of violence? Who is allowed to give the order to protect? In whose name can such an order be given and under which circumstances?

We are living in a world where the circulation of images relies on the force of visibility. The visible, together with the visual, creates an order that not only privileges certain images over others, but also establishes a particular relationship between the spectator and the spectacle. In particular, the coding of violence relies extensively on the framework of the visible. The power of the coding of violence lies in its ability to transform its force into subject positions that organize conflict into alliances between protectors and the protected. Analyzing the ways in which violence and protection are linked together through race and gender is key to understanding modern regimes of knowledge and power. It is vital that we interrogate the relationships that exist between the spectator and the visual, as well as between the spectator and the visible, in order to expose and reconfigure the underpinnings of violence and power in the postcolonial/neocolonial, global world order.

I wish to examine the relationship between the process of globalization and the coding of violence in the discourse of protection. I am especially interested in the process by which the discourse of protection enables speaking subjects to render violence visible while simultaneously concealing the framework against which violence is measured, a framework that constitutes certain positions of power as both nonviolent and invisible. I would like to interrogate the discursive formations that create these fields of visibility and that enable the production, circulation, and consumption of violence as an important signifier in the nation-state and other highly globalized societies. Such discursive formations are important, because they textualize violence by framing specific forms of representation that institute and demand the subject's compliance with identifiable subject-positions. I will consider the transnationality of such discourses—fellow travelers, as it were, alongside capital and labor—as well as their national production through the institutionalization of a gendered, racialized citizenship.

I would like to suggest that universalizing discourses based on key dichotomies such as West/non-West, civilized/barbaric, and modern/traditional are major sites for the production and reproduction of semantic regimes that enable empowered and disempowered subject positions and that determine the horizons within which actions and behaviors are perceived as violence. I would further argue that, within neo- or postcolonial modernity, the effort to bring particulars under the sign of a universal intensifies the necessity of such dichotomies within the broader network of what Spivak refers to as epistemic violence in the attempt to constitute the colonial subject as Other (1988). In this process, violence as a signifier mobilizes another set of discourses—the discourses of protection—which are crucial to modern forms of governmentality and to the notion of gendered, racial citizenship. This process takes place in the context of old and new forms of globalization, as well as in the context of the transnational coding of violence in relation to the discourses of protection. I am referring here to what Zakia Pathak and Rajeswari Sunder Rajan describe as the creation of "an alliance between protector and protected against a common opponent from whom danger is perceived and protection offered or sought, and this alliance tends to efface the will to power exercised by the protector" (1989: 566). These discourses institute gendered, racialized subject positions in the very act of making the violence visible.

Uneven processes of subject formation characterize neo- or postcolonialism. Various geopolitical locations are accorded different status within the global hierarchy. Inside these locations, groups are recognized according to gender, sexuality, race, class, and nation. Discourses of violence and protection have become the most important tropes for the representation of the particular; they circulate in a semantic system that is beyond law and order. These discourses serve to distinguish an inside and an outside, which assign specific subject positions to the protected and the protectors. This positioning is defined by the gendered metaphors of the private and the domesticated, which are opposed to the public and the political. Their construction relies on the spatial and physical metaphor of home as both a territorial homeland and a domesticated, delimited space.

Within the postcolonial world order, the representation of women has been central to the framing of violence and protection. Inderpal Grewal traces the historical concept of home to class and gender formations and to the deployment of female bodies within the antagonistic, comparative framework of colonial epistemology and exposes the opposition of home and "away" as relational, nationalist, and imperialist constructions (1996: 4–5). In a recent article, Iris Young also refers to the notion of masculinist protection and its relationship to the current security state in the United States. She makes a connection between a particular logic of masculinism, "which is associated with the position of the male head of household as a protector of the family, and masculine leaders and risk takers as protectors of a population" (2003: 3). While I agree with Young in her emphasis on the need to analyze the logic of masculinist protection, I would argue that such an understanding cannot limit itself to gender relations, but must take into consideration the role of race and nation and the ways in which violence is represented in the context of the national and transnational circulation of knowledge.

The metaphor of home is clearly gendered, since it is defined as the main location of women. However, home has served to define modern notions of nation as well as of family. As a spatial metaphor, it stands for the inside that is protected from the outside, in both spatial and affective terms. Lauren Berlant's elaboration of the coupling of suffering and citizenship sheds light on the importance of affective domination in the shaping and reshaping of U.S. citizenship (1997). The protection of the inside, construed as family or nation, requires the mobilization of not only political signifiers but also emotional signifiers. For example, the metaphors of guest and host, which define and regulate the labor force of immigrant and diasporic bodies in contemporary societies, establish a logic that naturalizes the movement of capital and labor for dislocated subjects while denying them the protection of a home space. The host/guest logic places the possibility of citizenship outside of the realm of politics through the presupposition that a guest can never be at home in the host place. Indeed, the very notions of "peoplehood" and "we-ness" create sites of agency for the protection of an "us" in its relation to an "other."

The institutionalization of both state regimes of surveillance (borders, prisons, mental institutions) and patriarchal family ideologies depend on these temporal and spatial metaphors, as well as on the discourses of protection. In the broader Western mode of dualistic and dichotomous thinking about the relationship between space and time, Doreen Massey argues that it is time that is coded masculine, while space is being represented as feminine, signifying absence or lack (1996: 6). As a consequence, gender positions and their meanings define agency within the discourses of protection.

Although submission to normative respectability is fundamental for all members of the nation-state, gender ideology assigns men the position of protectors and women the position of protected. As Inderpal Grewal and Caren Kaplan have noted, the insinuation of a "horrified gaze" in depicting female circumcision, veiling, suttee, arranged marriages, and so on has a long representational history in Western cultures. They argue that "within modernity, First World discourses of the Third World as well as nationalist discourses about its female or subaltern subjects continue such representational practices in a variety of historical contexts" (1996: 14). As Rajeswari Sunder Rajan has demonstrated, for example, the invocation of the subject in pain/of pain in the discursive field of Sati has created a gendered ground for the construction of the female subject as victim, thus equating victimhood with helplessness (1993: 34–35).

These discourses not only define particular aspects of women's lives through violence, but also give authority to those who claim the power to decide what counts as violence. For example, many Western global feminists rely on an abstract notion of gender violence in an attempt to protect non-Western women from their patriarchal societies. One of the problems that arise from the act of defining violence solely through gender categories is that, in constructing women and men as transcendental signifiers, we erase the historical and geopolitical forms of violence that stem from racism, colonialism, and current neo/postcolonial relations. These efforts converge with cultural, nationalist projects aimed at silencing women by producing and reproducing semantic fields that are organized around the concepts of violence and nonviolence. Such framing has been essential in the production and reproduction of both Eurocentrism and masculinist citizenship in the context of colonial modernity and postcolonial nationalisms.

In summary, then, violence as a signifier, an act, or an event cannot be separated from the representational practices that are produced in the historical context of modernity and postmodernity and that are circulated in a transnational context of unequal power relations. The representation of violence cannot be separated from cultural struggles over the meaning of identity, security, and protection and must be understood historically. The question of why some acts, events, signifiers are brought to visibility/vocalization and others are ignored remains central to efforts to expose the geopolitical underpinnings of the discourse of violence and protection.

Works Cited

Berlant, Lauren. 1997. *The Queen of America Goes to Washington City: Essays on Sex and Citizenship*. Durham: Duke University Press.

Butler, Judith. 1997a. *Excitable Speech: A Politics of the Performative*. New York: Routledge.

Butler, Judith. 1997b. *The Psychic Life of Power: Theories in Subjection*. Stanford: Stanford University Press.

Djebar, Assia. 1993. *Fantasia: An Algerian Cavalcade*. Trans. Dorothy S. Blair. Portsmouth, N.H.: Heinemann.

Grewal, Inderpal. 1996. *Home and Harem: Nation, Gender, Empire, and the Cultures of Travel.* Durham: Duke University Press.

Grewal, Inderpal, and Caren Kaplan. 1996. "*Warrior Marks:* Global Womanism's Neo-Colonial Discourse in a Multicultural Context." *Camera Obscura* 39: 5–33.

Massey, Doreen. 1994. *Space, Place, and Gender.* Minneapolis: University of Minnesota Press.

Pathak, Zakia, and Rajeswari Sunder Rajan. 1989. "Shahbano." *Signs: Journal of Women in Culture and Society* 14: 558–82.

Spivak, Chakravorty Gayatri. 1988. "Can the Subaltern Speak?" In *Marxism and the Interpretation of Culture,* ed. Cary Nelson and Lawrence Grossberg, 271–97. Urbana: University of Illinois Press.

Sunder Rajan, Rajeswari. 1993. *Real and Imagined Women: Gender, Culture and Postcolonialism.* New York: Routledge.

Young, Marion Iris. 2003. "The Logic of Masculinist Protection: Reflections on the Current Security State." *Signs: Journal of Women in Culture and Society* 29: 1–25.

Chapter 7

Is Secularism Less Violent than Religion?

Janet R. Jakobsen

Is secularism less violent than religion? In my research on this topic I began with a typically academic answer of "yes and no." But the more research and reading that I've done on the topic, the less accurate this answer has seemed, and finally I came to the conclusion that the answer must simply be "no." The secular is not less violent than the religious; in fact, it is more so. It is a source of greater, more intense, and more intractable violence than are religious practices, communities, or worldviews and commitments. So, given that this conclusion is somewhat counterintuitive in today's world, with its focus on the religious roots of terrorism, how did I get there?

The question was originally posed to me by a student in my "Religion, Gender, and Violence" course in the fall of 2002.[1] I had been asked by the chair of the religion department to develop this course the previous spring, in the hope of providing a venue to consider some of the issues that had come to the fore of public debate after the attacks of September 11, 2001. The student's question was part of a larger set of questions prompted by the media discussion of the attacks. Is religious "fundamentalism" the root of the problem? Is religion a particular source of violence in the world? If so, is secularism the answer to this violence? Is the spread of secularism a road to peace? There is a standard answer to all of this for those of us who study religion, one that it is important to reiterate: religion in and of itself does not promote violence anymore than secularism in and of itself promotes peace. Just as some of the most horrendous militarism and violence in the history of our ever smaller world has been religiously motivated, so has some of the most grand and most successful efforts for peace and peaceful social change been religiously grounded. Similarly, the most horrific and deadly wars of the twentieth century, particularly the two world wars, were pursued by putatively secular nation-states. Moreover, religion is not always and everywhere conservative. In the United States, we need only think of the religious roots of the civil rights movement to see that religion can be a force for progressive as well as for conservative social change. It is important to state these facts clearly because they run counter to the dominant narratives of the mainstream media.[2] And to state them is not to dismiss the issue of religious violence: I have also spent much of my scholarly energy considering the various forms of violence that have been legitimated and sustained in the name of religion.

The question of violence was crucial to take up in a course on gender because of the fact that women are often the objects of violence, both religious and secular. Women are increasingly the victims of war, and they are also frequently the targets of violence in patriarchal religions. Importantly, the secular state frequently takes up violence in the name of protecting these women. Protecting women from the Taliban was part of the justification for the recent U.S. war in Afghanistan, and this rhetorical gesture is merely the latest installment in a long history of such justifications for violence.[3] But it remains debatable whether secular violence aimed at "protecting" women actually contributes to their well-being. The U.S. government seemed unconcerned with the oppression of Afghan women before September 11, and this disregard has returned now that the United States has directed its attention elsewhere. In addition to the loss of life incurred in war, the U.S. bombing was hugely destructive of basic infrastructure in Afghanistan, including hospitals and schools, and yet United States promises in aid for rebuilding Afghanistan remain inadequate and unfulfilled. In other words, secular violence may have different, but nonetheless horrifying, consequences for women's lives. Given this reality, what position should feminists take? Is it possible to recognize and resist both religious and secular violence against women simultaneously?

My original thoughts on how religion both is and is not a less-violent discourse than is secularism were informed by the set of readings for "Religion, Gender, and Violence." In a week organized around the question, "Why Religion?" which asked why religion is implicated in violence so frequently and in such profound ways, we read two essays with viewpoints that were in certain ways opposing: the chapter "Pain and Truth in Medieval Christian Ritual" from Talal Asad's (1993) *Genealogies of Religion: Discipline and Reasons of Power in Christianity and Islam,* and David Bromley's "Dramatic Denouements" from the collection of essays *Cults, Religion, and Violence* (Bromley and Melton 2002). Both make arguments that are put to progressive political purposes, and yet they do so along virtually opposite lines. Asad argues that in order to understand practices of power, we need to recognize the ways in which violence goes to the core of medieval Christian practice. In other words, we make a political mistake if we see violence such as the judicial torture as practiced by the medieval church as an external imposition on an otherwise peaceful Christianity. Neither can we interpret this violence as simply a mistake that has been overcome as both legal proceedings and Christianity have become more rational. Rather, Asad argues modern secular reason is built, in part, on the rationalized violence that medieval judicial torture represented. I will return to this point in a moment.

Conversely, Bromley argues that to realize progressive political goals, one must not assume that religions in general, and religious cults in particular, are especially violent. Bromley is particularly concerned with cases of conflict between the state and religious cults, a case of particular importance because the very category of religious "cult" often implies irrationality and a tendency toward violence. Such assumptions are likely to contribute to what Bromley terms "dramatic denouements," such as the horrific outcome at Waco, Texas in the government's conflict and standoff with the Branch Davidians. Assuming that cults are particularly violent induces secular actors, particularly those in government like law enforcement officials, to view conflicts as unlikely to be resolvable by peaceful means and to treat dramatic denouements and violent conflicts as virtually inevitable. This sense of inevitability then leads government officials to hesitate to pursue nonviolent resolutions as actively as they might otherwise, and concomitantly to be willing to undertake risky and potentially dangerous means of ending the situation. Moreover, government officials can express a certain intransigence in relation to religious actors that leads the religious actors to escalate conflict from their side as well, setting off a cycle that all too often produces the "dramatic denouement."

These are both arguments that I have found myself making. In other words, both these positions—that it is crucial to recognize the violence in religion, and that we should not assume that religion is inherently violent—can be held by the same person (hence, my initial "yes and no" answer). If both of these positions are correct—and I will argue that they are—what do we make of the apparent contradiction?

To address this question, I would like to consider briefly some of the evidence for each side of the contradiction—the view that religion is inherently violent and the view that assumptions of inherent violence are misleading and can produce and intensify the violence they would hope to avoid. First, the evidence for religion as the greatest source of violence: The popular narrative, one that is deeply indebted to the progress narrative of modernity, argues that those societies that have not fully embraced modernization and its attendant secularization produce forms of religious belief that are impervious to modern reason. This means that these societies do not resolve conflict through the deliberative discussion that reason is supposed to provide. As a result, these societies are more prone to violent conflict. This argument is mostly directed from western sources toward nonwestern societies, which are seen as either resistant to modernity or as behind the times in terms of modern development. But, this argument has sometimes recently been deployed against the religious strains of the United States government, which are seen as fueling the government's willingness to go to war. In this version, it is supposedly the religiosity of the Bush administration, rather than its politics, that is the fundamental problem. In the end, though, this narrative is not particularly helpful. It frequently subscribes to colonialist and racist notions of who-is-ahead and who-is-behind in modern "development," and it tells us very little about when and why religious discourses become implicated in both nonstate violence like terrorism and state-based violence like that enacted by the United States government. This failure leaves us without good analytic resources in terms of how to address or stop these very real violences.

But, there is other, more compelling evidence for the contribution that religion makes to the persistence of violence in our contemporary world, and a few examples are worth exploring in more detail. E. Valentine Daniel, in a paper that he gave at a Barnard College symposium on religion and violence in October 2001, argues that his study of the dramatic violence in Sri Lanka in the 1980s (Daniel 1996) convinced him that once certain types of violence are named as religious violence—once they are implicated in the discourse of religion—they become intractable in ways that they would not be were they not constructed and constrained by being named "religious." Daniel traces the ways in which supposedly immutable categories, like "ethnicity," that become the names for violence are constructed. In the Sri Lankan case, the violence was most frequently termed "ethnic" violence between the majority Sinhalas and the minority Tamils, but Daniel shows that these ethnic groups were not always the primary means by which people understood themselves. Currently, Sinhalas and Tamils are most frequently defined through the Sinhala and Tamil languages, and violence is most frequently organized around concepts of linguistic nationalism. This linguistic nationalism, Daniel reports, is often described as interethnic conflict in the press and in everyday conversation among Sri Lankans. But, Daniel argues, from the nineteenth through the early twentieth centuries, locality rather than linguistic identity was the most important marker of difference, and distinctions between Buddhists and Christians were more important than those between Sinhalas and Tamils (1996, 14–17).

Religion now most frequently enters as a support for linguistic identity. Sinhalas are identified as primarily Buddhist and Tamils as primarily Hindus, and other religious groups—Christians and Muslims—are glossed over. Although linguistic nationalism "leads with its banner" in the conflict, "race, religion, and language have formed an unholy alliance that is charged by its claimants, adherents and speakers, respectively, with the mission of dividing the nation's citizens" (Daniel 1996, 14). Daniel expanded on this concept in his post–September 11 reflections, arguing that while the conflict was not religious but was rather political in origin, religion acts as a support to linguistic nationalism, which makes linguistic difference—because tied to religion—seem more eternal and unchangeable. The tie to religion makes it more difficult to see the ways that linguistic differences have been constructed, and hence it becomes more difficult to see the ways in which conflict between linguistic groups might be shifted, negotiated, or ended. The *naming* of the conflict in terms that included religion made it seem more intractable, more impervious to reason and hence resistant to peace.

We should note, here, that there is in the modern world much intertwining of the discourses of religion and race/ethnicity (sometimes race/ethnicity is understood in linguistic terms and sometimes it is not), and this intertwining may allow them to become mutually reinforcing discourses in maintaining violence. We saw this intertwining in the conflict in Bosnia-Herzegovina, a conflict named in the United States media as one between Serbs, an ethnic group, and Muslims, a religious group. Of course, if both groups had been named in religious terms, the American public would have had to acknowledge that the aggressors in this case were Christians—Orthodox Christians, but Christians nonetheless. We see similar confusions between "religious" identity and "ethnic" identity in Northern Ireland, and in the current public discourse of the United States, in which frequently Arab=Muslim or Muslim=Arab, and Arab/Muslim=Terrorist. There were, for example, several reports in U.S. newspapers after September 11 of Arab Christians being threatened, harassed, or attacked as "Muslims" and "terrorists."

I would suggest that these confusions can be deployed in mutually reinforcing ways that work to hold violence in place. When conflict around ethnic differences appears resolvable, religion can be brought in to heighten the sense of absolute difference between the parties to the conflict. This is part of what Daniel is arguing in the Sri Lanka case: The infusion of religious discourse takes the conflict to another plane. Similarly, in moments and places where religion proves to be less of an intensifier, ethnicity can be injected to maintain or heighten conflict. In the United States, for example, where racism is such a profound and foundational discourse, the equation of Islam with Arabs allows for responses and government policies grounded in racial profiling, while the government maintains its official line of religious tolerance.

One final example of the ways in which religion contributes to violent conflict shows that if we fail to take religion into account, we may also fail to resolve conflicts. This example is provided by Linda Beck, a political scientist who has worked on the civil war in Senegal and in particular on the role of women in the conflict and their exclusion from the peace process (Beck 2002). The civil war in Senegal is now two decades old. Since 1982 a southern separatist group in Senegal has waged a sporadic civil war. Several times peace talks have been organized; several times treaties have been produced; and several times these treaties have failed. How to explain this failure?

Beck argues that one reason that the conflict has proven so persistent is that this (wholly unsuccessful) peace process has been based on a secular, masculine, and governmental model of peace building. In this case, part of the problem, Beck's research shows, is that many of the combatants have taken religious vows to continue fighting—vows presided over in local religious traditions by women religious leaders. The fact that women have been central in sustaining the conflict shows that any assumption that women are inherently peaceful is mistaken, but it also means that if women are part of the problem, they must also be part of the resolution. Instead, these women religious leaders have been largely ignored in the governmental peace talks. The process has run along lines with which we're all familiar: You hold talks among leaders (who are all men); these leaders come to some agreement about what's going to happen; they sign a treaty to that effect; and then they try to enforce the treaty through governmental, or at least hierarchical, means. They fail. The combatants continue to fight.

Religion is a powerful legitimating force for conflict in this case, and if not addressed, certainly an impediment to peace. Beck suggests that in order to find the road to a lasting peace, we should not eschew religion in favor of secularism as if religion were somehow a natural source of violence. Rather we need to take both religion and gender more seriously—recognizing the complexity of people's religious commitments and recognizing women as leaders and including them in the peace process.

These examples (and we could undoubtedly find many more), make a persuasive case that religion can indeed contribute to, intensify, extend, expand, or maintain violent conflict, including some of the most intractable conflicts in the contemporary world; and that attention to religion and its role in violent conflict is an important part of any process that hopes to bring violent conflict successfully to an end. Conflicts that are legitimated in part by religion, like those in Sri Lanka and Bosnia-Herzegovina, have been some of the most brutal in our world, producing true horrors, including general-ized violence against civilians, mass rape, and even genocide.

If this is the case, why argue that secularism is even more violent? Shouldn't we instead be arguing that one of the major problems of today's world is that radical religious discourses are spreading and that their legitimation of horrific violence is increasing? I would have to say that part of the answer is certainly, "yes." The implication of religion in violence is a serious problem. Therefore, my argument about secular violence should not be taken to mean that religion is truly peaceful and religious violence is somehow a misreading or lie. As Asad argues, and as our world amply demonstrates, religion and violence are intertwined.

So, is not the answer to this problem the intervention of secular powers that can loosen the religious legitimation of violence, replace religious difference with common humanity, and bring negotiable reason to conflict resolution? No. Here is where I part company from the dominant story. Although religious support for violence is a very real problem in our world today, the answer that is usually given as a response to this reality—that we must replace religion with secularism—is misguided. As Linda Beck's example shows, replacing religious legitimation with secular peace processes does not necessarily increase the likelihood of peace (Beck 2002).

The idea that secularism is the best response to religious violence is part of the progress narrative that organizes modernity. In this story, progress is marked by an advance from religious faith to secular reason. Secularism is an advance over religion because reason provides a means of resolving conflict without violence. The central historical example in this narrative is the description of reason as the force that could bring an end to the "wars of religion" sparked by the Protestant Reformation. This ascension of secular reason marks the modern period as distinctive. This story, however, makes secular reason seem to be only a force for peace, and it leaves us without a full explanation of why wars—both religious and secular wars—have been so central to modern life. In fact, because of technological innovations, modern warfare has been incredibly destructive of human life. We cannot simply claim that modernity—or modern secularism—has led to the end of violence or the loss of human life.[4] But how then do we intervene in this continuing violence, whether religious or secular?

Let me return for a moment to the examples provided by Asad and Bromley. Asad's argument is not just about medieval Christianity; he is also interested in the ways in which religious discourse—and its violence—is taken up in modern discourses of reason, specifically in the secular discourse of the law. Asad demonstrates that the institution of the law is not so much an advance in rationality, and hence in nonviolence, as it is an extension of discipline—and, yes, violence—through new techniques of what social theorist Michel Foucault has called "governmentality." In other words, Asad argues that modern reason doesn't necessarily bring an end to religious violence; it just produces different—more rationalized—forms of violence. In fact, Asad is so interested in medieval religious violence because he sees this violence as a central aspect in the genealogy not just of "religion," but also of modern secularism.

This extension of Asad's analysis places it in a different relation to Bromley's argument than the apparent opposition with which I began my essay. Bromley is specifically concerned about the state—and the state violence of law enforcement—in relation to religious cults. Putting Bromley and Asad together, law enforcement is an example of a particular type of violence—a violence that, if Asad is right, we should call the violence of Christian secularism, and a violence that, if Bromley is right, can also induce more extreme forms of violence from religious groups in reaction.

Thus, in order to answer the question of whether secularism is less violent than religion, we need to be more specific. We need to understand the specific differences between a socially dominant religion like Christianity, which is intertwined with the state, and religions like those studied by Bromley and his colleagues, which are the object of state violence. And, in the end, we need to develop some sense of the mutual implication of these terms of analysis, coming to see the intertwining of secularism and religion à la Asad.

We also need to name the missing player in the secular-religious comparison: the secular state. In my estimation the state is the crucial, but obfuscated, piece of the puzzle surrounding religious and secular violence in the modern world.

In the dominant narrative, the secular state acts on behalf of peace over and against mostly nongovernmental religious actors. Not only is this supposedly what happened in the origin story for modern secularism, when the modern state in its establishment brought a peaceable end to the "wars of religion" sparked by the Protestant Reformation, but this is also supposedly what is happening now as the United States pursues its war on terrorism over and against the nongovernment forces of al Qaeda.

But there are problems with each of the main elements that make up this story in which the secular state is the agent for peace. I would like to briefly explore each of these elements—secularism, peace, and the state—in turn.

Secularism

The secularization narrative depends on the triumph of the secular state over religion, a triumph that supposedly involves a move to the universality of reason over the particularity of any specific religious belief. Yet this triumph of universality is also grounded in a particular history—that of Christian Europe—and its dependence on this history produces an understanding of secularism that is fundamentally intertwined with and in fact dependent upon Christianity. This history of European secularization is also part of the national story of the United States. The notion that the U.S. government is simultaneously a Christian and a secular state was made imminently clear in an essay by Andrew Sullivan (2001) for the *New York Times Magazine* in October 2001, entitled "This *Is* a Religious War." Sullivan takes up the moment directly after September 11 to argue that the United States must undertake a war against terrorism and, despite abjuring to the contrary, this war should be recognized as a "religious war." He makes this argument by drawing a contrast between "Western civilization" and "Islamic civilization." In the structure of his argument he draws on a common imbalance in our national thinking about cross-cultural engagement: While we often see the complex character of our own culture, we can have difficulty recognizing this same complexity in others. When thinking of others we tend to take a single part as representative for the whole.

He begins the article with the requisite acknowledgment that the terrorist attacks were not simply direct expressions of religious belief in Islam, just as the Christian Coalition is not simply a straightforward expression of Christian faith. Sullivan also acknowledges Christian terrorism in the United States—noting specifically violence around abortion clinics and the killing of doctors who perform abortions—but importantly, this terrorism tells us nothing about U.S. society or Christianity more broadly. Despite these acknowledgments, Sullivan goes on to argue that although the attacks cannot be taken as representative of all Islam, they are representative of a deep strain in what he refers to as "Islamic civilization." Sullivan uses the idea that this politicized Islam is, although not representative of all Islam, nonetheless connected to "Islamic civilization" as the basis for the claim that the United States is embarked on an "epic" battle akin to that against Nazism and Communism. In fact, this epic struggle is even greater because the secular claims of Nazism and Communism were "built on the very weak intellectual conceits of a master race and a Communist revolution," whereas "Islamic fundamentalism is based on a glorious civilization and a great faith" (53).

The relation that Sullivan draws between Christian terrorism and the history of Christianity is quite different, however. Christian terrorism, rather than representing a strain of "Christian civilization," is an exception to a broader Christian history that leads to religious tolerance. He points specifically to John Locke's "Letter of Toleration" as a fundamental document demonstrating how Christianity learned from centuries of religious war to live in civil peace.[5] Thus there is a point of slippage in Sullivan's argument. Sullivan makes the claim that the United States is the land of religious freedom because it is the descendant of a specifically Christian history. The United States is posed as simultaneously tolerant and superior. Here he is able to have his logical cake and eat it, too. The United States is superior because it represents religious freedom, because it separates religion from politics—the cake—and because it is specifically Christian—eating it too.

There is a very interesting moment when this argument displays itself: "With Islam, this has worse implications than for other cultures that have had rises and falls. For Islam's religious tolerance has always been premised on its own power. It was tolerant when it controlled the territory and called the shots. When it lost territory and saw itself eclipsed by the West in power and civilization, tolerance evaporated" (52). The referent for "this" in the above quote is not entirely clear, but it seems to be the loss of the Ottoman Empire, so that Islam no longer "controlled territory and called the shots." Sullivan associates this shift away from dominance with a subsequent rise of extremist Islam. In other words, the connection between religious culture and extremism has worse implications for Islamic civilization than for Christian cultures like the United States

Given events in the United States since September 11—vigilante violence against Muslims and racial profiling of Arabs and Muslims by the U.S. government, for example—there is good reason to question whether or not, as Sullivan claims of predominantly Muslim societies, the United States or other Christian societies are most tolerant only when they are in power, and whether this tolerance evaporates once the dominant society is threatened. But it is also important to recognize the ways in which Christianity and secularism are intertwined in Sullivan's argument: Secularism and, perhaps even more importantly, religious tolerance, are not separate from religious identity but are specifically tied to Christianity and distanced from Islam.

Let me be clear about the stakes here. When we say that the horror that was experienced in New York on September 11 is somehow reflective of "Islamic civilization," whereas Christian terrorism is an exception to an otherwise tolerant history of Christianity, then the violence of terrorism justified in the name of Islam takes on a particular meaning and a particular terror. It is frightening not just because of the massive loss of life, not just because of the innocence of those whose lives were lost, not just because of the randomness of their loss, but also because the violence represents a massive threat to our society itself. Moreover, with this narrative the violence that is undertaken by the United States in response takes on a particular meaning. It becomes violence only in the service of peace rather than in the service of domination. It becomes necessary and, no matter what the horror that might have been visited on the Afghan people or the Iraqi people, our violence is lesser than that directed against us. Our violence literally becomes less violent. It is about tolerance and peace rather than about war.

Peace

How do we create peace? What is the relationship between war and peace? It is now commonplace to criticize the repeated claim of governments that war is undertaken on behalf of peace. The tremendous brutality of World War I, which was supposed to be "the war to end all wars," followed in such quick succession by the even more horrific and deadly World War II, put an end to at least some of the naïveté that war was a good way to produce peace. Yet, in the spring of 2003, the United States went to war again in the name of protecting freedom, spreading democracy, and, yes, creating peace. One of the things that the war in Iraq was supposed to do was reconfigure political relations in the entire Middle East so as to promote both peace and security. Why, when so many other wars undertaken in the name of peace have failed in this stated purpose, does this ideology remain so strong that it is taken up time and again? The reason may lie at the core of the modern conceptualization of peace.

We can see this by looking at the roots of our Western conceptions of peace in the Middle Ages. Tomaž Mastnak (2002) has written a brilliant new study of the roots of the Christian Crusades against Islam that may shed some light on this topic. He argues that the Church's willingness to pursue conflict with Islam was rooted not just in Christian understandings of the fundamental differences between Christians and Muslims but also in the Church's understanding of peace. Specifically, the Church's willingness to use violence was rooted in a peace movement of the end of the tenth and the beginning of the eleventh centuries. The *"pax Dei"* or Peace of God movement was carried out by clerics in the area that is now central France, and the movement eventually succeeded in bringing the Church to institute to the *"treuga Dei"* or Truce of God. But, as Mastnak says, "these peace-making efforts together resulted in the crusade at the end of the eleventh century" (2002, 1). The idea that a peace movement should be the origin of what became one of the bloodiest chapters in Christian history is a profound one, but Mastnak makes a compelling case.

The purpose of the peace movement was to end extragovernmental and extralegal raids on property and persons. During a period without a strongly established state, groups of bandits would support themselves by raiding farms and villages. Both the bandits and their victims were Christians, and the Church stepped into the vacuum in the hope of protecting both its property and the putatively defenseless villagers. In particular, the Church invoked the need to protect women and children. The Church moved both to restrict and to rationalize the violence. The peace movement within the Church demanded a moratorium on fighting on Sundays and holy days (in a religious calendar full of holy days), and through this effort, fighting was reduced precipitously. And yet, once the Church had taken the authority for itself to control violence through the deployment of its own violent forces (even if these forces were intended to be preventative), then the rationalization and elaboration of the Church's use of violence began.

In the end, Mastnak argues, the Church brought a cessation to the initial type of fighting among Christians. It produced peace. But this peace among Christians was produced through the projection of the violence outward against Islam. A unified identity among Christians was established by projecting a fundamental difference between Christians and Muslims. Voluminous treatises were written promoting the idea that Christians should never use violence against each other, but that violence against Muslims was of a wholly different order and would purify both Christians and the world. Thus in one sense the desire for peace produced the very problem that we moderns hope to solve. Our modern concern is that social differences, whether religious or ethnic or other differences, will be taken to be fundamental and will seem resolvable only through violence. We search for peace as a means of avoiding violence like that in Bosnia-Herzegovina. And yet Mastnak's argument implies that Western conceptions of peace developed in conjunction with the concept that such fundamental differences should be addressed by violence like that of the Crusades. Small wonder, then, that we see violence as a road to peace, and even smaller wonder that this path so often leads only to more violence.

The Secular State

Mastnak's argument also raises questions about our third term: *the secular state*. We could read his narrative, as I do, as a cautionary tale that requires us to interrogate the presumption that violent means produce peace; or we could read it as the prehistory of modernity in which the secular state must replace religious authority as the agent of peace. As we have seen, one of the most common narratives about the shift from the Middle Ages to the modern world is that in modernity, the secular state takes over rationalized violence from religious actors and in so doing produces a new and more reasoned approach to peace.

But, as with the view that violence is the path to peace, there is plenty of evidence to show that the modern state is the origin of, rather than the solution to, most of the contemporary world's violence. Take the example of Rwanda's 1990s genocide, the origin of which was supposedly the profundity of ethnic differences in civil society that prompted a mania of violence based on fear and loathing of the "other." This hatred was supposed to be so deep and the mania so extreme that the world's governments stood by impotently and failed to intervene with rationalized violence to stop the bloodshed. In fact, ethnicity is no more foundational—and probably less so—in Rwandan society than elsewhere. In Rwanda, intermarriage and long-standing social connections meant that ethnic differences were clearly the constructed product of class and political systems rooted in colonialism.[6] Timothy Longman (2002), in his contribution to the October 2002 "Responding to Violence" conference at Barnard College (on which the current volume is based), argues that instead of focusing on ethnicity, we should look to the Rwandan state as the source of the problem. Longman argues that the problems that induced the genocide were political in nature. Ethnicity was not the cause of this violence. Instead, ethnicity was presented by the state as the solution to political problems that the country faced. The Hutu-dominated state presented the genocide—and forced many citizens to participate in the killing—with the rationale that the eradication of Tutsi would put an end to struggles over economic resources and political power. If the state can be the generating force for such tremendous violence, only an empowered civil society—one less subject to the manipulations of the state—can serve as the basis for rebuilding society in a manner that will prevent history from repeating itself. Thus, Longman argues that we should not focus on ethnicity or fear civil society in trying to rebuild Rwandan society.

This dynamic, in which ethnic or religious differences, conflict, and violence are offered by states as solutions to political problems, is not restricted to Rwanda alone. We see it, in part, in Sri Lanka—hence Daniel's concern about what happens when a conflict gets *named* as religious. The conflict may not be religious in origin, yet naming it as a religious conflict or as a matter of religious differences may both intensify the conflict and obscure its origins so as to make it more intractable. And we can see this in the United States, where as much as officials may say that the current U.S. wars are not against Islam, the public discourse certainly focuses on Islam as a source of the problem. Given the lack of hard evidence to tie Saddam Hussein to al Qaeda, how much legitimacy was added to claims of Iraqi responsibility by the fact that, despite its secular government, Iraq is a predominantly Muslim country?

This is not to get religion off the hook; religion is not just a front for something that is "really" political. But it is to say that we have to look to the secular state—the supposed purveyor of peace—as a major source of violence. And it is to say that the solutions to this violence are not necessarily an extension of secularism. An end to religious discourse will not necessarily bring about an end to violence. We are more likely to find sources for peace in changes in the political relations that encourage both state-based and religiously based violence.

While there are currently many arguments about whether the state is becoming less important in this age of globalization, we still need to take the state—and its capacity for violence—seriously. It is true that terrorist organizations like al Qaeda are nongovernmental organizations, and they may represent the wave of the future. But, are these nongovernmental (often religious) actors more violent than (secular) states? If we are asking a quantitative question, we must recognize that since the horrible day of September 11, 2001 we have witnessed a massive storm of governmental violence in relation to a smaller wave of terrorist attacks. In terms of numbers, we can have no doubt that more people have died in the wars in

Afghanistan and Iraq than in isolated terrorist attacks, and that many of these people have been civilians. And, we must remember that this last war was pre-emptive. If the question is one of quantity—of "less" and "more"—we have to say that states, and modern secular states in particular, have the lock on "more." They have the weapons, and they use them.

More importantly, the progress narrative, including the assertion that secularism is less violent than religion, obscures these facts. The narrative that secularism is less violent than religion makes state violence look necessary: If irrational religions produce intractable violence, the story goes, who else can protect us from it but the state? In addition, this narrative makes state-based violence look nonviolent—like peace—or at least like a road to peace. But my analysis suggests that violence generated by the state is not a road to peace, but a road to more violence. And this increasing cycle of violence will probably include more religious violence in reaction to state actions. The point of this comparative analysis is not to excuse religiously based violence but to recognize that, if we hope to reduce the level of violence in the world, we must look at *all* the sources of violence.

This is why I have come to find it important to say that we must answer "no" to the question: Is the secular less violent than the religious? The answer "no" is not only true in quantitative terms; it is also important to assert "no" because the usual answer of "yes" is part of the discourse that produces, maintains, extends, and intensifies a cycle of violence. If we can stop this narrative—the one in which religion is always the problem and the secular state is always the answer—then we will have taken at least one step toward finding new solutions to the problem of violence in our times.

We cannot turn our backs on religious violence. We should not use our refusal of modern narratives and their violences to obscure the fact that religious violence is real—states don't just use religion to extend their violence. As Asad points out and Sullivan confirms, religion and secularism are intertwined, and they are intertwined specifically at the point of legitimating violence. The violence of the modern state, including that of the U.S. government in particular, is religious as well as secular. Those who blame the Bush administration's religiosity for its willingness to use violence are not all wrong. They just miss two points: We must also look at the political relations that are intertwined with this religiosity; and we must recognize that the problem is not simply limited to a single administration. Christianity has been a legitimating force in the use of violence throughout the history of the United States.

Thus, in the caveat—in the equivocal "yes" and "no" that forces us to look at multiple sources of violence—we may find our best hope for activism and intervention. We may be able to figure out when modern discourses of democracy and secularism contribute to peace and when they serve not to resolve our problems but to extend them. Perhaps with this knowledge we can seek to change the social relations that make violence so much a part of the modern world.

Notes

1. I would like to thank all of my students in this course for the seriousness and insight with which they engaged such difficult issues. I learned a great deal from them. I would also like to thank the audiences at both the Center for Women's and Gender Studies at the Graduate Center, City University of New York and at the Feminist, Gender, and Sexuality Studies program at Cornell University for their comments on earlier versions of this paper.

2. For a clear statement of this dominant media narrative, see Andrew Sullivan's 2001 essay in the *New York Times Magazine*, which I discuss at length below. The widespread acceptance of this dominant narrative is indicated by the fact that the letters to the editor published about Sullivan's essay were uniformly laudatory.

3. For an in-depth exploration of this history see Chaudhuri and Strobel 1992.

4. For a more extensive argument about secularism and the progress narrative see Jakobsen and Pellegrini 2000.

5. He ignores that fact that Locke was not interested in toleration among all religions or all possible religious beliefs, but was primarily concerned with relations among a dominant Protestantism and Protestant dissenters. He is ambivalent on the question of Catholicism and was very clear to exclude Jews. And, although the circle of those religions tolerated by a dominant Protestantism has expanded, if Sullivan can argue that we are engaged in an epic struggle, an argument that implies military action that extends beyond arresting the particular people who committed these heinous crimes, because Christian and Muslim history differ, how far removed are we from the widely criticized and obviously intolerant comments of the Italian prime minister that Christian civilization is superior? (See Associated Press 2001.) For more on the contrast between this type of hierarchical religious tolerance and religious freedom see Jakobsen and Pellegrini 2003.

6. For a synopsis of this history see Mamdani 2001.

Works Cited

Asad, Talal. 1993. *Genealogies of Religion: Discipline and Reasons of Power in Christianity and Islam.* Baltimore: Johns Hopkins University Press.

Associated Press. 2001. "Italian Leader Says West Can 'Conquer' Islam." *Washington Post*, September 26, A15.

Beck, Linda. 2002. "Beyond Peace Marches: Women and Conflict Resolution (in Senegal)." Public Lecture. Barnard College. New York.

Bromley, David and J. Gordon Melton. 2002. *Cults, Religion, and Violence.* Cambridge: Cambridge University Press.

Chaudhuri, Nupur and Margaret Strobel. 1992. *Women and Western Imperialism: Complicity and Resistance.* Bloomington: Indiana University Press.

Daniel, E. Valentine. 1996. *Charred Lullabies: Chapters in an Anthropography of Violence.* Princeton: Princeton University Press.

Jakobsen, Janet R. and Ann Pellegrini. 2003. *Love the Sin: Sexual Regulation and the Limits of Religious Tolerance.* New York: New York University Press.

Jakobsen, Janet R., with Ann Pellegrini. 2000. "Introduction: World Secularisms at the Millennium." *Social Text* 64: 1–27.

Longman, Timothy. 2002. "State, Society, and Violence." Responding to Violence Conference. Barnard College. New York. October. http://www.barnard.edu/bcrw/respondingtoviolence/longman.htm

Mamdani, Mahmood. 2001. *When Victims Become Killers: Colonialism, Nativism, and the Genocide in Rwanda.* Princeton: Princeton University Press.

Mastnak, Tomaž. 2002. *Crusading Peace: Christendom, the Muslim World, and Western Political Order.* Berkeley: University of California Press.

Sullivan, Andrew. 2001. "This *Is* a Religious War." *New York Times Magazine,* October 7: 44–53.

Part II

Violence and the U.S. Political Regime

Chapter 8

Biblical Promise and Threat in U.S. Imperialist Rhetoric, Before and After 9/11[1]

Erin Runions

Given that conservative Protestantism is all too apparently alive and well in the United States, it may be prudent to consider how common interpretations of the Bible become part of the political calculus. Many people on the Left bemoan the Christian Right without paying attention to precisely how biblical interpretations get incorporated into right-wing discourse, and what recognizing biblical influence on politics might mean for engaging bellicose, imperialist rhetoric such as that of the younger Bush administration. In other words, I am urging consideration of the way in which the primacy of the Bible—particularly, belief in the absolute, inerrant truth and authority of the Bible, and adherence to "fundamentals" of the faith therein—affects policy and military decisions on the part of government, and acceptance of those decisions by the American people. The public's response to the U.S. wars since 9/11 may be affected by the overlap between longstanding, biblically inflected, national discourses on the one hand, and personalized understandings of the Bible popular in conservative Protestant circles on the other.

My point is to think about how the language of the Bush administration cleverly accesses congealed past discourses in its sacred posturing,[2] bringing the national past and the individual present together in securing support for war. The convergence of national and personal religious language prompts people to understand themselves and their nation through scriptural images—such as Israel entering the promised land—so that expansionist positions appear divinely ordained and therefore incontestable. In my view, the emotional and political force of such religious identifications should not be underestimated, even when the connections to contemporary politics are not always conscious or made explicit. These kinds of identifications form the framework in which events are understood, and they give spiritual pitch (and therefore emotional weight) to people's political convictions. Further, as I will discuss here, the power of biblical language in the United States increases exponentially when it intersects with prevalent understandings of gender and of the U.S. role in the world. In this essay I examine how biblical tropes of covenant (the promise of the land and blessing) and apocalypse (the internal and external threat of evil against that promise) are mobilized in the support of aggressive foreign policy, and how the gendering of these tropes may subtly affect the public's response to military aggression.

As scholars of religion and American history have repeatedly shown, American national identity has been shaped by the biblical language chosen by the first settlers, leaders, and preachers to emphasize both covenant and apocalypse. Of particular appeal to early Americans—from the Puritans to the architects of the American constitution—was the text of Deuteronomy, outlining the covenant between God and Israel (Conner 2002; Lutz 1988; Lutz 1992, 136). The Deuteronomic covenant provided a hopeful and motivating narrative upon which to model a perceived calling in the world and a relationship to God. For instance, as sociologist of religion Robert Bellah recalls in his study of covenant and the American myth of origin, the Puritans who were to form the Massachusetts Bay Colony had already forged an "agreement" between each other and God before they departed England for the new world (1975, 15–16). Covenant became the template for documenting and justifying communal decisions.

Like the Israelites, early Americans understood themselves to be entering into the Promised Land. Following the covenantal pattern outlined in Deuteronomy of prescribed moral and legal obligations to be kept by the people of Israel in return for God's blessing, the settlers understood themselves to be obligated to do God's will in return for God's blessings. The threat within both Deuteronomic and American covenantal thinking lay in the prospect of divine punishment for breaking covenant. Bellah points to John Winthrop's oft-cited sermon "A Model of Christian Charity" as a prototypical instance in early covenantal thinking, strongly influenced by Deuteronomy. Given while still aboard ship in 1630, Winthrop's sermon urged the people to live according to God's will, in order that the "city on the hill" might prosper. Patterning his sermon along the biblical lines of promise of blessings for kept covenant and curses for broken covenant, Winthrop suggested that if the people kept their side of the covenant with God, they would be blessed, but if covenant were broken, they would be punished (Bellah 1975, 13–15; Bercovitch 1983, 221–22; Ingebretsen 1996, 11–12). Thus, Winthrop's covenantal exhortation was accompanied by the warning, "But if our hearts shall turn away so that we will not obey, but shall be seduced and worship . . . other Gods, our pleasures, and profits, and serve them; it is propounded unto us this day, we shall surely perish out of the good land wither we pass over this vast sea to possess it" (cited in Bellah 1975, 15).

The Puritans and their covenantal documents have had a lasting influence on American political life. As Sacvan Bercovitch, scholar of American literature, puts it, "Their influence appears most clearly in the extraordinary persistence of a rhetoric grounded in the Bible, and in the way that Americans keep returning to that rhetoric, especially in times of crisis, as a source of cohesion and continuity" (1983, 219). Some scholars have gone as far as to argue that the covenantal model was foundational for American political theory and practice (see Elazar 1995; Elazar and Kincaid 1980).[3] Political scientist Donald Lutz makes the argument that many of the early documents of the settlements prefigure the constitution in their covenantal nature, even where they were not specifically named as covenants (1980, 1990a, 1990b). Bellah shows that the idea of covenant between America and God persisted even once church and state were officially separated, with covenantal thinking manifesting itself in presidents' speeches in what Bellah calls the tradition of American civil religion. Presidents from Jefferson to Reagan have drawn on the analogy between the United States and Israel to affirm the status of the United States as the chosen people of God. The United States has consistently been described as the new Israel, divinely appointed by God to bring light to the nations (Bercovitch 1983, 221–24; Bellah 1970, 175).

Within the tradition of American civil religion, the United States takes on a messianic role with respect to the rest of the world. From the mid-nineteenth century on, national self-understanding includes the notion of a special mission, a "manifest destiny," to lead all humanity toward civilization and progress (Stephanson 1995, xii–xiv). Professor of American studies Amy Kaplan suggests that it is precisely this understanding of the mission to save the world from various dangerous aggressions and dictators that grounds the notion of American exceptionalism. As long as the United States can present itself as safeguarding freedom for the world, its own pretensions to empire can be ignored. As Kaplan puts it, "imperial politics denied at home are visibly projected onto demonic others abroad, as something only they do and we do not" (1993, 13).

Covenantal thinking in early America was accompanied by an apocalyptic narrative. The Hebraic fear of curses for breaking covenant was amplified in the Christian context of the settlements by apocalyptic thinking about sin and judgment, as found in the New Testament. In the apocalyptic narrative that grew up around New Testament texts such as Matthew 24, Mark 13, and the book of Revelation, time is suddenly interrupted by the return of Christ and the judgment of all people who are divided between eternal reward and eternal punishment (i.e., heaven and hell). Apocalypse becomes the guarantor of covenant, providing the vivid imagery of the everlasting consequences for keeping or breaking covenant. So while entry into the Americas was understood as the reward of paradise, a new world, a new order (Bercovitch 1983, 222–24), this promise was not without an accompanying threat of evil that might disrupt this utopic trajectory.

As scholar of American literature Edward Ingebretsen (1996) has suggested—and his work is foundational to my argument here—the Puritan settlers' calling as divinely favored was accompanied by an apocalyptic belief that evil might at any moment creep in, steal all the things held most dear, and destroy the community. Sin was warned against as that which might destroy not only the present communal life, but also the individual's future afterlife. Early Americans were constantly reminded that hell and all forms of evil threatened to intrude at any moment, and of individual susceptibility to entertaining evil. For the Puritans and their successors, Ingebretsen argues, a most terrifying aspect of evil was its ability to creep into the lives of individuals or their neighbors; thus constant guard was kept against it. Interior scrutiny formed good citizens, whose good behavior banished evil and fear. He suggests that many times this scrutiny bled into real life, generating suspicion of anyone or anything different (1996, 21–28).[4] Here early preachers like Cotton Mather or Jonathan Edwards were instrumental in shaping consciousness of the invisible world and the ever-present threat of fire and brimstone. The threat of smoldering otherworldly punishment for moral corruption was even dramatized, in the case of the Salem witch hunts, in the burning of heretics.[5]

Ingebretsen highlights the colonial context in which apocalyptic thought shored up a covenantal "right" to the land. The threat of individual sinfulness to the covenant was amplified by the evil already residing in the land. In Ingebretsen's words, "the agents of imagined [moral] decline were many—and the Indians, those 'swarthy demons,' were always on hand as potential scapegoats to channel this negative energy" (1996, 21). Within this context, captivity stories of literal and spiritual bondage flourished, reminding settlers of the aboriginal people who seemed to threaten the nation's destiny (1996, 22–27). Yet, clearly the aboriginal peoples were more than just scapegoats. As historian Anders Stephanson shows, early Americans viewed the elimination of aboriginal peoples and the acquisition of new territory as an affirmation of their divine calling to bring civilization and progress to the world. He gives as early examples Winthrop's assessment of the smallpox epidemic among aboriginal peoples as "miraculous plagey," and Benjamin Franklin's assessment of rum as "'the appointed means' by which 'the design of Providence to extirpate these savages' was fulfilled 'in order to make room for the cultivators of the earth'" (1995, 11). The genocide of aboriginal people was justified through analogy to the biblical promise of Israelite victory over the original Canaanite inhabitants of the promised land who, like the aboriginal people of the Americas, were understood as idolatrous, seductive, and covenant-threatening (Warrior 1991, Donaldson 1996, Bercovitch 1983). In a Christian apocalyptic context, conquest of the land's inhabitants was also seen as victory over cosmic forces of evil.

Ingebretsen's work shows the longstanding connection between the expansion of borders by banishing external threats and the reinforcement of borders through scrutiny of individual moral shortcomings. Captivity stories, with their thematics of external threat and deliverance, fed more general apocalyptic anxieties about something lurking internally, needing to be caught, uncovered, scrutinized, banished. Ingebretsen goes on to show that apocalyptic fear has remained a politically productive part of the cultural imagination of the nation for centuries. He argues that fear has been both created and managed through religious confessions, devout obsessions with apocalyptic end times and judgments, and in secularized versions through gothic and science-fiction horror stories and films. In his words, "without obvious force or coercive violence, a mythologized religious framework . . . controls without seeming to control; shapes a political order while seemingly indifferent to shape" (1996, 201).

Ingebretsen's description of the controlling functions of apocalyptic thought points to the relationship, to which I will return presently, between an externalized fear of the Other and an internalized shame, working together in the imperialist project of expanding borders and maintaining control of those within them.[6] Biblically inflected national discourse, along with attendant hopes and fears, has persisted, perhaps because apocalyptic and covenantal images are expedient both in motivating governments' foreign-relations policy and action and in enforcing compliant behavior at home. Not only have these discourses consistently authorized colonialism in general[7] and American acquisition of territory and resources in particular, but at the same time they impart an aura of familiarity, historicity, and moral authority, to which much of the population is sure to submit.

Like prior national leaders, George W. Bush, his speechwriters, and members of his administration tap deeply familiar biblical images in the rhetoric motivating various military tactics. The position taken by the Bush administration with respect to the rest of the world clearly falls within the tradition of covenantal, messianic chosenness by God. In his speech on the first anniversary of 9/11, Bush was able to make the same claim about the United States that the writer of John's gospel makes about Christ: "America is the hope of all mankind. . . . That hope lights our way. And the light shines in the darkness. And the darkness will not overcome it" (Bush 2002b).[8] In the happy marriage of covenant and apocalypse, the impinging darkness must be fought. The light of the world requires darkness, in order to vanquish it. Throughout the Bush administration's rhetoric, the United States is described as using its military strength in the role of fulfilling, and ensuring, certain moral obligations for the rest of humanity, thus (both apocalyptically and paradoxically) creating a "new era" of peace and justice. To give but one example, the September 2002 *National Security Strategy,* known best for advocating "pre-emptive strikes," claims that the U.S. duty is "to help make the world not just safer but better" (White House 2002, 1) and to "defend liberty and justice because these principles are right and true for all people everywhere" (White House 2002, 2). Here the United States polices "universal" moral obligation for the world. The rhetoric recalls the longstanding tradition of manifest destiny in U.S. nationalism that, as Stephanson argues, "constitut[es] itself not only as prophetic but also universal" (1995, xiii).

In the 2002 *National Security Strategy,* and throughout Bush's speeches, the United States is apocalyptically chosen by "history" to fulfill its calling in the world. As scholar of religion Elizabeth Castelli observes (2003), in the 9/11 anniversary speech, history actually converges with God. Castelli's observation can be extended to the rest of the discourses produced by the Bush administration: Throughout their documents "history" seems to be a thinly veiled, secular substitution for "God."[9] History chooses the United States to lead the world to safety (resulting, of course, from enforced moral conformity): "History has called our nation into action. History has placed a great challenge before us: Will America—with our unique position and power—blink in the face of terror, or will we lead to a freer, more civilized world? There is only one answer: This great country will lead the world to safety, security, peace and freedom" (Bush 2002a). The rhetoric is well crafted. It is, to many minds, as Castelli names it, an "unsettling juxtaposition of nationalism and theological determinism," but its purpose is, of course, to settle the matter. There is a certain inexorability in having been chosen: "We" (and here individual members of the population are interpellated into a single national mind) must not refuse the call of history/God, "we" must only accept.

The cosmic duty of the chosen nation is, as the fight with "darkness" and terror suggests, accompanied in this rhetoric by the urgency of cosmic battle with evil itself. The current rhetoric provoking fear of terrorism seems clearly to be rooted in the apocalyptic heritage of the nation. The language used by Bush, of terrorists in their caves and hiding places, evokes the image of lurking evil threatening the nation at every turn. The evil terrorists are those who (like Satan, presumably) "seek to master the minds and souls of others," over and against which stand "the defenders of human liberty" (2002b). Evil is fearful precisely because of its ambitious, murderous irrationality: "Our greatest fear is that terrorists will find a shortcut to their mad ambitions when an outlaw regime supplies them with the technologies to kill on a massive scale" (2002c).[10] Thus, the rooting out of "hidden evil" and "mad ambition" makes palatable rhetoric that continually demands scrutiny, as for example in the weapons inspection in Iraq.

Moreover, within the discourse of the Bush administration, external threats are portrayed as having infiltrated the borders of the nation, thus motivating the need for increased internal scrutiny. Fear of "evil among us" ensures acquiescence with a demand for intensified domestic policing. Many proposals, both formal and informal, go uncontested, encouraging people to watch for and report anything suspicious, in short, to spy on their neighbors. Such an apocalyptic fear of an internal hidden threat clearly grounds and justifies the disappearances of those who look Arab, Muslim, or South Asian in the United States after 9/11. The Patriot Act allows individual's (mainly people of color's) rights to be suppressed in the name of exposing perceived hidden threats.

And to turn the eye to gender for a moment, perhaps the U.S. impulse to save the world from hidden threat is somewhere at work behind the sudden urge to save Afghan women from the veil.[11] Here gender is the site on which imperialist, apocalyptic, and covenantal discourses converge. Postcolonial feminist critics point out how the discourse of protection harms Afghan and Muslim women. Lila Abu-Lughod, on the panel "Responding to War," convened at Columbia University shortly after 9/11, suggested that the rhetoric of liberating Afghan women was just one more case—in Gayatri Spivak's words (1988)—of white men trying to save brown women from brown men. Taking this postcolonial critique as a premise, I would like briefly to consider the rhetoric whereby white men both assume savior complexes and use the fear of hidden threats to assure public support. To be very clear, I am in no way arguing that Afghan women should not have self-determination. But I am suspicious that the American will to "free them" is consistent with the rest of the apocalyptic and covenantal discourses being mobilized, and therefore operates from a base of fear and misogyny.

Evidently, the trope of rescuing women has played a major role in shutting down resistance to the attacks on Afghanistan, even though it has been well recognized that the discourse of saving women is only a front for ongoing U.S. military activity in that country. The urgent need to rescue Afghan women is successful as a front because it necessarily interacts with many other of the discourses on war with pretensions to "saving." As a front, however, it plays the important rhetorical role of tapping into the senses of inexorability and urgency that the prevalent apocalyptic and covenantal discourses carry. There is an urgency to "do something" to save the women of Afghanistan from the evil that they face. The "something" that is accepted as the only option is American military aggression because it fulfills expectations about the U.S. saving role in the world.

I wonder, though, whether the ready acceptance of this mission to save Afghan women has also to do with the apocalyptic underside of the U.S. covenantal savior complex. Misogynist portrayals of female sexuality through apocalyptic imagery have in the past been used as motivations and justifications for the subjugation of women (as internal and external threats) in colonial contexts. Fear of women's "secret" powers are typified by apocalyptic figures such as the Whore of Babylon (Revelation 17–18), and her more "secreted" latter-day Wiccan offspring, whose evil was "exposed" in the Salem witch hunts (Vander Stichele 2000; Pippin 1999; Ingebretsen 1996). Professor of English Mary Wilson Carpenter (1995) has suggested that the fear of women demonstrated by misogynist tropes in apocalyptic discourse bolsters male homosocial utopic visions such as the apocalyptic vision of finding, conquering, and controlling new, "heavenly" lands (see also Pippin 1999; Keller 1996; Quinby 1994). Along these lines, religious studies scholar Catherine Keller draws the connections between Columbus' apocalyptic vision of the new world, his description of the new world as a woman's nipple, and the corollary violation of the new world's women and children.[12]

In other words, the fear and subsequent violation of women's chosen mode of comportment is a theme familiar to feminist critics of the colonial uses of apocalyptic language. Certainly, the "freeing" of women has justified homosocial conquest after 9/11. Is there anything more homosocial than the father-son war competition? As Castelli suggests with characteristic acumen, "It is perhaps not incidental that the efforts of Bush-the-Son since September 11 have had a decidedly Oedipal cast. One doesn't need to be Freud or Fellini to understand Bush-the-Son's assertion that *his* war will be bigger and longer than his father's" (2003). But beyond justifying the war and saving brown women from brown men, the United States has also "saved" the world from a mode of dress—one which hides women's bodies from prying eyes—distinct from that prescribed by "universal" values. In a talk given in New York City in March of 2002, on a panel sponsored by War Is Not the Answer, feminist academic and activist Silvia Federici made the point that there may be *a fear of veiled women as the Other* operating in the demand to free Afghan women (Federici 2002). Federici derived her argument from Franz Fanon's suggestion that the French were concerned about Algerian women unveiling, not because they cared about women's freedom, but because it inhibited their proprietal gaze. If, on some level, a perceived *threat* of veiled women influenced the public's acceptance of the bombing of Afghanistan, it was a perception consistent with apocalyptic misogyny.

It is not enough, however, to show that biblical subtexts are at work in describing and justifying U.S. imperialism in the name of protection.[13] It is crucial to explore the way in which biblical images in political discourse are able to interact with a substantial portion of the population's faith commitments. Not only do images of promise and threat recall familiar, historical, nation-building language, but they also gain strength by connecting with personal piety and individualized ways of reading the Bible. Biblically based national rhetoric easily becomes personalized truth. Indeed, biblically infused rhetoric is effective precisely because it can blur the lines between individuals' identities as Christians and their identities as citizens of the United States. American civil religion is not explicitly Christian, as Bellah points out (1970, 175); the analogy, however, between the United States and Israel that serves as its rallying point was evidently born out of Christian beliefs, and continues readily to accommodate, even invite, Christian interpretations. Christians are able to identify with Israel, through the equivalence that has been drawn by early Christian writers, as well as contemporary theologians, between the "old" Deuteronomic covenant, and the "new" covenant inaugurated by Christ. Like Israel under the "old covenant," the individual member of the Church under the "new covenant" is understood to be chosen and redeemed by God. Many Christians consider themselves part of the new, spiritual, Israel by virtue of accepting their part in the new covenant. Such an identity can easily be conflated with membership in a nation that is also the "new Israel," in the slightly different sense of inheritor of the Promised Land.

Such a conflation of spiritual and political identity takes on new gravity for any persons who also subject themselves to moral scrutiny in keeping with the demands of their faith. In conservative Protestant circles especially, redemption is thought to bring with it a personal relationship with Christ in which all aspects of life and decision making are submitted to Christ for approval and help, through prayer and study of the scripture. In this view, individuals (members *and* citizens of the new Israel) must also always seek to do God's will, in accordance with scripture. And yet, for individual Americans "to do God's will" in the world of foreign affairs, they must necessarily rely on national leaders; they must follow, or oppose, those leaders as their conscience and reading of scripture leads them. If then, the president also prays and submits his decisions to the will of Christ, as George W. claims to do (Fineman 2003), the identification between Christian leader and Christian individual is made all the more easily.[14] Indeed, the President's claim to an intimate relationship with Christ makes it possible and likely for the American Christian who strives to be Christ-like to go beyond simply identifying as a member of the new (spiritual/national) Israel, to identifying with its leader (Christ/Bush) as well.

The importance of moral scrutiny, both before and after the individual's choice to accept the new, Christian covenant is amplified by apocalyptic thinking. Thousands of American Christians avidly await the "rapture," the sudden return of Christ and the ascension of true believers into the heavens, as made manifest by the popularity of the fictional representation of that drama in the *Left Behind* series.[15] The preponderance of Internet sites devoted to the rapture attests to the activity of the apocalyptically minded faithful in scrutinizing current events as indicators of the proximity of the end times. Because the final return of Christ is expected imminently, cutting short any time remaining before the final reckoning, apocalyptic thought is accompanied by a sense of urgency, a sense that moral decisions must be made and that lives must be staked upon those decisions. Action—to root out evil and avoid destruction—must be taken. The suddenness of the rapture is, as ever, used as a leverage point for encouraging conversion or rededication to the Christian life.

Personal apocalyptic belief can, therefore, quickly become conflated with national discourses, when evils to be guarded against suddenly appear—on television and confirmed by the president—in the form of Middle Eastern dictators. Fear of moral ill quickly moves from interior shame to external threat. National moral obligation becomes of utmost importance. And as recent presidents have so aptly modeled, personal moral shame is quickly exonerated by national banishment of external fears.

As a strange counterbalance to the sense of urgency imparted by apocalyptic need to combat evil, however, there is a certain strand of predestination in much of contemporary apocalyptic thinking. God's unchangeable plan is fully prescribed and described in scripture; the Christian's job is simply to understand God's plan as it unfolds and to be ready for the end. In the Reverend Jerry Falwell's assessment, "It is impossible to stop the march of prophecy" (1999, 273). There is, therefore, a certain fatalistic compliance embedded within the exigency of apocalypse. In more extreme representations of this viewpoint, the prophecies of the Hebrew Bible, in particular, are scrutinized for their possible fulfillment in today's world. So, for instance, multiple Internet sites interpret Iraq as the modern-day geographic and moral equivalent of ancient Babylon: "The anti-christ will get into war with Egypt, and take the spoils back to Iraq (Daniel 11:25). They will try to settle things; have peace talks. . . . He will come against Egypt again. In Daniel 11:30, it says the ships of Chittim, the U.S., shall come against him. He shall be grieved and return, and have indignation against the Holy covenant" (Rogers 2003).[16] In these literalist apocalyptic readings, world events turn around a third "Israel," the actual "holy land" which must be restored in some way before Christ is to return. God's plan as dictated by the Hebrew prophets, therefore, entails the convergence of all three Israels—geographic, spiritual, and national (i.e., the United States)—providing the perfect and uncontestable rationale (within this logic) for U.S. involvement in the Middle East.[17]

In more allegorical readings of scripture, God's plan for the future can be understood on the level of analogy between a biblical character and a reader, as can be seen in the autobiography of George W. Bush, where he likens his call to national leadership to that of Moses's call to lead the children of Israel (1999, 8–9). Bush is challenged to accept the call in a sermon, which begins with the need to "spend" and "consume" time immediately and responsibly, before it runs out (1999, 2). Here, clearly, the covenantal notion of divine calling joins with an apocalyptic understanding of the necessity to fulfill that calling before it is too late. When the demand for (personal and national) submission to God's unchanging plan is combined with expectation of the sudden end, the outcome is pressing conformism. The president must adhere to God's "plan," and so, therefore, must the people.

In short, these twin discourses of covenant and apocalypse have produced a national identity in which the nation's actions in the world are seen as inexorably urgent. Because the United States understands itself as a nation chosen and commanded by God, its path seems singular and unalterable (at least if the nation is to fulfill its covenantal obligation). But its task, because it functions on both human and cosmic levels, is of the utmost exigence. The future, not only of the United States, but of the world hangs in the balance. For the conservative Protestant Christian especially, this language resonates at a personal level with the urgent need to fight evil, internal and external, in order to prepare for the return of Christ. What works so effectively in Bush's rhetoric is that although it does not really stray too far, as Fred Barnes of the *Weekly Standard* points out (2003), from the mainstream confines of civil religion, it takes on a greater significance within the interpretive traditions of conservative Protestantism, to which much of the population adheres, and with which Bush's personal commitment to Christ corresponds.

There may also be other, subtler, factors at work in the public's favorable response to the Bush administration's rhetoric, only one of which I am able to touch on here. I am interested in how prevalent understandings of gender roles become part of the equation when covenantal and apocalyptic national discourses are integrated into a particular faith perspective and taken to heart as personal truth. For example, contemporary conservative *and* mainstream readings of biblical covenant are often imbued with a heteronormative understanding of gender. In other words, these biblically based discourses contain an embedded conceptualization of gender as a binary set of heterosexual relations and distinctions (Butler 1993), which, in the present context, idealizes masculinity as heroic and active, and femininity as receptive and maternal. Interpreted through this kind of thinking about gender roles, the covenantal and apocalyptic rhetoric of war is made to appear, like gender, as "natural."

Culpability for this gendered reading of covenant lies in part with the Hebrew prophets, who more than once depict Israel as an unfaithful woman in need of rescue. The prophets consistently chastise Israel for breaking covenant, taking political matters into her own hands (described as sexual infidelity), and suffering for it; if only she would leave things up to her male leaders (Yahweh and his approved king). Contemporary interpreters amplify this image of Israel by reading prophetic texts through gender stereotypes even when the Hebrew constructions are difficult, unclear, or ambiguous.[18] Some contemporary versions of this story, built from prophetic texts such as Ezekiel and Hosea, build a whole theology around Israel, the unfaithful-wife-turned-prostitute, who must be reclaimed by Yahweh. The title of Raymond Ortlund's book *Whoredom: God's Unfaithful Wife in Biblical Theology* (1996) speaks volumes about the way that this image can get taken up in contemporary interpretations. Thus, in biblical scholarship and in writing for lay people, Israel is commonly described as a damsel in distress (the distress is of course her fault for sleeping with the enemy), who must wait to be rescued by Yahweh or his divinely appointed ruler.

This language of gender in the prophetic writing and its interpretation dovetails with a particular kind of biblical colonial discourse. The hope for rescue of Israel from her sexualized sin takes the form of expectation that she will be *led* into *triumph over*—as opposed to *alliance with*—other nations. Israel is instructed by God, some interpreters insist, that she must not work in any way on her own terms, for to do so would be a grave sin. This gendered depiction of Israel's hope for political dominance both condones Israel's colonial aspirations but disavows responsibility for them at the same time. Israel's active, aggressive colonialism of surrounding nations is disavowed by the story of a more passive, ladylike colonialism, in which Israel must be chastised and then led into domination by the divinely appointed (masculine) ruler, who does only Yahweh's bidding. Israel is not to take the initiative, credit, or blame for her colonialism. She is merely a conduit for Yahweh's will; she is not responsible for these conquests, rather, Yahweh is.[19]

When the gendered biblical narrative is transposed into the present, it also takes on an apocalyptic quality. In the prophetic narrative, Israel's suffering, when it occurs, is her own fault; it is the consequence for breaking covenant. Here the trope of the sexually sinful woman is a connection point between the two discourses that is easily exploited by rhetoricians. As a backslidden "harlot" the spiritual/national Israel paradoxically becomes, for politically minded evangelists like Pat Robertson, her own mortal enemy, the apocalyptic Whore of Babylon. Says Robertson in an interview, "I frankly think that the United States of America stands on the brink of really terrible judgment. . . . America is like Babylon, the Mother of Harlots. So that is cause, in my opinion for a righteous God to bring His wrath against us" (1999, 258). With an apocalyptic understanding of the new covenant framing the image of the United States, the negative consequences for covenant breaking through sexual transgression (metaphoric and literal) are of a cosmic order.

Such divine wrath upon the sinful woman, America, was evident to Roberston's friend Falwell in the events of 9/11. It is Falwell's belief that "the Abrahamic covenant—the promise that God gave to Abraham that he would bless those who blessed him and curse those who cursed him—is a fundamental ethic for the success of any society" (1999, 284). Such an interpretation of national ethics undoubtedly led him—on Robertson's *700*

Club television show, two days after the towers fell—infamously to attribute
9/11 to a God angry with those who, to Falwell's mind, broke covenant.
Notable in Falwell's accusation of "the pagans, and the abortionists, and the
feminists, and the gays and the lesbians" was his attempt to shame alternative forms of gender expression and sexual identity. A fear of contravened
gender roles thus manifests itself through an apocalyptic interpretation of
covenant.

But importantly, within both old and new covenantal frameworks,
punishment for sexual deviance is a precursor to repentance, forgiveness,
and triumph. The only acceptable response following national disaster,
within this logic, is to wait passively to be led into dominion over other
nations by Yahweh. American international triumph—as in the devastation
of Afghanistan or the deposing of Saddam Hussein—can be seen as a sign of
God's favor.

If—and here I am only sketching an idea—this rather dominant interpretation of the prophetic view of Israel becomes conflated with the Israel of
American civil religion, then those who put their stock in the image of the
United States as Israel might identify (even unconsciously) with an image of
the shameful, feminine, passive people of God. If so, they would be
positioned to do nothing in the face of their nation's imperialist mission, in
fact, to welcome it as God's favor, and to feel no responsibility for it, since it
must all be left to God. Insofar as such identifications might be operating in
the American populace, however, they work in complicated ways, because
as I have suggested above, identification as the people of God can move
toward an identification with a messianic figure (divinely appointed leader).
So on one hand, American people, identifying as the feminized people of
God, feel it is not up to them to do anything one way or another, as they
ought to be passive. And on the other hand, a self-styled divinely appointed
leader and his armed forces do the masculine work of rescuing the United
States, the world, and Afghan women from "evil men," at the same time
achieving control over other nations.[20] With the strange sort of cross-
identification that goes on between Israel and God, the U.S. population and
its president, an apathetic authorization of imperialism sets in. Though the
call to aid the rest of the world must be heeded, it is well enough to leave it up
to the president to heed it. People passively wait for the president in their role
as damsel in distress, but at the same time they feel that it is they who are
avenging 9/11, or helping Afghan women, or oppressed Iraqis, in their
identity as divine leader on the world scene.

Now, as in the past, apocalypse and covenant have been represented
through misogynist, gendered imageries which worked in tandem to authorize American dominance. Where apocalyptic language feeds a sense of
urgency with respect to national policies and military action, covenantal
understandings of American identity feed the public's willingness to go
along with the specifics of its government's actions. Even if the present
administration were not to be re-elected, the prevalence of biblically rooted
discourses in American culture and politics suggests that after a brief
remission these discourses would soon resurface, given their emotional and

spiritual currency. The question is, can this kind of deeply rooted rhetoric be effectively resisted? Though this essay is necessarily only one small contribution to what I hope is a larger collective project of strategizing resistance, it would point to thinking about how to dismantle conscious and unconscious identifications with misogynist biblical images and discourses that may create emotional attachments to political positions in favor of war. Of course, any such attempt must also take account of how attachments to biblical images and ideas work into positions of resistance.[21] Those who wish to engage the rhetoric of the United States as savior, judge, and harlot, must carefully and self-critically intercept these discourses. The challenge lies, perhaps, in creating a rhetoric and a discourse that counteracts any sense of purpose and entitlement to save a helpless world from evil.

Notes

1. Much of the analysis of the apocalyptic nature of the rhetoric discussed here was initially worked out in the preparation of an arrested piece of street theatre called "the burning bush," conceived with Michael Casey, Daniel Lang/ Levitsky, and Meredith Slopen. My development of these ideas has been greatly assisted through conversations with Elizabeth Castelli and Jennifer Glancy, and through the critical eyes, cast upon earlier drafts, of Michael Casey, Tanya Erzen, and Scott Kline.

2. To read a line or two with Guy Debord, the "sacred contemplation" with which the Bush administration shrouds itself promotes no less than "spectacular consumption which preserves congealed past culture" (1983 [1967], #25, #192). One of the most disturbing "missions" of the present administration—as proposed by the Project for the New American Century, a think tank whose statement of purpose is signed by Donald Rumsfeld, Dick Cheney, Jeb Bush, and Paul Wolfowitz, among others—is framed in the language of spectacle: "to fight and decisively win multiple simultaneous major theatre wars" (Donnelly 2000, iv).

3. For more tentative statements of the similarities between the biblical notion of covenant and the American Constitution, as well as American constitutional law, see Gaffney 1985, Riemer 1980.

4. Tina Pippin (1999, 2002), Stephen O'Leary (1994), and Lee Quinby (1994) have also shown how apocalypse forms a deeply seated layer within American culture.

5. Mather's tract *Wonders of the Invisible World* (1950 [1692]) also details his involvement with the Salem witch hunts.

6. The twinning of external threat and internal shame is something like introjection in Freud's description of melancholia; it is also similar to what Bhabha identifies in colonial and postcolonial contexts as the uncanny (*unheimlich*), i.e., the repressed fear of the Other, who uncannily reemerges as the stranger within, and who represents a shameful threat to internal order (i.e., homeland security), and must then be exposed (1994, 10, 166–67).

7. The covenantal/apocalyptic quest for a new land, and the apocalyptic rooting out of "evil" inhabitants and their practices, is very much a part of Western colonizing identity (see Keller 1996, Milhou 1999, Smolinski 1999). Daniel

Elazar argues (with no sense of irony) that "frontiersmen . . . that is to say, people who have gone out to settle new areas where there were no established patterns of governance . . . are to be found among the most active covenanters" (1980, 13). In short, covenant, apocalypse, and colonialism are habitual bedfellows.

8. For a brilliant reading of the apocalyptic logic of this citation, see Elizabeth Castelli (2003).

9. Tony Blair is also fond of deifying history. For instance, during his speech to the U.S. Congress, July 17, 2003, as reported in the BBC News, July 18, 2003, Blair made assertions about what history would forgive (being wrong about weapons of mass destruction in Iraq) and what it would not forgive (hesitation in the face of menace).

10. Putting this speech (Bush 2002c) together with the *National Security Strategy's* assertion that the United States is above the jurisdiction of the International Criminal Court (White House 2002, 31), and with the U.S. record of arms dealing, Bush seems to be acknowledging that the United States is the "outlaw regime" that provides "shortcuts to mad ambition." Such a blatant unconscious self-indictment is perhaps to be expected in such flamboyant accusation.

11. There is a large body of literature on the complex set of colonial and postcolonial relations behind the problem of a Western drive to "unveil" Muslim women, and on Muslim women's political and social agency in wearing the veil, with which I cannot engage within the scope of this essay. See for instance, Ahmed 1992; Sullivan 1998; Moghissi 1999; Moallem 1999, 2001; Hoodfar 2001.

12. For a critique of Keller's proposed alternatives to apocalyptic language, see Donaldson 2002.

13. Here my argument is informed by Moallem's discussion of the discourses of protection (1999). Moallem cites Pathak and Sunder Rajan, who observe that the service of protection "tends to efface the will to power exercised by the protector" (2001, 200).

14. Thanks to Tanya Erzen for this insight into the appeal of Bush's own commitment to those of faith. Along these lines, Gutterman gives an extensive analysis of the language Bush uses to describe his conversion experience in such a way as to transform his weaknesses, which might hinder political success, into "signifiers of divine strength" (2001, 31).

15. For analyses of the *Left Behind* series, and of other conservative Protestant writing, see the website *Proselytizing Media: Conservative Christian Media Encounters the World,* ed. Tanya Erzen, http://www.nyu.edu/fas/projects/vcb/ ChristianMedia. See also McAlister 2003.

16. See also A Voice in the Wilderness 2003.

17. For an entertaining account of Reagan's apocalypticism, see Vidal 1993; for a more theoretical discussion of Reagan's rhetoric, see O'Leary 1994.

18. For the way scholars reinscribe the misogyny of the prophets, see Exum 1996, 101–28.

19. Several examples of the gendering of colonial language in scholarly readings of the prophets can be taken from interpretations of the prophetic text of Micah. Delbert Hillers glosses the text of Micah (5:6–14)—in accounting for a strange poetic shift between Israel's aggression and defeat—as follows, "Israel's rights have already in the past been violated by other nations, but she cannot and should not avenge herself. Instead the supreme power will step in to vindicate her rights by punishing her adversaries" (1984, 73). Some scholars are so insistent on the point of Israel's feminine passivity that they gloss over aspects of

the text that do not quite bear out such a reading. For instance, in Micah 4:13, Zion is figured as an active, ambiguously gendered, colonizing force. Using language usually reserved for kings, Zion (modified by feminine verb forms) is depicted as having an iron horn (a rather phallic image) and copper hooves, trampling other nations. Yet scholars explain this active colonizing role away. For instance, Mays calls the image a later addition to the original prophecy, in order to amplify what he sees as the (colonial) purpose of the book: "a promise which looks *for the peoples [i.e. other nations] to be brought under the reign of YHWH* by the divine power of Israel" (1976, 109, emphasis mine). Wolff interprets likewise, "the 'daughter of Zion' herself becomes the agent of Yahweh's punishment of his enemies, but she is empowered and authorized to do this only by the word and deed of Yahweh" (1990 [1982], 133); so also McKane, "the defeat of the mighty nations by the daughter of Zion is a miracle wrought by Yahweh (v. 13) and cannot be accounted for by weight of armour" (1998, 12). For further detailed analysis, see Runions 2001, 182–209.

20. In my own experience after 9/11, in antiwar efforts to talk to people on the street, I was astounded by the number of people who were willing to trust the president, even when they were not sure that war on Afghanistan was the best solution.

21. For instance, the apocalyptic images of "the beast" and "the belly of the beast" are often invoked by the Left to speak of capitalism and its institutions.

Works Cited

Ahmed, Leila. 1992. *Women and Gender in Islam: Historical Roots of a Modern Debate*. New Haven: Yale University Press.

Barnes, Fred. 2003. "God and Man in the Oval Office." *Weekly Standard* 8(26) (March 17): 11–12.

Bellah, Robert N. 1970. *Beyond Belief: Essays on Religion in a Post Traditionalist World*. Berkeley: University of California Press.

Bellah, Robert N. 1975. *The Broken Covenant: American Civil Religion in Time of Trial*. Chicago: University of Chicago Press.

Bercovitch, Sacvan. 1983. "The Biblical Basis of the American Myth." In *The Bible and American Arts and Letters*, ed. Giles Gunn, 221–32. Philadelphia: Fortress; Chico, CA: Scholars.

Bhabha, Homi K. 1994. *The Location of Culture*. London: Routledge.

Bush, George W. 1999. *A Charge to Keep: My Journey to the White House*. New York: Perennial.

Bush, George W. 2002a. "Remarks by the President in Address to the Nation." Washington D.C., June 6. http://www.whitehouse.gov/news/releases/2002/06/20020606–8.html.

Bush, George W. 2002b. "President's Remarks to the Nation." Ellis Island, NY, September 11. http://www.whitehouse.gov/news/releases/2002/09/20020911–3.html.

Bush, George W. 2002c. "Remarks by the President in Address to the United Nations General Assembly." New York, NY. September 12. http://www.whitehouse.gov/news/releases/2002/09/20020912–1.html.

Butler, Judith. 1993. *Bodies That Matter: On the Discursive Limits of "Sex."* New York: Routledge.

Carpenter, Mary Wilson. 1995. "Representing Apocalypse: Sexual Politics and the Violence of Revelation." In *Postmodern Apocalypse: Theory and Cultural Practice at the End,* ed. Richard Dellamora, 107–35. Philadelphia: University of Philadelphia Press.

Castelli, Elizabeth A. 2003. "Globalization, Transnational Feminisms, and the Future of Biblical Critique." Paper presented at the conference The Global Future of Feminist New Testament Studies at Scripps College, Claremont, Calif. February 28.

Connor, George E. 2002. "Covenants and Criticism: Deuteronomy and the American Founding." *Biblical Theology Bulletin* 32(1): 4–10.

Debord, Guy. 1983 [1967]. *Society of the Spectacle.* Trans. Black and Red. Detroit: Black and Red.

Donaldson, Laura E. 1996. "Postcolonialism and Biblical Reading: An Introduction." *Semeia* 75: 1–14.

Donaldson, Laura E. 2002. "The Breast of Columbus: A Political Anatomy of Postcolonial and Feminist Religious Discourse." In *Postcolonialism, Feminism, and Religious Discourse,* ed. Laura E. Donaldson and Kwok Pui-lan, 41–61. New York: Routledge.

Donnelly, Thomas. 2000. *Rebuilding America's Defenses: Strategy, Forces and Resources for a New Century.* Washington, D.C.: Project for the New American Century. http://www.newamericancentury.org/Rebuilding AmericasDefenses.pdf

Elazar, Daniel J. 1980. "The Political Theory of Covenant: Biblical Origins and Modern Developments." *Publius: The Journal of Federalism* 10(4): 3–30.

Elazar, Daniel J. 1995. *Covenant and Polity in Biblical Israel: Biblical Foundations and Jewish Expressions.* Covenant Tradition in Politics 1. New Brunswick, NJ: Transaction.

Elazar, Daniel J., and John Kincaid, eds. 1980. *Covenant, Polity, and Constitutionalism.* Vol. 10(4) of *Publius: The Journal of Federalism.* Philadelphia: Center for the Study of Federalism.

Exum, J. Cheryl. 1996. *Plotted, Shot, and Painted: Cultural Representations of Biblical Women.* Journal for the Study of the Old Testament Supplement Series 215. Gender, Culture, Theory 3. Sheffield: Sheffield Academic Press.

Falwell, Jerry. 1999. Interview by Cal Thomas. In *Blinded by Might: Can the Religious Right Save America?* by Cal Thomas and Ed Dobson, 259–78. Grand Rapids, MI: Zondervan.

Federici, Silvia. 2002. Panel presentation, "Women and War." Judson Memorial Church. New York City. March 15.

Fineman, Howard. 2003. "Bush and God." *Newsweek* 141(10) (March 10): 22–30.

Gaffney, Edward McGlynn. 1985. "The Interaction of Biblical Religion and American Constitutional Law." In *The Bible in American Law, Politics, and Political Rhetoric,* ed. James Turner Johnson, 81–106. Philadelphia: Fortress; Chico, CA: Scholars.

Gutterman, David S. 2001. "Presidential Testimony: Listening to the Heart of George W. Bush." *Theory and Event* 5(2) http://muse.jhu.edu/journals/theory_and_event/v005/5.2gutterman.html.

Hillers, Delbert R. 1984. *Micah: A Commentary on the Book of the Prophet Micah.* Hermeneia. Philadelphia: Fortress.

Hoodfar, Homa. 2001. "The Veil in Their Minds and on Our Heads: Veiling Practices and Muslim Women." In *Women, Gender, Religion: A Reader,* ed.

Elizabeth A. Castelli with Rosamond C. Rodman, 420–46. New York: Palgrave.

Ingebretsen, Edward J. 1996. *Maps of Heaven, Maps of Hell: Religious Terror as Memory from the Puritans to Stephen King.* Armonk, N.Y.: M.E. Sharpe.

Kaplan, Amy. 1993. "'Left Alone with America': The Absence of Empire in the Study of American Culture." In *Cultures of United States Imperialism,* ed. Amy Kaplan and Donald E. Pease, 3–21. Durham, N.C.: Duke University Press.

Keller, Catherine. 1996. *Apocalypse Now and Then: A Feminist Guide to the End of the World.* Boston: Beacon.

Lutz, Donald S. 1980. "From Covenant to Constitution in American Political Thought." *Publius: The Journal of Federalism* 10(4): 101–34.

Lutz, Donald S. 1988. *The Origins of American Constitutionalism.* Baton Rouge: Louisiana State University Press.

Lutz, Donald S. 1990a. "The Mayflower Compact, 1620." In *The Roots of the Republic: American Founding Documents Interpreted,* ed. Stephen L. Schechter, 17–23. Madison, WI: Madison House.

Lutz, Donald S. 1990b. "The Declaration of Independence, 1776." In *The Roots of the Republic: American Founding Documents Interpreted,* ed. Stephen L. Schechter, 138–49. Madison, WI: Madison House.

Lutz, Donald S. 1992. *A Preface to American Political Theory.* Lawrence: University Press of Kansas.

Mather, Cotton. 1950 [1692]. *The Wonders of the Invisible World.* Mount Vernon, N.Y.: Peter Pauper.

Mays, James Luther. 1976. *Micah: A Commentary.* Old Testament Library. Philadelphia: Westminster.

McAlister, Melani. 2003. "Prophecy, Politics, and the Popular: The *Left Behind* Series and Christian Fundamentalism's New World Order." *South Atlantic Quarterly* 102: 773–98.

McKane, William. 1998. *The Book of Micah: Introduction and Commentary.* Edinburgh: T and T Clark.

Milhou, Alain. 1999. "Apocalypticism in Central and South American Colonialism." In Vol. 3 of *The Encyclopedia of Apocalypticism,* ed. Stephen J. Stein. *Apocalypticism in the Modern Period and the Contemporary Age,* 3–35. New York: Continuum.

Moallem, Minoo. 1999. "The Textualization of Violence in a Global World: Gendered Citizenship and Discourse of Protection." *Review of Japanese Culture and Society* 11–12 (December 1999–2000): 9–17.

Moallem, Minoo. 2001 [1999]. "Transnationalism, Feminism, and Fundamentalism." In *Women, Gender, Religion: A Reader,* ed. Elizabeth A. Castelli with Rosamond C. Rodman, 119–45. New York: Palgrave.

Moghissi, Haideh. 1999. *Feminism and Fundamentalism: The Limits of Postmodern Analysis.* London: Zed Books.

O'Leary. Stephen D. 1994. *Arguing the Apocalypse: A Theory of Millennial Rhetoric.* Oxford: Oxford University Press.

Ortlund, Raymond C. 1996. *Whoredom: God's Unfaithful Wife in Biblical Theology.* New Studies in Biblical Theology. Grand Rapids, MI: Eerdmans.

Pathak, Zakia, and Rajeswari Sunder Rajan. 2001. "Shabano." In *Women, Gender, Religion: A Reader,* ed. Elizabeth A. Castelli with Rosamond C. Rodman, 195–215. New York: Palgrave.

Pippin, Tina. 1999. *Apocalyptic Bodies: The Biblical End of the World in Text and Image.* London: Routledge.

Pippin, Tina. 2002. "Of Gods and Demons: Blood Sacrifice and Eternal Life in *Dracula* and the Apocalypse of John." In *Screening Scripture: Intertextual Connections Between Scripture and Film,* ed. George Aichele and Richard Walsh, 24–41. Harrisburg: Trinity Press International.

Quinby, Lee. 1994. *Anti-Apocalypse: Exercises in Genealogical Criticism.* Minneapolis: University of Minnesota Press.

Riemer, Neal. 1980. "Covenant and the Federal Constitution." *Publius: The Journal of Federalism* 10(4):135–48.

Robertson, Pat. 1999. Interview by Cal Thomas. In *Blinded by Might: Can the Religious Right Save America?,* by Cal Thomas and Ed Dobson, 248–58. Grand Rapids, MI: Zondervan.

Rogers, Jerry and Dena. 2003. "God's Plan for the End-Time Harvest," http://www. planetkc.com/nnnel/GODS_PLAN.htm.

Runions, Erin. 2001. *Changing Subjects: Gender, Nation and Future in Micah.* Playing the Texts 7. London: Sheffield Academic Press.

Smolinski, Reiner. 1999. "Apocalypticism in Colonial North America." In Vol. 3 of *The Encyclopedia of Apocalypticism,* ed. Stephen J. Stein, *Apocalypticism in the Modern Period and the Contemporary Age,* 36–71. New York: Continuum.

Spivak, Gayatri Chakravorty. 1988. "Can the Subaltern Speak?" In *Marxism and the Interpretation of Culture,* ed. Cary Nelson and Lawrence Grossberg, 271–313. Urbana: University of Illinois Press.

Stephanson, Anders. 1995. *Manifest Destiny: American Expansionism and the Empire of Right.* New York: Hill and Wang.

Sullivan, Zohreh T. 1998. "Eluding the Feminist, Overthrowing the Modern? Transformations in Twentieth-Century." In *Remaking Women: Feminism and Modernity in the Middle East,* ed. Lila Abu-Lughod, 215–42. Princeton: Princeton University Press.

Vander Stichele, Caroline. 2000. "Apocalypse, Art and Abjection: Images of the Great Whore." In *Culture, Entertainment and the Bible,* ed. George Aichele, 124–38. Sheffield: Sheffield Academic Press.

Vidal, Gore. 1993. "Armageddon?" In *Gore Vidal: United States Essays 1952–1992,* 995–1006. New York: Random House.

A Voice in the Wilderness. 2003. "Iraq War: Gulf War II." http://www.a-voice.org/ main/iraq-war.htm. March.

Warrior, Robert Allen. 1991. "A Native American Perspective: Canaanites, Cowboys, and Indians." In *Voices from the Margin: Interpreting the Bible in the Third World,* ed. R. S. Sugirtharajah, 287–95. Maryknoll, NY: Orbis.

White House. 2002. *The National Security Strategy of the United States of America.* Washington, D.C.: Government Printing Office, http://www.whitehouse.gov/ nsc/nss.pdf.

Wolff, Hans Walter 1990 [1982]. *Micah: A Commentary.* Trans. Gary Stansell. Minneapolis: Augsburg.

Chapter 9

The Best Defense?

The Problem with Bush's "Preemptive" War Strategy

Neta C. Crawford

In December 1837 British military forces based in Canada learned that a private American ship, the *Caroline,* was ferrying arms, recruits, and supplies from Buffalo, New York, to a group of anti-British rebels on Navy Island on the Canadian side of the border. On the night of December 29, British and Canadian forces together set out to the island to destroy the ship. They did not find the *Caroline* berthed there, but they tracked it down in U.S. waters. While most of the crew slept, the troops boarded the ship, attacked the crew and passengers, and set it on fire. They then towed and released the *Caroline* into the current headed toward Niagara Falls, where it broke up and sank. Most on board escaped, but one man was apparently executed and several others remained unaccounted for and presumed dead.

In a letter to Secretary of State Daniel Webster, British ambassador Henry Fox defended the incursion into U.S. territory and the raid on the *Caroline.* British forces were simply acting in self-defense, he said, and protecting themselves against "unprovoked attack"[1] with preemptive force. In his eloquent reply to Fox, Webster rejected the British argument and articulated a set of demanding criteria for acting with a "necessity of self-defense"—in particular for a legitimate use of preemptive force. Preemption, Webster said, is justified only in response to an imminent threat; moreover, the force must be necessary for self-defense and can be deployed only after nonlethal measures and attempts to dissuade the adversary from acting had failed. Furthermore, a preemptive attack must be limited to dealing with the immediate threat and must discriminate between armed and unarmed, innocent and guilty. The British attack on the *Caroline* failed miserably by these standards:

> It will be for that Government [the British] to show a necessity of self-defence, instant, overwhelming, leaving no choice of means, and no moment for deliberation. It will be for it to show, also, that the local authorities of Canada,—even supposing the necessity of the moment authorized them to enter the territories of the United States at all,—did nothing unreasonable or excessive; since the act, justified by the necessity of self-defense, must be

limited by that necessity, and kept clearly within it. It must be shown that admonition or remonstrance to the persons on board the "Caroline" was impracticable, or would have been unavailing; it must be shown that daylight could not be waited for; that there could be no attempt at discrimination between the innocent and the guilty; that it would not have been enough to seize and detain the vessel; but that there was a necessity, present and inevitable, for attacking her in the darkness of night, while moored to the shore, and while unarmed men were asleep on board, killing some and wound[ing] others, and then drawing her into the current above the cataract, setting her on fire, and, careless to know whether there might not be in her the innocent with the guilty, or the living with the dead, committing her to a fate which fills the imagination with horror. A necessity for all this the government of the United States cannot believe to have existed.

Webster concluded that "if such things [as the attack on the *Caroline*] be allowed to occur, they must lead to bloody and exasperated war."[2]

In September 2002 the Bush administration announced a fundamental shift in the official American "national security strategy." The new strategy relies heavily on the preemptive use of force, and in defending it National Security Adviser Condoleezza Rice referred to Daniel Webster's "famous defense of anticipatory self-defense" (quoted in Sanger 2002, B7). But Rice missed Webster's point. Webster sought precisely to limit the resort to preemption, even in the name of self-defense. Preemption, after all, initiates violent conflict, so it must meet demanding strictures. By drawing a sharp line between legitimate preemption and illegitimate aggression, Webster sought to avoid "bloody and exasperated war."

New World, New Doctrine?

The new Bush security strategy contrasts sharply with the official cold war strategy of *deterrence*. The old idea was to protect the country by telling opponents—particularly the Soviet Union—that any attack would be met with devastating retaliation, and by building military forces sufficient to make the threat of retaliation credible. The new strategy is not so much to deter threats as to *preempt* them, to nip them in the bud, to "act against such emerging threats [from our enemies] *before they are fully formed*" (Bush 2002a, ii, emphasis added). "Our best defense," in short, "is a good offense" (*National Security Strategy* 2002, 6). But the new doctrine goes well beyond what might be considered justified preemption; rather, it is a preventive offensive war strategy.

This shift in strategy emerged soon after September 11. In October 2001, Secretary of Defense Donald Rumsfeld said, "There is no question but that the United States of America has every right, as every country does, of self-defense, and the problem with terrorism is that there is no way to defend against the terrorists at every place and every time against every conceivable technique. Therefore, the only way to deal with the terrorist network is to take the battle to them. That is in fact what we're doing. That is in effect self-defense of a preemptive nature" (Rumsfeld 2001).

The U.S. *National Security Strategy* released in September 2002 draws out more fully the case for preemption. The argument begins from the permissibility of preemption for the sake of self-defense:

> For centuries, international law recognized that nations need not suffer an attack before they can lawfully take action to defend themselves against forces that present an imminent danger of attack. Legal scholars and international jurists often conditioned the legitimacy of preemption on the existence of an imminent threat—most often a visible mobilization of armies, navies, and air forces preparing to attack. (*National Security Strategy* 2002, 15)

Greater reliance on preemption, in a wider range of circumstances, is now necessary, the administration argues, because the nature of war has changed: "It's a different world," according to Colin Powell. "It's a new kind of threat" (Dao 2002, 18).

The world is different in particular, the administration argues, because "terrorists" seek "martyrdom" and leaders of "rogue states" are often risk-prone and willing to sacrifice the lives of their people; because preparations to attack the United States will often not be visible (they may use "weapons of mass destruction" that "can be easily concealed, delivered covertly, and used without warning"); and because attacks may be devastating. For these reasons we need to revise our understanding of when a threat is "imminent": "We must adapt the concept of imminent threat to the capabilities and objectives of today's adversaries" (*National Security Strategy* 2002, 15). The United States cannot wait for a "smoking gun" if it comes in the form of a mushroom cloud. Therefore, "The greater the threat, the greater is the risk of inaction—and the more compelling the case for taking anticipatory action to defend ourselves, even if uncertainty remains as to the time and place of the enemy's attack. To forestall or prevent such hostile acts by our adversaries, the United States will if necessary, act preemptively" (*National Security Strategy* 2002, 15).

I do not dispute the administration's moral premise: that the right to self-defense sometimes permits preemption. But even in the new environment, distinctions between short- and long-term threats and between different sorts of potential adversaries remain fundamental. Denying the importance of these distinctions, as the administration does, is morally unacceptable and will lead to greater instability.

Preemption

The distinction between immediate threats and long-term potential threats underpins the classical distinction between preemption and preventive war.

Although preemption is not mentioned in the United Nations charter, where under Article 51—apart from collective uses of force authorized by the Security Council—individual states may only act in self-defense in the case of attack. Yet preemption has historically been considered a particular kind of self-defense against *immediate* threats.

Conventional just-war theory proposes standards for legitimate preemption close to those that Webster argued for in 1837. That theory has two elements. *Jus ad bellum* criteria describe conditions for legitimately undertaking a war: The cause must be self-defense, war must be a last resort and necessary in the sense that no other methods would work, the attack must be proportionate, and the war must have a chance of success. In such cases, political theorist Michael Walzer argues "states may use military force in the face of threats of war, whenever the failure to do so would seriously risk their territorial integrity or political independence" (Walzer 2000, 85). *Jus in bello* criteria concern the legitimate conduct of war and include injunctions of proportionality and discrimination between combatants and noncombatants, where noncombatants are not legitimate targets.

Preemptive war is directed against an opponent who has not yet attacked or harmed anyone. So, it is a grave step and should only be undertaken if it is both prudent and morally justified. Building on Webster and just-war theory, I argue that a legitimate preemptive use of force must meet four conditions:

Self to Be Defended Narrowly Defined

The party contemplating preemption should have a narrow conception of the "self" to be defended. On the face of it the self-defense criterion seems clear. When our lives are threatened we must be able to defend ourselves, using force if necessary. But self-defense could come to have a thicker sense, that our "self" is expressed not only by mere existence but also by our free and prosperous existence. For example, even if a tyrant would allow us to live, but not under institutions of our own choosing, we may justly fight to free ourselves from political oppression. But how far do the rights of the self extend? What values may actors legitimately defend with military force? If someone threatens our access to food, fuel, or shelter, can we use force? Or, if they allow us access to the material goods necessary for our existence but charge such a high price that we must make a terrible choice—between food and health care, or between mere existence and growth—are we justified in using force to secure access to a good that would enhance the self? With economic interests and vulnerabilities understood to be global, and the moral and political community of democracy and human rights defined more broadly than ever before, the self-conception of great powers expands. But a broad conception of self is not obviously legitimate, nor are the values to be defended apparent. When the self is defined too expansively, too many interests become vital. But war itself—and certainly preemption—is not justified to protect imperial interests or assets taken in a war of aggression.

The United States has increasingly defined its "self" in broad terms. According to the most recent *Report of the Quadrennial Defense Review*, the "enduring national interests" of the United States that are to be secured by force if necessary include "contributing to economic well-being," which itself includes "vitality and productivity of the global economy" and "access to key markets and strategic resources" (U.S. Department of Defense 2001, 2). Further, the goal of U.S. strategy is to maintain "preeminence." As President Bush said at West Point, "America has, and intends to keep, military strengths beyond challenge" (U.S. Department of Defense 2001, 30 and 62; Bush 2002b). The *National Security Strategy* also fuses ambitious political and economic goals with security: "The U.S. national security strategy will be based on a distinctly American internationalism that reflects the fusion of our values and our national interests. The aim of this strategy is to help make the world not just safer but better" (*National Security Strategy* 2002, 1). And, perhaps most strikingly, the Bush administration claims that "today the distinction between domestic and foreign affairs is diminishing" (*National Security Strategy* 2002, 31). But if the self is defined very broadly and threats to this greater "self" are met with military force, self-defense will look, at least to outside observers, like aggression. As Richard Betts argues, "When security is defined in terms broader than protecting the near-term integrity of national sovereignty and borders, the distinction between offense and defense blurs hopelessly. . . . Security can be as insatiable an appetite as acquisitiveness—there may never be enough buffers" (Betts 1982, 142, 143).

Justified Fear of Imminent Attack

To justify preemption there must to be strong evidence that war is inevitable and likely in the immediate future. Immediate threats are those that can be made manifest within hours or weeks unless action is taken to thwart an attack. This requires clear intelligence showing that a potential aggressor has both the capability and intention to do harm in the near future. Capability alone is not a justification.[3]

As Michael Walzer argued persuasively in *Just and Unjust Wars*, simple fear cannot be the only criterion for launching a preemptive attack. Fear, already omnipresent in world politics, increases in the context of a terrorist campaign. The nature of fear in the wake of a devastating assault may be that a government and people will, justifiably, be vigilant. Indeed, they may out of this heightened fear be hypervigilant about threats—seeing small threats as large and brutally squashing potential threats. The fearful may then overreact to threats that do not risk the territorial integrity or political independence of a state. Or, the threat of "uncertainty" may trigger preemptive attacks.

The threshold for credible fear is necessarily lower, then, in the context of contemporary counterterror war, in which terrorists have the advantage of surprise. But the consequences of lowering the threshold of fear may be increased instability and the premature use of force. If simple fear justifies preemption, then preemption will have no limits since, according to the Bush administration's own arguments, we cannot always know with certainty what the other side has and where it might be located or when it might be used. And if fear of a surprise attack was once clearly justified, when and how will we know that a threat has been significantly reduced or eliminated?

If simple fear does not suffice, then how much of what kind of fear justifies preemption? We need to tread a fine line. The threshold of evidence and warning cannot be too low: Simple apprehension that a potential adversary might be out there somewhere and may be acquiring the means to do harm cannot trigger the offensive use of force. This is not preemption but paranoid aggression, and it promises endless war. We must—stressful as it may be psychologically—accept some vulnerability and uncertainty. We must also avoid the tendency to exaggerate threats and inadvertently heighten our own fear. For example, though nuclear weapons are more widely available than in the past, as are delivery vehicles of long range, nuclear weapons and long-range delivery vehicles are not yet in the hands of hundreds or even dozens of terrorists. A policy that assumes such a dangerous world is, at this point, paranoid. Rather than assuming that we live in such a world, or soon will, we should work to make this outcome less likely.

On the other hand, the threshold of evidence and warning for justified fear cannot be so high that those who might be about to do harm get so far along in their preparations that they cannot be stopped or the damage limited. Assuming a substantial investment in intelligence gathering, assessment, and understanding of potential adversaries, what we need is a policy that both maximizes our understanding of the capabilities *and* intentions of possible adversaries and simultaneously minimizes our physical vulnerability. While uncertainty—about intentions, capabilities, and risk—can never be eliminated, it can be reduced.

Aggressive intent coupled with a capacity to do immediate harm is the right threshold for legitimate preemption. We should judge intent by considering two questions: First, have potential aggressors harmed us in the recent past or said they want to harm us in the near future? And second, are potential adversaries moving their forces into position to do significant harm? While it might be tempting to assume that secrecy on the part of a potential adversary is a sure sign of aggressive intentions, it may simply be a desire to prepare a deterrent force that might itself be the target of a preventive offensive strike. For example, consider the September 11 attacks. On these criteria it would have been entirely permissible to arrest the hijackers of the four aircraft used as weapons. But prior to September 11, taking the war to Afghanistan to attack al Qaeda camps or the Taliban would not have been justified preemption unless it was clear that such action could have thwarted imminent terrorist attacks.

The Bush administration strategy has collapsed the distinction between imminent (immediate) threat and potential future threats. It assumes that grave threats are now always imminent. But such a view is both innaccurate and ultimately dangerous. In assuming that we are always in danger of immediate and grave assault, we lose precisely the time we need to distinguish between potential threats and likely threats; we also may tend to strike first, without much evidence. Further, we deemphasize diplomacy, arms control, and negotiation and turn to the use of force because we assume there is no time for these measures. But the assumption of imminent threat makes us less secure.

Preemption Likely to Succeed

Another criterion for preemption to be justified is that it must be likely to succeed in reducing or eliminating the threat. Specifically, there should be a high likelihood that the source of the military threat can be found and that the damage it was about to do could be greatly reduced or eliminated by a preemptive attack. If preemption is likely to fail on either of those counts it should not be undertaken. The prosecution of a successful counterterror war is very difficult. Terrorist operatives are hard to find because they are generally few in number, mostly inactive and concealed, and tend to be co-located with civilians. Preemption may be easier against states simply because the preparations of governments, even for surprise attacks, tend to involve larger-scale mobilizations that often are more visible.

Military Force Required

For military preemption to be justified, force must be necessary. There must be no time for other measures to work, or those other measures must be unlikely to avert a devastating attack, the preparations for which are already underway. If an attack can be thwarted by arresting a potential terrorist, for example, then military strikes should not be used, even if they would also be effective. The requirement that military force be necessary thus puts the onus on defenders to work to resolve conflicts with potential adversaries. The problem with the Bush administration's logic, as noted above, is in assuming that the threat is imminent, they assume that force is required.

Conduct of Military Preemption

Even if these four criteria for undertaking a justified preemptive strike are met, the use of preemptive force must also meet *jus in bello* criteria of proportionality and discrimination. Specifically, the damage caused by the preemptive strikes should not exceed what was put at risk by the attack that is preempted. Thus, when the administration suggests that nuclear weapons might be used to preempt the acquisition of chemical and biological weapons, it proposes a disproportionate response ("National Strategy to Combat Weapons of Mass Destruction" 2002).

Preemptive action should also avoid killing innocents and using measures that harm the prospects of future peace. As Immanuel Kant argued more than two hundred years ago, "Some level of trust in the enemy's way of thinking must be preserved, even in the midst of war, for otherwise no peace can ever be concluded and the hostilities would become a war of extermination" (Kant 1983, 110). Discrimination is extremely difficult in the case of counterterrorist preemption because terrorists do not live in separate garrisons as regular armies do but among civilian populations who may be unaware of their presence. Civilian deaths are thus both unavoidable and foreseeable even if the preemptive strike involves the use of precision guided weapons or commando raids.

Preemptive actions must also have limited military objectives, and the preemptive action should cease when the threat is eliminated or significantly reduced. A legitimate preemptive motive does not give license to actions that go beyond reducing or eliminating an immediate threat.

Preventive Wars?

If preemption may sometimes be legitimate, is the Bush administration right to extend the case of justified preemption to preventive offensive wars? If all threats are considered imminent and unavoidable without the use of force, then yes. But although war has been transformed along many of the lines the administration suggests, not all threats are immediate and unavoidable. The threat posed by terrorism is significant. Unconventional adversaries, prepared to wage unconventional "asymmetric" war, can conceal their movements, weapons, and immediate intentions and may conduct devastating surprise attacks.[4] Nuclear, chemical, and biological weapons, though not widely held, are more readily available than they were in the recent past. And of course the "everyday" infrastructure of the United States can be turned against the country, as were the hijacked planes on September 11. Terrorists in particular are extremely flexible. Unlike conventional militaries, they can project power with great efficiency: They do not have to develop weapons and delivery vehicles; they may live among their target populations; and they require comparatively little in the way of logistical support. It is also true that although physical risk to terrorism could certainly be reduced in many ways, as Rumsfeld acknowledges, it is impossible to achieve complete invulnerability.[5] And though the United States was open to serious threats in the past, Americans are perhaps more emotionally aware of that exposure today since, as Condoleezza Rice says, "9/11 crystallized our vulnerability" (Rice 2002). In sum, when combined with the advantage of surprise, terrorism is a formidable military strategy that costs many times more to defend against than it costs terrorists to conduct.

On the other hand, terrorists do not hold all the cards. For example, their sources of funding, often tied to illicit transactions and black market economies, are vulnerable to disruption through determined law enforcement. And while terrorists can piggyback on the infrastructure of their targets, they are also vulnerable to detection via that same infrastructure as they use phones, faxes, the Internet, and other electronic media. Finally, although there are far too many leaks in the containment of technologies and weapons of mass destruction, many of those weapons are still relatively expensive to acquire and difficult to produce in any quantity. Still, if we imagine all possible scenarios, the potential for devastation seems limitless and it ostensibly makes great sense to get them before they get us.

Perhaps for this reason Bush administration defense planners made a shift, even prior to September 11, from basing military planning on intentions and likely threats to what they call a "capabilities-based approach," which attempts to "anticipate the capabilities that an adversary might employ" and "focuses more on how an adversary might fight than who the adversary might be and where war might occur" (U.S. Department of Defense 2001, 14). Indeed, the scenarios proliferate, according to General Ralph Eberhart, in charge of the military's role in homeland security: "The list goes on and on. We can all envision the terrible things that might happen" (quoted in Shenon and Schmitt 2002, A12).

But in estimating potential threats, the intentions of a likely adversary are much more important than capabilities that "might" be employed by someone. So the assertion that the United States faces rogue enemies who "hate everything" about it must be carefully evaluated. While there is certainly compelling evidence that al Qaeda members desire to harm the United States and American citizens, the *National Security Strategy* makes a questionable leap when it assumes that "rogue states" also desire to harm the United States and pose an imminent military threat. Moreover, the administration blurs the distinction between "rogue states" and terrorists and essentially erases the difference between terrorists and the states in which they reside: "We make no distinction between terrorists and those who knowingly harbor or provide aid to them" (*National Security Strategy* 2002, 5). But these distinctions make a difference when a country is deciding whether or not to initiate the use of force.

Current U.S. policy does not, however, respect these distinctions. As President Bush said at West Point: "We must take the battle to the enemy, disrupt his plans and confront the worst threats before they emerge. . . . Our security will require . . . a military that must be ready to strike at a moment's notice in any dark corner of the world. And our security will require all Americans to be forward-looking and resolute, to be ready for preemptive action when necessary to defend our liberty and to defend our lives." Indeed, since September 11 and the administration's gradual articulation of its new security doctrine, the United States has sent troops to fight terrorists not only in Afghanistan but in the Philippines, Yemen, Indonesia, and former Soviet Georgia and has confronted both Iraq and North Korea over the issue of weapons of mass destruction. A limitless preventive offensive doctrine thus entails an expanding list of force commitments that might spread U.S. military forces thin at the same time that it risks escalating military conflicts.

Such uses of force, while seeming sensible in an atmosphere of perceived heightened vulnerability, may at best be unnecessary. At worst there is risk of backlash fueled by fear and resentment, not least because discrimination between combatants is difficult in preventive war. Indeed, because they have not yet made an aggressive act, nearly all those killed or injured by a preventive war will be noncombatants.

To see how the administration has blurred the distinctions between preemption and preventive offensive war, consider their arguments about the threat posed by Iraq's potential to acquire weapons of mass destruction. Vice President Cheney argues that Iraq poses a threat to the United States: "Many of us are convinced that Saddam Hussein will acquire nuclear weapons fairly soon. . . . Deliverable weapons of mass destruction in the hands of a terror network or murderous dictator or the two working together constitutes as grave a threat as can be imagined. The risks of inaction are far greater than the risks of action" (Cheney 2002, A8). But here we must recall the distinction between preemptive war and preventive war. There is no *imminent* threat supposed or cited in this case since Iraq has no nuclear weapons at this point.

Moreover, while other so-called rogue states present more imminent nuclear threats, the administration still insists that Saddam's potential future capability justified immediate action. As one Bush administration official told the *New York Times* after North Korea announced that it would remove monitoring equipment on both its nuclear reactor and plutonium stockpiles—enabling it to produce several more nuclear weapons within a few months—"We still think Saddam is the bigger threat, but there is no question that the North Koreans, who already have superior firepower, may soon be in a position to threaten to deploy or sell its nuclear capability. Iraq is a long way from that" (quoted in Sanger and Dao 2002, A1, A10).

Thus, the administration's arguments about Iraq reveal both their tendency to conflate preemption and prevention and the weakness of their factual, legal, and moral claims. The new *National Security Strategy* is not actually "preemption" in the manner described by the just-war tradition or any of the other "legal scholars and international jurists" that the administration might be referring to. Rather, the policy is more accurately described as one of waging preventive war. But preventive war is not justified under just-war theory, nor is it likely to be judged legal under international law. The trend has been quite the opposite: to equate preventive war, such as was launched by Japan against the United States in 1941 and by Germany against Russia and the Soviet Union in World Wars I and II, with aggression. In any case, it threatens a world of "bloody and exasperated war."

Prudence

Foreign policies must be judged not only on grounds of legality and morality but also on grounds of prudence. Preemption is only prudent if it is limited to clear and immediate dangers and if there are constraints on its conduct—proportionality, discrimination, and limited aims. If preemption becomes a strategy—or if it becomes the cover for a preventive offensive-war doctrine—it may become self-defeating as it increases instability and insecurity.

Specifically, a legitimate preemptive war requires that states show that the potential aggressors have the capability *and* the intention of doing great harm. But while capability may not be in dispute, the motives and intentions of a potential adversary may be misinterpreted. Specifically, states may mobilize in what appear to be aggressive ways because they are fearful or because they are aggressive. Some states may defensively arm because they are afraid of the "preemptive/preventive" state; others may arm offensively because they resent the preventive-war aggressor who may have killed many innocents in a quest for total security. A preemptive doctrine that has—because of great fear and a desire to control the international environment—become a preventive-war doctrine is likely to create both more fearful states and more aggressor states.

In either case, whether states and groups arm because they are afraid or because they have aggressive intentions, instability is likely to grow as a preventive war creates the mutual fear of surprise attack. In the case of the U.S. preemptive/preventive-war doctrine, instability is more likely to increase because that doctrine is coupled with the goal of maintaining global "preeminence," and the United States has said that it will discourage any military rivals from challenging it (U.S. Department of Defense 2001, 30, 62).

Further, a preventive-war doctrine undermines international law and diplomacy, both of which can be useful—even to hegemonic powers. Preventive war short-circuits nonmilitary means of solving problems. If all states reacted to potential adversaries as if they faced a clear and present danger of imminent attack, tensions would escalate along already tense borders and regions. Article 51 of the U.N. charter would lose much of its force. In sum, a preemptive/preventive-war doctrine moves us closer to a state of nature than a state of international law.

Moreover, while preventive-war doctrines assume that today's potential rival will become tomorrow's adversary, diplomacy or some other factor could work to change the relationship from antagonism to accommodation. As Bismarck said in 1875, "I would . . . never advise Your Majesty to declare war forthwith, simply because it appeared that our opponent would begin hostilities in the near future. One can never anticipate the ways of divine providence securely enough for that" (quoted in Craig 1955, 255).

In sum, one can understand why any administration would favor preemption and why some would be attracted to preventive war if they think it could guarantee invulnerability. But this psychological reassurance is at best illusory and the effort to attain it may be counterproductive. Preventive wars are imprudent, because they bring wars that might not happen and increase resentment. They are also unjust, because they assume, as Bismarck said, perfect knowledge of an adversary's ill intentions when such presumptions may be premature or false. The temptation to slide over the line from preemption to preventive war is great because that line is vague and because of the extraordinary stress of living under the threat of terrorist attack or war. But that temptation should be resisted. Vulnerability is a fact of life. And the stress of living in fear should be reduced by true prevention—arms control, disarmament, negotiations, confidence-building measures, and the development of international law.

Notes

1. British Ambassador to the United States Henry S. Fox in a letter to the U.S. Secretary of State Daniel Webster, March 12, 1841, in Shewmaker 1983, 42.
2. Webster in a letter to Fox, 24 April 1841, in Shewmaker 1983, 62, 67–68.
3. Yet current U.S. military doctrine is to defend against potential and actual military capabilities, not against likely threats.
4. I spell out the nature of this transformation in Crawford 2003. Also see Betts 2002.
5. Critics of U.S. foreign policy will say that much of this vulnerability is of America's own making because it financed, armed, and trained some of the individuals, groups, and governments that have turned on the United States. But these issues of responsibility are perhaps beside the point now—assuming, that is, that the United States is wise enough to halt current and future support for such unsavory characters. This, of course, remains to be seen.

Works Cited

Betts, Richard K. 1982. *Surprise Attack: Lessons for Defense Planning*. Washington, D.C.: Brookings Institution.

Betts, Richard K. 2002. "The Soft Underbelly of American Primacy: Tactical Advantages of Terror." *Political Science Quarterly* 17(1) (spring): 19–36.

Bush, George W. 2002a. "Preface." *The National Security Strategy of the United States of America*. Washington, D.C.: Office of the President. September.

Bush, George W. 2002b. "Remarks at Graduation Exercise of the United States Military Academy, West Point, New York." June 1. White House Transcript. http://www.whitehouse.gov/news/releases/2002/06/20020601-3.html

Cheney, Dick. 2002. "In Cheney's Words: The Administration Case for Removing Saddam Hussein." *New York Times*. August 27. A8.

Craig, Gordon A. 1955. *The Politics of the Prussian Army, 1640–1945*. New York: Oxford University Press.

Crawford, Neta C. 2003. "Just War Theory and the U.S. Counterterror War." *Perspectives on Politics* 1(1): 5–25.

Dao, James. 2002. "Threats and Responses: Perspectives; Powell Defends a First Strike as Iraq Option." *New York Times*. September 8.

Kant, Immanuel. 1983. "To Perpetual Peace: A Philosophical Sketch." In *Perpetual Peace and Other Essays on Politics, History and Morals*, 107–43. Indianapolis: Hackett Publishing Co.

National Security Strategy of the United States of America. 2002. Washington, D.C.: Office of the President. September. http://www.whitehouse.gov/nsc/nss.pdf.

National Strategy to Combat Weapons of Mass Destruction. 2002. December. http://www.whitehouse.gov/news/releases/2002/12/WMDStrategy.pdf.

Rice, Condoleezza. 2002. "Wriston Lecture: President's National Security Strategy." October 1. New York.

Rumsfeld, Donald H. 2001. "Remarks at Stakeout Outside ABC TV Studio." October 28. www.defenselink.mil/news/Oct2001/t10292001_t1028sd3.html.

Sanger, David E. 2002. "Beating Them to the Prewar." *New York Times.* September 28.

Sanger, David E., and James Dao. 2002. "North Korea Says It Regains Access to its Plutonium." *New York Times.* December 23.

Shenon, Philip, and Eric Schmitt. 2002. "At U.S. Nerve Center, Daily Talks on the Worst Fears." *New York Times.* December 27.

Shewmaker, Kenneth E., ed. 1983. *The Papers of Daniel Webster: Diplomatic Papers, Volume 1, 1841–1843.* Hanover, N.H.: University Press of New England.

U.S. Department of Defense. 2001. *Report of the Quadrennial Defense Review.* Washington, D.C.: Government Printing Office. September 30.

Walzer, Michael. 2000. *Just and Unjust Wars: A Moral Argument with Historical Illustrations.* New York: Basic Books.

Chapter 10

The Erosion of Democracy in Advancing the Bush Administration's Iraq Agenda

Government Lies and Misinformation and Media Complicity[1]

Jody Williams

Overview

The terrorist attacks of September 11, 2001, against the Twin Towers in New York City and the Pentagon are said to have changed everything in the world. I do not agree. What may have changed as a result of September 11 is the American psyche and its newfound sense of vulnerability in the world. In my view, for the Bush administration it has been very much "business as usual" in the sense of those in power taking advantage of uncertainties and fear to advance their own political and ideological agendas.

I believe that the Bush administration took advantage of the fear and uncertainty engendered by the horrific attacks of September 11 to put forth a national security policy of preemptive self-defense as if it were a direct response to September 11 instead of just one element of a longer-standing, post–cold war political vision of unrivaled U.S. power long developed by members of the administration. They then used that policy as a justification to remove Saddam Hussein from power.

In order to achieve those foreign policy goals, the Bush administration relied on outright lies, distortions, and manipulation of information to push the American public to support an invasion of Iraq. Domestically, major media outlets acted more like public relations firms for the administration's agenda than objective news sources that supposedly are the underpinnings of the much-lauded American free press. Meaningful public debate was stifled and the press largely ignored opposition to the war. Those who did dare to speak out were publicly attacked and vilified. In this post–September 11 environment, people across the country who did not agree with policy direction felt isolated and unsure of their own concerns about the dramatic press for war and the attacks on civil liberties at home.

Internationally, the administration tried to use similar manipulations, coupled with intense political and economic pressure, to achieve international support for the invasion. They had hoped to build upon the surge of global sympathy toward the United States in the aftermath of September 11 and the international cooperation that developed in the administration's war on terrorism resulting from those attacks. Instead, in the process of taking the United States to war, the Bush administration alienated some of its closest allies and much of the Arab world.

Its policy of preemptive self-defense threatens to dramatically destabilize international security and international law and has set a dangerous precedent, the ramifications of which will be felt for years if not decades. In using the violence of September 11 to advance their foreign policy agenda, the Bush administration has made the United States more vulnerable and has eroded civil liberties, further diminished free expression in America, and threatened the very fabric of our democracy.

Iraq: The Spin and the Lead-Up to War

The Bush administration—and its primary ally, British Prime Minister Tony Blair—spun the case that the Iraqi regime posed such an overwhelming and immediate threat to national and global security that "preemptive self-defense" gave cause for a just war against Saddam Hussein. This doctrine is spelled out in its policy document entitled the *National Security Strategy of the United States* released on September 17, 2002.[2]

The primary justifications for a war of preemptive self-defense against Iraq were that Hussein's regime supported terrorists in general, had links to al-Qaeda in particular, and was continuing to develop weapons of mass destruction (WMD).[3] As that argument spun out, the administration consistently stated that there was a direct link between Saddam Hussein and al-Qaeda, implying that, through that link, Hussein was responsible either directly or indirectly for the attacks of September 11.

The administration sought to soften the image of the invasion by also arguing that it was seeking regime change to free the Iraqi people from decades of despotic rule, to provide them the right to form their own government and use the riches of Iraqi oil to benefit all the people of the country. In particular, the administration used this argument to play to the best side of the American psyche—the belief that most Americans share that this country really does stand for freedom and justice and democracy and self-determination for all under all circumstances.

These were the essential elements that the administration used to try to rally both the U.S. Congress and the United Nations for war against the Hussein regime. On September 12, 2002, Bush addressed the UN in the push for a new UN resolution requiring the regime to give up WMD and stop support for terrorism in order to avoid war.[4] On October 11, 2002, both Houses of the U.S. Congress voted to authorize an attack on Iraq if the regime refused to give up WMD as required by UN resolutions. On November 8, the Security Council unanimously passed Resolution 1441, which established an enhanced inspection regime to disarm Iraq, to be carried out by the UN Monitoring, Verification, and Inspection Commission (UNMOVIC) and the International Atomic Energy Agency (IAEA).[5]

Even as the weapons inspectors were resuming their activities, the Bush administration increased rhetorical and real pressure on the Iraqi regime, and began to move troops into the region. Hussein grudgingly began to cooperate with the inspectors, but the Bush administration, under pressure from its primary ally British Prime Minister Tony Blair, agreed to press for another UN resolution to grant international legitimacy to the war.

On January 27, 2003, Mohamed ElBaradei, Director General of the IAEA, reported to the UN Security Council that after the first sixty days of the resumed weapons inspections, "We have to date found no evidence that Iraq has revived its nuclear weapons programme since the elimination of the programme in the 1990s. . . . With our verification system now in place, barring exceptional circumstances, and provided there is sustained proactive cooperation by Iraq, we should be able within the next few months to provide credible assurance that Iraq has no nuclear weapons programme."[6]

Yet as if operating in a vacuum, and essentially disregarding ElBaradei's report, on February 5, 2003, in a dramatic bid to convince a skeptical world of the imminent need for war, U.S. Secretary of State Colin Powell presented the administration's case to the United Nations as prelude to its push for a second UN resolution for war.[7] In arguing that the Iraqi regime had not abandoned its WMD programs, much of the evidence he presented was based upon undisclosed sources, and documents and intercepts were subject to various interpretations.[8] Many of the administration's claims made by Powell have subsequently unraveled, as described below. While Powell made an eloquent presentation, the evidence he presented did not convince a skeptical world of the need for immediate action. With little support, the US withdrew its bid for a resolution to endorse its war with Iraq.

On March 17, 2003, in an address to the nation, President Bush gave Saddam Hussein an ultimatum: Leave Iraq within forty-eight hours or face war. Two days later the United States launched its invasion of Iraq with a "decapitation attack" aimed at Saddam Hussein and his two sons.

The Spin—Myth or Reality

On May 1, 2003, after a dramatic photo-op fighter jet landing on the aircraft carrier the USS Abraham Lincoln, standing before a huge banner hung on the ship which read "Mission Accomplished," Bush declared major combat operations of the war to be over.[9] However, on July 16, a little less than three months later, as organized attacks on occupation forces were on the rise, the new commander of U.S. Central Command General John Azibaid acknowledged that U.S. occupying forces in Iraq were facing a "classical guerrilla-type campaign."[10] No weapons of mass destruction have as yet been found in the occupied country and the administration's arguments for war have been rapidly losing currency—a currency that many believe they never should have had in the first place.

The Bush administration was helped tremendously in advancing its war agenda domestically by the U.S. media. Embracing the administration's arguments for its post–September 11 policies, both at home and abroad, media outlets gave virtually no room for dissent or even objective discussion—particularly in the lead up to the Iraq invasion and during the war itself, when U.S. reporters were "embedded" with advancing U.S. troops. The "embedding" of media was only the most overt aspect of the administration's policy of misinformation and propaganda to achieve its goals vis-à-vis Iraq.

Almost as soon as Bush began his rhetorical assault on the imminent threat of Saddam's WMD, time after time it would be revealed that evidence he cited was false, nonexistent, or distorted. One of the first examples was his October 2002 statement that an IAEA report on Hussein's nuclear capacity alleged that the regime was "six months away" from developing a nuclear weapon. Almost immediately the IAEA refuted the allegation, pointedly noting that no such report existed at all. While Bush's claims were put out loud and clear, the subsequent disclaimer by his spokesperson Ari Fleischer was barely noted by the media. It still remains a piece of misinformation little touched upon by the media.[11]

Other WMD evidence used both by Bush and high-ranking members of his administration has also proven to be either completely false or to have been made "more forward leaning" in order to bolster the position that the administration wanted to prove.[12] The most notorious example of the use of false information is Bush's statement in his January 28, 2002, State of the Union Address that Hussein sought uranium in Africa for nuclear weapons.[13] The CIA had successfully argued for removal of a similar statement from an earlier speech given in October by Bush because it knew the "evidence" to not be credible. It also has stated that it pressed the White House to drop such allegations from Bush's address.[14]

An example of making information "more forward leaning" is the case of aluminum tubes bought by Iraq that the administration declared would be used for producing nuclear bombs. Although numerous experts stated that the tubes were not for nuclear production, administration officials presented the issue as yet more proof of its case for war. One intelligence analyst who had participated in the aluminum-tubes debate said, "You had senior American officials like Condoleezza Rice saying the only use of the aluminum really is uranium centrifuges. She said that on television. And that's just a lie."[15]

It has been widely reported that Vice President Cheney, his chief of staff, Lewis "Scooter" Libby, and others went repeatedly to CIA headquarters to press for interpretations of information to support the push for war.[16] One senior administration official said, "Nearly every day, Cheney and Scooter hammered the agency on Iraq or terrorism. Over time, the agency got tired of fighting."[17] But apparently, even this pressure did not satisfy the needs of the administration. Defense Secretary Donald Rumsfeld set up a shadow agency, the Office of Special Plans (OSP), to compete with the CIA and its military counterpart, the Defense Intelligence Agency, in interpretation of data.[18]

The other primary argument for the invasion was the "bulletproof" evidence, as declared in September 2002 by Donald Rumsfeld, that Saddam Hussein had ties with al-Qaeda.[19] President Bush and his advisors repeatedly talked of these ties, with the barely veiled implication that because of the links Hussein was in some way responsible for the attacks of September 11. Yet, these claims proved even weaker, if possible, than the evidence provided regarding the WMD in Hussein's possession.

On June 15, 2003, retired General Wesley Clark was interviewed on NBC television's *Meet the Press,* where he stated that the Bush administration began trying to implicate Hussein immediately after the September attacks. Clark said, "Well, it came from the White House, it came from people around the White House. It came from all over. I got a call on 9/11. I was on CNN, and I got a call at my home saying, 'You got to say this is connected. This is state-sponsored terrorism. This has to be connected to Saddam Hussein.' I said, 'But—I'm willing to say it, but what's your evidence?' And I never got any evidence."[20]

According to the nonprofit media watchdog Fairness and Accuracy in Reporting, "Clark's assertion corroborates a little-noted CBS Evening News story that aired on September 4, 2002. As correspondent David Martin reported: 'Barely five hours after American Airlines Flight 77 plowed into the Pentagon, the secretary of defense was telling his aides to start thinking about striking Iraq, even though there was no evidence linking Saddam Hussein to the attacks.' According to CBS, a Pentagon aide's notes from that day quote Rumsfeld asking for the 'best info fast' to 'judge whether good enough to hit SH at the same time, not only UBL.' (The initials SH and UBL stand for Saddam Hussein and Osama bin Laden.) The notes then quote Rumsfeld as demanding, ominously, that the administration's response 'go massive . . . sweep it all up, things related and not.'"[21]

Others in and around the Bush administration began publicly trying to connect Hussein to al-Qaeda and thus to the September 11 attacks. On behalf of the administration, James Woolsey, a former director of the CIA and a current member of the Defense Policy Board, went to Europe to seek evidence to back the claim. His evidence—that Mohamed Atta, the leader of the 9/11 attacks, had met with an Iraqi intelligence official in Prague—was not supported by U.S. intelligence or by Czech officials.[22] In February 2003, the *New York Times* reported that an FBI official said, "We've been looking at this hard for more than a year and you know what, we just don't think it's there."[23] Additionally, a classified British intelligence report seen by BBC News stated, "There are no current links between the Iraqi regime and the al-Qaeda network."[24] Moreover, the 9/11 Commission, which completed its hearings in the summer of 2004, came to a similar conclusion.

U.S. Media Bias, the Administration's "Information Warfare," and the Stifling of Public Debate

It can be difficult to understand why much of the American public still wants to believe the nearly mythological justifications for the invasion. It is easy to see why people outside the United States cannot understand the "gullibility" of the American public and are confused by the claims of seemingly uniform support for the Bush administration's policies. But from inside the country, it is easier to understand.

Particularly since September 11, the mainstream American media has largely supported an aggressive war on terrorism and a "muscular" U.S. foreign policy. In the immediate aftermath of the September attacks, it was considered "unpatriotic" at best and "treasonous" at worst to publicly ask any questions about the root causes of terrorism or the appropriate responses to terrorism.

The assault on such questioning began almost immediately after the attacks and helped foster an environment of fear of public discourse. One particularly high-profile case was that of late night television's Bill Maher, then host of *Politically Incorrect*. Maher's commentary on U.S. military responses to terrorism might have been ill timed, but the response to it helped feed into a traumatized American psyche and contributed to stifling public questioning of administration policies. Sponsors withdrew support for the show, which was ultimately cancelled. According to Bush's spokesperson Ari Fleischer, what had happened to Maher was appropriate and a signal to Americans that they "need to watch what they say, watch what they do, and this is not a time for remarks like that—there never is."[25]

Another high-profile incident occurred during the invasion when the lead singer of the popular singing group the Dixie Chicks said she was embarrassed to be from the same state as Bush. Clear Channel, a corporation owning 1,200 radio stations in the United States, went immediately on the attack and called for all its stations to stop playing the band's music.[26] Clear Channel, whose stations helped organize prowar rallies around the United States, also organized an event in Louisiana where a 33,000-pound tractor smashed Dixie Chicks CDs, tapes, and other paraphernalia.[27]

The mainstream media has consistently presented positions that reinforced the administration's point of view and left little room for debate and discussion, particularly in the lead-up to the war and during the invasion itself. For example, one survey of 414 Iraq-related stories on the three major U.S. networks between September 2001 and February 2002 found that all but 34 of the stories were sourced out of the White House, the Defense Department, or the State Department.[28]

The situation did not improve once the invasion started. Fairness and Accuracy in Reporting (FAIR), a nonprofit organization that monitors the media, began a three-week study on March 19, 2003, the day after the war began. They canvassed 1,617 on-camera sources in stories about Iraq on the evening newscasts of six U.S. television networks and news channels.[29] The major findings include the following: "Nearly two thirds of all sources, 64 percent, were pro-war, while 71 percent of U.S. guests favored the war. Anti-war voices were 10 percent of all sources, but just 6 percent of non-Iraqi sources and 3 percent of U.S. sources. Thus viewers were more than six times as likely to see a pro-war source as one who was anti-war; with U.S. guests alone, the ratio increases to 25 to 1.... Looking at U.S. sources, which made up 76 percent of total sources, more than two out of three (68 percent) were either current or former officials.... In the category of U.S. officials, military voices overwhelmed civilians by a two-to-one margin, providing 68 percent of U.S. official sources and nearly half (47 percent) of all U.S. sources. This predominance reflected the networks' focus on information from journalists embedded with troops, or provided at military briefings, and the analysis of such by paid former military officials."[30]

At the same time, despite the largest public protests in the streets of American cities since the height of the Vietnam War, the massive displays of opposition to official policy were barely acknowledged, let alone covered. Often, when there was coverage of antiwar events, it would be placed in inner sections of newspapers, as if they were entertainment or events of local significance rather than displays of massive public opposition to national policy. Further, the FAIR study cited above found, for example, that "just 3 percent of U.S. sources represented or expressed opposition to the war. With more than one in four U.S. citizens opposing the war and much higher rates of opposition in most countries where opinion was polled, none of the networks offered anything resembling proportionate coverage of anti-war voices."[31]

In the face of such a barrage of biased reporting, it is very difficult for individual citizens to believe that their opposition opinions, or even basic questioning of events, are anything but rare, isolated, and, perhaps, even "unpatriotic." As Chris Hedges, a nonpacifist war correspondent for about twenty years, writes in his recent book *War Is a Force That Gives Us Meaning,* "The effectiveness of the myths peddled in war is powerful. We often come to doubt our own perceptions. We hide these doubts, like troubled believers, sure that no one else feels them. We feel guilty. The myths have determined not only how we should speak but how we should think. The doubts we carry, the scenes we see that do not conform to the myth are hazy, difficult to express, unsettling. And as the atrocities mount, as civil liberties are stripped away (something, with the 'War on Terror,' already happening to hundreds of thousands of immigrants in the United States), we struggle uncomfortably with the jargon and clichés. But we have trouble expressing our discomfort because *the collective shout* [emphasis added] has made it hard for us to give words to our thoughts. This self-doubt is aided by the monstrosity of war."[32]

Another aspect of the assault on freedom of expression has been the passage of the USA Patriot Act, rushed through a panicked Congress and signed into law on October 26, 2001, allegedly to strengthen U.S. intelligence tools to fight terrorism.[33] The act actually makes it much easier to spy on U.S. citizens in general, through "roving wiretaps," which can follow the target rather than be confined to a specific telephone; through surveillance of computer use; and through investigation of an individual's library records.[34] Just as the media largely ignored public opposition to the invasion of Iraq, it has given scant coverage to opposition to the Patriot Act. Librarians and local governments across the country have been taking increasing action in opposition to the act. Librarians, for example, are organizing to repeal Section 215 of the act, which allows the FBI to secretly obtain court orders for access to library and bookstore records.[35] By March 2003, at least 160 municipalities and county governments in the United States had passed resolutions in opposition to the act.[36]

The above outlines just the domestic public face of the attempts to mold U.S. public opinion. In a presentation in April 2003 in Washington, D.C., one university professor analyzing the situation noted the administration's "attempts to assert 'full spectrum dominance' over all levels of wartime communication . . . effacing the traditional boundary between battlefield deception and public sphere propaganda."[37] Further, he stated, "According to defense analyst William Arkin, the Bush strategy lays out goals for information warfare that pursue D5E: 'destruction, degradation, denial, disruption, deceit, and exploitation.' Arkin notes that the wide array of sites and practices of information control brought into the range of this policy 'blurs or even erases the boundaries between factual information and news, on the one hand, and public relations, propaganda and psychological warfare on the other.'"[38]

The administration sought to carry out this strategy through an office in the Pentagon called the Office of Strategic Influence (OSI), created shortly after September 11 to generate support for the war on terror.[39] The OSI considered a range of options from standard public relations to the covert planting of disinformation in foreign media—an operation known as "black propaganda."[40] Yet when plans for OSI were leaked to the *New York Times,* it reported "even many senior Pentagon officials and congressional military aides say they know almost nothing about its purpose and plans."[41] With the leak of its creation to the press, the controversy generated resulted in Rumsfeld's shutting OSI down within one week[42]—the day after Bush proclaimed zero tolerance for lies by American officials and vowed to "tell the American people the truth."[43]

While OSI might have been publicly closed, it is likely the policy itself continued. As a *Newsday* columnist wrote at the time of the closing, "But don't worry, Rumsfeld's people were whispering yesterday around the Pentagon. They'll keep on spreading whatever stories they think they have to—to foreigners especially. Call it the free flow of misinformation. Who needs a formal office for that?"[44] On November 18, 2002, en route to a meeting of defense ministers in Chile, Rumsfeld himself told reporters on his plane, "And then there was the Office of Strategic Influence. You may recall that. And 'oh my goodness gracious isn't that terrible, Henny Penny the sky is going to fall.' I went down that next day and said fine, if you want to savage this thing fine I'll give you the corpse. There's the name. You can have the name, but I'm gonna keep doing every single thing that needs to be done and I have."[45] Despite the controversy generated when the creation of OSI was revealed, these comments about the continuation of the policy went essentially unreported. As reported by FAIR, "A search of the Nexis database indicates that no major U.S. media outlets—no national broadcast television news shows, no major U.S. newspapers, no wire services or major magazines—have reported Rumsfeld's remarks."[46]

In the period leading up to a possible second UN resolution to endorse the war in early 2003, when it was revealed that the administration's National Security Agency was "conducting a secret 'dirty tricks' campaign against UN Security Council delegations in New York as part of its battle to win votes in favor of war against Iraq," much more concern was generated in the international media than in the U.S. press.[47] The activities included intercepting the home and office phone calls as well as e-mail of country representatives to the United Nations in order to gather information as to how they might vote on the resolution.[48]

Conclusion

As I stated in the opening paragraphs of this piece, I believe the Bush administration played upon the vulnerability of an American public traumatized by September 11 to advance a post–cold war political and military agenda long under development by members of the administration. As one senior administration official reportedly observed, inside the government, the terrorist attacks were "a transformative moment" not because they revealed a threat previously unknown to the government, but because of the drastically reduced resistance of the American public to military action abroad. With the attacks on the United States, "the options are much broader."[49] One of those options was the invasion of Iraq.

In order to justify the invasion, administration officials lied, and distorted and manipulated information to push the American public to support an invasion of Iraq as "preemptive self-defense." While the Bush administration's post–September 11 national security strategy based on preemption did not stir much debate inside the United States, it did abroad. Many argued that it would create precedents that would make the world much less, rather than more, secure.

To now find that the evidence used to justify its first preemptive action—the invasion of Iraq—was based not just on uncertain intelligence, but on "forward-leaning" interpretation of intelligence as well as outright lies to justify policies already in motion puts U.S. credibility further at risk. The strategies and tactics used by the Bush administration to achieve its ends left, in the words of one commentator, "diplomacy in ruins." The impact of its increasingly tattered credibility on both U.S. and global security remains to be seen.

In addition to the erosion of domestic civil liberties through legislation such as the Patriot Act, democracy in the United States has been threatened by the stifling not just of the freedom of speech of individuals but of public discussion and debate about policies that have an impact on the course of our nation. Major U.S. media outlets have been complicit in the erosion of our freedoms by acting more like public relations firms for the Bush agenda than objective news sources that supposedly are the underpinnings of the much-lauded American free press.

There have been a few journalistic voices that have spoken out, including one of the foremost in contemporary America, Walter Cronkite. In discussing his decision in mid-2003 to begin to write a regular column, he stated, "In my years as a journalist I have known only a single time as critical as this, when it seemed that the future of our democracy hung in the balance. . . . We all know the issues that today threaten a seismic change in this land we love and our relations with each other and the rest of the world: Our bellicose military policy, our arrogant foreign policy, our domestic security policy that threatens our freedom of speech, press and person. . . . As a witness to most of our 20th century history, I have a few ideas that might at least be provocative. And a little provocation with perhaps some original ideas can't hurt as we put the issues and their possible solutions on the table for discussion."[50]

Only if more and more of us continue to find and exercise our public voices can the violence wrought upon our democracy through the lies and distortions of the current administration, coupled with the complicity of much of the mainstream media, be countered. As this situation demonstrates, the use of violence in all forms to counter violence only serves to erode our liberties and make us all less secure—both in the United States and around the globe.

Notes

1. This article is an adaptation of a larger piece, entitled "Iraq and Preemptive Self-Defense," I wrote for inclusion in *The Iraq War and Its Consequences* (Singapore: World Scientific Publishing Co.), scheduled for publication in September 2003. That article, in addition to some of the elements explored here, discusses the real reasons for the invasion of Iraq.
2. "The National Security Strategy of the United States of America," The White House, Washington, D.C., September 17, 2002, available at: www.whitehouse. gov/nsc/nss.html; see also "National Strategy to Combat Weapons of Mass Destruction," U.S. Department of Defense, December 2002, available at: www.defenselink.mil/pubs/.

3. As a result of the first Gulf War, through a series of UN resolutions, the regime was required to get rid of its WMD. UN weapons inspections were carried out between 1992–1998, when they were suspended.

4. "Remarks by the President in Address to the United Nations General Assembly New York, New York," The White House, Office of the Press Secretary, September 12, 2002, available at: www.whitehouse.gov/news/releases/2002/09/20020912–1.html.

5. United Nations Security Council Resolution 1441, S/Res/1441/2002, November 8, 2002, available at: www.un.org/documents/scres.htm.

6. Mohamed ElBaradei, "The Status of Nuclear Inspections in Iraq," Statement to the United Nations Security Council on behalf of the International Atomic Energy Agency, New York, January 27, 2003, available at: www.un.org/News/dh/iraq/elbaradei27jan03.htm.

7. Secretary Colin L. Powell, "Remarks to the United Nations Security Council," The U.S. State Department, February 5, 2003, available at: www.state.gov/secretary/rm/2003/17300.htm.

8. The White House, "US Secretary of State Colin Powell Addresses the UN Security Council," February 5, 2003, available at: www.whitehouse.gov/news/releases/2003/02/20030205–1.html. For a point-by-point discussion of the elements of the speech, see "Powell's Feb. 5th Presentation to the UN," Center for Cooperative Research, available at: www.cooperativeresearch.org/wot/iraq/colin_powell_february_5_presentation_to_the_un.html.

9. "Bush to Declare Major Combat Over in Iraq," *Associated Press*, April 30, 2003.

10. Jonathan Marcus, "US faces up to guerrilla war: It has taken a change in command for senior US officers to utter the 'G' word about Iraq," *BBC* News, July 17, 2003, available at: news.bbc.co.uk/1/hi/world/middle_east/3074465.stm; Vernon Loeb, "'Guerrilla' War Acknowledged: New Commander Cites Problems," *Washington Post,* July 17, 2003, p. A1.

11. Dana Milbank, "For Bush, Facts Are Malleable," *Washington Post,* 22 October 2003; Fairness & Accuracy in Reporting, "MEDIA advisory: Bush Uranium Lie is Tip of the Iceberg: Press should expand focus beyond '16 words,'" July 18, 2003, at: http://www.fair.org/press-releases/beyond-niger.html. For an analysis of sixteen major distortions by the administration to justify the invasion, see: Council for a Livable World, "Iraq: 16 Distortions, not 16 Words," July 31, 2003, available at: www.clw.org/16distortions.html.

12. John W. Dean, "Missing Weapons of Mass Destruction: Is Lying About The Reason For War an Impeachable Offense?" *FindLaw,* June 6, 2003; James Risen and Douglas Jehl, "Expert Said to Tell Legislators He Was Pressed to Distort Some Evidence," *New York Times,* June 25, 2003.

13. Articles and analyses of the evidence presented by the Bush administration to justify attacking Iraq abound. See, for example: William M. Arkin, "A Hazy Target; Before going to war over weapons of mass destruction, shouldn't we be sure Iraq has them?" *Los Angeles Times,* March 9, 2003; Seymour M. Hersh, "Offense and Defense," *The New Yorker,* April 7, 2003; Robin Cook, "Shoulder to Shoulder and Stabbed in the Back," *Los Angeles Times,* June 6, 2003; John W. Dean, "Missing Weapons Of Mass Destruction: Is Lying about the Reason for War an Impeachable Offense?" *FindLaw,* June 6, 2003; John B. Judis and Spencer Ackerman, "The Selling of the Iraq War: The First Casualty," *The New Republic,* June 30, 2003; Dana Milbank, "White House Didn't Gain CIA Nod for Claim on Iraqi Strikes: Gist Was Hussein Could Launch in 45

Minutes," *Washington Post,* July 20, 2003; Dana Priest, "Uranium Claim Was Known for Months to be Weak: Intelligence Officials Say 'Everyone Knew' Then What the White House Knows Now about Niger Reference," *Washington Post,* July 20, 2003.

14. Edward T. Pound and Bruce B. Auster, "The Plot Thickens: New Evidence fails to resolve mystery of Bush's State of the Union misstep on Iraq," *US News and World Report,* July 28–August 4, 2003. See also, Robert Sheer, "A Diplomat's Undiplomatic Truth: They Lied," *Los Angeles Times,* 8 July 2003.

15. John B. Judis and Spencer Ackerman, "The Selling of the Iraq War: The First Casualty," *The New Republic,* June 30, 2003.

16. John B. Judis and Spencer Ackerman, "The Selling of the Iraq War: The First Casualty," *The New Republic,* June 30, 2003; Julian Berger, "The Spies Who Pushed for War," *The Guardian* (London), July 17, 2003; Jim Lobe, "The Other Bush Lie," *TomPaine.com,* July 15, 2003; Ray McGovern, "Not Business as Usual: Cheney and the CIA," *Alternet,* June 30, 2003. In this piece McGovern writes, "As though this were normal! I mean the repeated visits Vice President Dick Cheney made to the CIA before the war in Iraq. The visits were, in fact, unprecedented. During my 27-year career at the Central Intelligence Agency, no vice president ever came to us for a working visit."

17. Edward T. Pound and Bruce B. Auster, "The Plot Thickens: New Evidence fails to resolve mystery of Bush's State of the Union misstep on Iraq," *US News and World Report,* July 28–August 4, 2003.

18. Julian Berger, "The Spies Who Pushed for War," *The Guardian* (London), July 17, 2003.

19. John B. Judis and Spencer Ackerman, "The Selling of the Iraq War: The First Casualty," *The New Republic,* June 30, 2003.

20. Fairness and Accuracy in Reporting, "MEDIA ADVISORY: Media Silent on Clark's 9/11 Comments: Gen. says White House pushed Saddam link without evidence," June 20, 2003. http://www.fair.org/press-releases/clark-iraq.html.

21. Fairness and Accuracy in Reporting, "MEDIA ADVISORY: Media Silent on Clark's 9/11 Comments: Gen. says White House pushed Saddam link without evidence," June 20, 2003.

22. John B. Judis and Spencer Ackerman, "The Selling of the Iraq War: The First Casualty," *The New Republic,* June 30, 2003.

23. James Risen and David Johnston, "Split at C.I.A. and F.B.I. On Iraqi Ties to Al Qaeda," *New York Times,* February 2, 2003.

24. "Leaked Report Rejects Iraqi al-Qaeda Link," *BBC News,* February 5, 2003. http://news.bbc.co.uk/2/hi/uk_news/2727471.stm.

25. Mark Armstrong, "White House Politically Corrects Maher," *E! Online News,* September 27, 2001.

26. Norman Soloman, "Media Nix: From Blix to Kucinich to the Dixie Chicks," Global Policy Forum, April 24, 2003, available at: www.globalpolicy.org/security/issues/iraq/media/2003/0424medianix.htm.

27. Paul Krugman, "Channels of Influence," *New York Times,* March 25, 2003, available at: www.commondreams.org/views03/0325–03.htm.

28. In 2001, a total of 14,632 sources were interviewed by the three major network's evening news broadcasts. Of these sources, 92 percent were white, 85 percent were male, 75 percent were Republican, when party noted, and 9 percent were the president himself; see "The Usual Suspects," *Utne,* Nov–Dec 2002. See also Fairness and Accuracy in Reporting, available at: www.fair.org, particularly the section devoted to "Iraq and the Media."

29. The news programs studied were ABC World News Tonight, CBS Evening News, NBC Nightly News, CNN's Wolf Blitzer Reports, Fox's Special Report with Brit Hume, and PBS's NewsHour with Jim Lehrer.

30. Steve Rendall and Tara Broughel, "Amplifying Officials, Squelching Dissent: FAIR study finds democracy poorly served by war coverage," FAIR, May/June 2003, available at: www.fair.org/extra/0305/warstudy.html.

31. Steve Rendall and Tara Broughel, "Amplifying Officials, Squelching Dissent: FAIR study finds democracy poorly served by war coverage," FAIR, May/June 2003, available at: http://www.fair.org/extra/0305/warstudy.html. The antiwar percentages ranged from 4 percent at NBC, 3 percent at CNN, ABC, PBS, and FOX, and less than 1 percent—one out of 205 U.S. sources—at CBS.

32. Chris Hedges, *War Is a Force That Gives Us Meaning* (New York: Public Affairs, 2002).

33. "Uniting and Strengthening America by Providing Appropriate Tools Required to Intercept and Obstruct Terrorism (USA PATRIOT ACT) Act of 2001," US Congress, HR 3162, October 24, 2001, available at: www.epic.org/privacy/terrorism/hr3162.html.

34. Much analysis has been written about the impact of the USA Patriot Act. See, for example, Mary Minnow, "The USA Patriot Act and Patron Privacy on Library Internet Terminals," *Law Library Resource Xchange,* February 15, 2002, available at: www.llrx.com/features/usapatriotact.htm; Center for Constitutional Rights, "The State of Civil Liberties: One Year Later. The Erosion of Civil Liberties in the Post 9/11 Era," 2002, available at: www.ccr-ny.org/v2/reports/docs/Civil_Liberties.pdf.

35. Chris Finnian, "Opposition to the USA Patriot Act is Growing," American Booksellers Association, November 14, 2002, available at: news.bookweb.org/freeexpression/943.html.

36. Brian Seals, "Watsonville joins opposition to Patriot Act," *Santa Cruz Sentinel,* 26 March 2003, available at: www.santacruzsentinel.com/archive/2003/March/26/local/stories/02local.htm.

37. Gordon R. Mitchell, "Legitimation Dilemmas in the Bush National Security Strategy," paper presented at the Eastern Communication Association Conference, Washington, D.C., April 23–26, 2003.

38. William M. Arkin, "Defense Strategy: The Military's New War of Words," *Los Angeles Times,* November 24, 2002, cited in Gordon R. Mitchell, "Legitimation Dilemmas in the Bush National Security Strategy," paper presented at the Eastern Communication Association Conference, Washington, D.C., April 23–26, 2003.

39. "New Pentagon Office to Spearhead Information War," CNN.com, February 20, 2002, available at: www.cnn.com/2002/US/02/19/gen.strategic.influence/.

40. Tom Carver, "Pentagon Plans Propaganda War," BBC World News, February 20, 2002, available at: news.bbc.co.uk/1/hi/world/Americas/1830500.stm. In this article Carver wrote, "Some generals are worried that even a suggestion of disinformation would undermine the Pentagon's credibility and America's attempts to portray herself as the beacon of liberty and democratic values."

41. James Dao and Eric Schmitt, "Pentagon Readies Efforts to Sway Sentiment Abroad," *New York Times,* February 19, 2002, available at: www.commondreams.org/headlines02/0219–01.htm.

42. For a full transcript of Rumsfeld's remarks to the press at the announcement of the closing of OSI, see "US Closes Office of Strategic Information: Says effectiveness damaged by media," U.S. Department of State, International

Information Programs, February 27, 2002, available at: usinfo.state.gov/regional/nea/sasia/text/0227rmfd.htm.

43. Norman Soloman, "Pentagon's Silver Lining May be Bigger Than Cloud," Media Beat, Fairness and Accuracy in Reporting, February 28, 2002, available at: www.fair.org/media-beat/020228.html.

44. Norman Soloman, "Pentagon's Silver Lining May be Bigger Than Cloud," Media Beat, Fairness and Accuracy in Reporting, February 28, 2002, reporting on *Newsday* column by Ellis Henican, available at: http://www.fair.org/media-beat/020228.html.

45. Fairness and Accuracy in Reporting, "Media Advisory: The Office of Strategic Influence is Gone, but Are Its Programs in Place?" November 27, 2002. The full transcript of Rumsfeld's remarks are available at the U.S. Department of Defense website at: www.dod.gov/news/Nov2002/t11212002_t1118sd2.html. For discussion of the continued programs, despite closing of OSI, see NPR's *On the Media*, "Global Information War in the Works?" an interview with William Arkin on WNYC on December 13, 2002, available at: www.wnyc.org/onthemedia/transcripts/transcripts_121302_information.html.

46. Fairness and Accuracy in Reporting, "Media Advisory: The Office of Strategic Influence is Gone, but Are Its Programs in Place?" November 27, 2002.

47. Martin Bright, Ed Vulliamy, and Peter Beaumont, "U.S. National Security Agency Memo Reveals Spying on U.N. Delegates," *The Observer* (UK), 3 March 2003, available at: reclaimdemocracy.org/weekly.2003/spying_on_un.html.

48. Martin Bright, Ed Vulliamy, and Peter Beaumont, "U.S. National Security Agency Memo Reveals Spying on U.N. Delegates," *The Observer* (UK), March 3, 2003, available at: reclaimdemocracy.org/weekly.2003/spying_on_un.html.

49. Nicholas Lemann, "The Next World Order: The Bush Administration may have a brand-new doctrine of power," *The New Yorker*, April 1, 2002.

50. Press release, "Walter Cronkite to Write Weekly Newspaper Column," *King Features*, undated, available at: http://www.kingfeatures.com/pressrm/PR129.htm.

Part III

Contexts and Locations of Violence

Chapter 11

Naming Enmity

The Case of Israel/Palestine

Gil Anidjar

For Joseph.

Enabling a naming of the enemy, three questions should and, for the most part, have emerged. *What is the enemy? Who is the enemy?*, and, finally, *What to do with (or to) the enemy?* When attending to the so-called Middle East conflict, the last two questions appear to have been answered repeatedly and with devastating clarity. Indeed, it would be hard to deny the overwhelming evidence that such is the case. Little room is thus left to displace the presumption of symmetry (the basic fact of mutual hostility) or to question the plain existence (if it can still be called such without obscenity) of adversaries or the deadly course of actions that have been taken (presumably, again, with parity). Yet hesitations and waverings remain as to the "proper" designations that would adequately name the past and current situation in Israel and Palestine. These designations, these names, are perhaps well known, and they say much about the agendas they serve, consciously or not. Who, after all, are the adversaries? Israelis and Palestinians? Jews and Muslims? Jews and Arabs? Political realists and religious extremists? Beyond an all-too-familiar, horrid, and seemingly inescapable "cycle of violence," what is it that maintains the distance and kindles the enmity named under these headings? What purposes are served by and what are the reasons for the naturalization of this distance, the naturalization of the opposition and the enmity between two adversaries (for there would be two and only two—no less, no more—parties involved), an enmity that, as prominent narratives would have us believe, goes back to ancient biblical times, the ineluctable legacy of "the Middle East," a region and a land eternally ravaged by war and conflict?

Apparently adjudicating on the substance of the enmity, the first set of terms (Israeli versus Palestinian) defines the substance as a political problem and more precisely as the result of two national and nationalist struggles over one territory. This forms the basis of more or less familiar (if hardly equal) narratives. Palestinians, yet to achieve national sovereignty, would be engaged in a struggle for a recognition of their national claims, claims contested (in part or *in toto*) by the Israelis, themselves successful heirs to a history of oppression and to a historical movement that strove to reach and establish a "national home," national consciousness, national settlement, finally fighting a "war of independence."[1] Alternatively, the conflict may be inscribed in the aftermath of World War II and the general struggle against Western colonialism, with the added misfortune of a lack of resolution resulting from colonial and postcolonial configurations, or, more likely, from the stubborn resistance to resolution by one or more of the parties involved. Finally, the terms may signify the infuriating victory of the last colonial-settler state, bastion of Western imperialism and its colonial aims, against whom natives are still engaged in a fierce liberation struggle.

The second set of terms (Jew versus Muslim) locates the conflict on a much older theological scene. The intolerance of Islam would have made it impossible for the Jews to live on equal and peaceful terms with the Muslims, an impossibility that would go back to the historical treatment of religious minorities in Islamic regimes, to competing narrative claims over the Abrahamic traditions, or simply to the increasing slide into extremism found in all religious communities (Jewish as well as Muslim, Hindu, and even Christian—but I digress) with different consequences at different historical periods. Finally, the last set of terms (political realism versus religious fanaticism) constitutes a division that rearticulates those considered so far, necessitating adjustments, not the least of which is historical. Here, a political program (national, secular, and democratic) would oppose a fanatically religious zealotry, making a resolution all the more unlikely because of the asymmetric planes upon which the parties encounter (or fail to encounter) each other. The adversaries would be at war over a theologico-political divide that is also a historical one. The dark age of religion would be resisting the (not-so-new) dawn of secular democracy.

It is perhaps ironically difficult to consider that, although such narratives are well entrenched within American discourse (even if the closest to truth are considered—if considered—"radical"), none of the terms mentioned so far have dominated the discursive scene such as has deployed itself over the "Middle East conflict." How, then, did these ostensible markers (Jew and Arab) come to inscribe themselves so forcefully on modern discourses of the most varied kind—political, religious, cultural, and so forth—even when accompanying distinct or even opposed political agendas, caveats and sophisticated analyses, critiques and debunkings? The terms only appear to maintain the symmetry of planes such as we have already encountered. "Jew" is primarily a religious term (it is as such that it appears above), whereas "Arab," although often confused and collapsed with a religious conviction, is more widely understood as an ethnic marker. In this perspective, war would again be thought across a double divide: a religious community with nationalist aspirations would be facing a massive ethnic body, the latter rejecting the former for allergic reasons, with no other visible goal than that of expelling the foreign intruder. Here, one could alternatively point out that, in modern times at least, Jews have insisted on defining themselves (and have certainly been defined by less-than-friendly others) as "more than a religion."[2] If this is true, and if Jews are, in fact, an ethnic community (a fact that "American Jews"—not "Jewish-Americans"—would perhaps want to deny at the manifest level), then the "Middle East conflict" can still be said to be thought and conducted on one ethnic plane.[3]

One of the ironies of the naming of enmity said to oppose Jew to Arab resides in the fact that the ethnic argument is, of course, rarely mentioned.[4] Among the numerous "ethnic conflicts" and instances of "ethnic violence" that have marked the twentieth century and its aftermath, none would seem to provide an adequate analogy to the situation at hand.[5] This could be made even clearer were one to suggest that, between Jews and Arabs, we are witnessing a racial and racist confrontation, comparable to South Africa. The analogy has, of course, been raised—and not without justification given the ideological, economic, and military convergences and collaborations between the apartheid state and the state of Israel.[6] Yet, it has rarely been pushed to the point of suggesting that two "races" are here at war. This too is a question of names, and more. Were Arabs and Jews deemed two races, the vocabulary of race, which has been inherited from the nineteenth century (and which continues to operate in different guises and contexts), would likely impose upon them both the term "Semites." Even taking into account the massive collusions surrounding the modern invention of Jews as an "ethnic" (and national) grouping at the time when racial and nationalist theories were being elaborated,[7] or debates as to whether Arabs were or not considered "Semites" in racial and racist discourse (Lewis 1999), the general acceptance of the term today (think of "Semitic languages") would make it difficult to separate, on ethnic, racial, or racist terms, Jews from Arabs without endeavoring to reconstruct a new and improved racial vocabulary, or worse, a racist science (or without attempting to render this endeavor invisible). Here lies another irony: the terms that continue to dominate the discursive field called "Israel and Palestine" (or better yet, "the Middle East") fail to revive (or at least to make explicit) the very history upon which they would seem to be predicated: the history of racism. For who, today, would dare to speak of the Jews as a race? More generally, who would dare to speak not of a "clash of civilizations" but of a "war of races"? Even the argument that new names might still designate the "same" phenomena (and there is cause for such concern), one would have to account for the discursive shift that has rendered race invisible or, more precisely, unnameable in the case of Jews and Arabs.

One rarely observed reason that "Jew" and "Arab" remain dominant markers is that they continue to determine the daily life of millions. Indeed, "ethnic" self-definition having been massively accepted by Jewish organizations across the Western world (with, among other factors, the unabashed emphasis on preserving Judaism by protecting it from miscegenation—or, in its more benign appellation, "intermarriage"), the terms "Jew" and "Arab" have gained institutional (and military) force precisely where the discourse of European racism would have presumably been, if not vanquished, at least avenged. In the state of Israel, as part of a larger apparatus of discriminating measures, government-issued, mandatory I.D. cards have been prescribed by the Israeli legislature for fifty years (the practice has now been interrupted for no less troubling reasons linked to the massive arrival of non-Jewish Russian immigrants). On these cards, which every citizen of the state must carry, Jew and Arab—embodiments of Althusserian interpellations—come before the law under two headings: "Nationality" (Jew, Arab) is thereby distinguished from "citizenship" (Israeli), and one can already note that, in one register of the "nationality" category, "Jew" is de-theologized, whereas "Arab" is simply maintained as distinct from any religious content, an ethnic or simply political marker. How has it become possible for the state that claimed reparations for one of the most horrifying chapters in the history of racism and state-sponsored racism to institutionalize a "national" (read, ethnic) distinction among its own citizens? What history is preserved, or worse, re-enacted in the naming of Jew and Arab as ethnic categories? In a proximate context, Bernard Lewis sketches an Eastern European genealogy for this distinction between nationality (i.e., ethnic nationality) and citizenship. Lewis confirms the terms of the debate as we have been exploring them by pointing out that the institutionalization of this distinction involved the transformation of religion into ethnicity (in our case, "Jew"), and a confinement, even a kind of eradication of religion (here, "Arab," which stands for, and erases, Muslim, or Christian) as an identity category. The significance of this "secular" institution that would leave religion behind is traced by Lewis to the Soviet Union, in particular, although Lewis could have referred to the general shift undergone in the changing (self-)perception of Jews in the West, from a "religious" minority to a "racial" one. The pragmatic, if not historical, reasons for that shift at the institutional level are made clear in Lewis's comment that "ethnic nationality, unlike religion, cannot be changed by an act of conversion."[8] Disciplined citizens, Foucault might say, cannot simply transform themselves. They must be locatable. (Imagine the conundrum the Jewish state would face if Arab Jews, Zionism's Jewish victims, as Ella Shohat has argued (1988), had insisted on being "nationalized" as Arabs, or if Palestinians had invoked Jewish roots—or better yet, converted en masse). But be that as it may, we may temporarily conclude from this simplifying survey that whether one speaks of Israelis and Palestinians (nationalism as the primary factor), Jews and Muslims (religion as the primary factor), or Jews and Arabs (with poised, so-called "democratic" politics, on one side and "fanatical" religion, on the other), one is never simply mistaken. One does, however, maintain and further sediment a violent state of affairs that, institutionalized by the state of Israel (among other institutions and organizations), reinscribes invisible or uninterrogated ethnic and racist distinctions, gaping distances and enmities between Jew and Arab.

Suspending the question of accuracy as to an analysis that would attempt to isolate the three spheres that have been recalled here (politics, religion, ethnicity)—surely, it is both contrived and inaccurate to engage in such analytical, isolating speculations in such a complex situation—one must still account for the enduring power of names; the hegemonic dominance of two among them, in particular; as well as for the answers they provide to questions of historical origins (clearly, each set of names embodies a distinct historical narrative, a particular array of inevitabilities) and, more urgently, to possibilities of a resolution, one that would admittedly have to answer the call of justice. At this juncture, I want to address the power of naming enmity, the sustaining role played by names such as "Jew" and "Arab," insofar as they constitute the terms with which both question and answer (cause and effect, origins and solutions) are thought. Within the general frame that they provide, as I have tried to elaborate it here, they are themselves answers of sorts to two of the questions with which we began regarding the enemy. Who is the enemy? (the Jew, the Arab) What to do with the enemy? (discriminate against, expel, occupy, harass, starve, shoot, bomb, deport, torture, kill, etc. but also eat like and eat with, speak and sleep with, dress like, listen to the music of, hire, exploit, collaborate with, imitate, admire, etc.). The first of the three questions mentioned (What is the enemy?) has not been answered for at least two reasons.

Until the twentieth century, within the Western discursive sphere that occupies us here, the question, What is the enemy?, had not been asked. No field of knowledge had claimed the enemy as one of its founding concepts (compare the discourse on love in philosophy or theology, or friendship and sovereignty in politics); no field of knowledge, no discipline, had claimed to provide an answer to the question: What is the enemy?[9] Today, there is ever less certainty as to what an enemy is, and although this enigmatic fact hardly constitutes an obstacle to the devastating treatment of enemies everywhere, it remains puzzling enough to call for a poised reconsideration. Second, the undeniable and continued investment (from theological and emotional, to political and economic) of the West in Israel and Palestine, in the Jew and the Arab, and most important in their categorization as enemies, remains at some level profoundly puzzling. (Compare, for example, the lesser media coverage of Chechnya or even Ireland at the time, and so not only in the United States.) Here, too, answers have yet to be formulated. As paradigmatic enemies of the West (mostly, but not only, of Christian Europe), Jews (as theological and later racial enemies) and Arabs (as political and military enemies, from the Saracens to the Turk, from despotism to terrorism) belong to a long, almost uninterrupted history of concern and fear about Muslim presence in Europe (today referred to as a "demographic threat" in Europe and in Israel), and a no less uninterrupted history of negotiating, more or less violently, the presence of Jewish populations. The Jew, the Arab, then, constitute the basic terms of a Western history of the enemy, a history that, were it written, would provide an elaborate answer as to how the enemy becomes what the enemy is (or was). This history, this enemy which is not *one*, partakes of Jew, of Arab, and of the West. It engages and confronts each of the terms in their mutual and co-constitutive relations. This history could also be named, with some anachronism, a history of the Semites (that Western construct that more or less lumped together Jews and Arabs, ancient Hebrews and "Middle Eastern" peoples). Itself a potentially significant answer to the question, What is the enemy?, the history of the Semites (the Jew, the Arab) has yet to be written. Alternatively, and more generously, one could consider that it has been partly (and partially) written as two discrete histories: that of Europe and the Jews (the history of anti-Semitism, for the most part) and that of Islam and the West (the history of Orientalism). Two histories, then, which, without a shred of evidence or simple justification that they should be treated as distinct, continue to obey the governing "principles" that have defined the entire set of terms we have considered thus far, all of which, without exception, treat as given the clear and distinct gap, the dangerous state of enmity that allegedly separates Jew from Arab (in whatever configuration one chooses from those depicted above). Put another way, the reductive and uninterrogated claim that what there is between Jew and Arab is enmity already sets the stage for a resolution by way of separation. (On that model, the solution to Apartheid would be to separate blacks from whites, that is to say, to preserve and maintain Apartheid).[10] More important, without answering the crucial question as to what the enemy is, the entire discursive sphere I have tried to describe massively occludes the after all not unlikely possibility that Western history (the history of Christian Europe in its temporal and geographical extensions) plays a constitutive role in the sedimentation of the enmity between Jew and Arab.[11] What that role continues to be, what accounts for the investment in both Jew and Arab, what the mediating links are between these terms when viewed from the perspective of Europe and of the West at large—these are questions that have yet to be explored, let alone answered. Even to begin to treat the question of the alleged enmity between Jew and Arab (if these terms are in fact naming anything of relevance to the issue) by isolating them as the polar and systemic site of conflict, as origin and goal of a historical given, as if they always already, and at any point in history, constituted an autonomous and meaningful unit of analysis, is to obfuscate everything.

There are, of course, some important exceptions to this general state of obfuscation (even laudable attempts to move beyond it).[12] And yet, one would have to explain their exceptional (and marginal) status. One would have to account for the absence of both a concept of enemy (an answer to the question: What is?) and a history of the enemy (the forms and objects the question of enmity has taken in the West—itself a unit that remains, of course, difficult to grasp insofar as it has failed to define itself rigorously enough to provide an answer to said questions). More modestly, one would have to address what continues to constitute obstacles to filling these absences. It is therefore not a matter of establishing guilt or even responsibility (at least not yet) nor of claiming reparations (all in due time). It is rather about lifting obstacles that prevent a consideration of (minimally) historical and conceptual pressures such as those that continue to frame and determine the debate, and indeed, the "conflict," that prevent a consideration not just of the "Jewish question" (as that famous chapter and export of European history is called) but of an "Arab question" as well. Not all such obstacles can be lifted, certainly not at once, and provisions must obviously be made for the fact that other pressures—contemporary or not—are at work, be they ideological, economic and financial, political and personal, and indeed, racist and religious. Some of these issues have been addressed. Some have not. Among those treated, some have gained currency in the public discourse, and some have not. At this point, and by way of a temporary conclusion, I want to leave these considerations aside and attend to the kind of politically imaginative work that may yet enable a different naming of Jew and Arab. Here, the terms are not yet thought of as one happy (or unhappy) togetherness of Arab and Jew, nor are they to be understood any longer as names of the enemy. Indeed, what these terms could name—and whether they are even to be preserved (but who could decide such a thing?)—remains to be discovered. In order to be new (but it may also be very old), what would thus be named would have to be other (the enemy is not the other), at least other than reductively oppositional. It may even overlap, producing and articulating different zones of indistinguishability, different planes of symmetry and asymmetry. More importantly, it may already be at work, today.

It is in this context that the Israeli historian Amnon Raz-Krakotzkin has suggested an original recasting of the concept of binationalism (borrowed in part from Hannah Arendt) in order, precisely, to avoid what currently constitutes an object of hegemonic consensus and was already at the center of the Oslo accords, namely, *separation*. As Arendt had pointed out, in the political program adopted by the Zionist leadership "the Arabs were simply not mentioned,"[13] and separation—the solution adopted by the UN in the partition plan of 1947—became and remained the only consistent agenda held valid or even viable by Zionism and its numerous supporters. But as Raz-Krakotzkin explains, the presupposition was always that "in order to establish a Jewish state and to ensure Jewish hegemony and Jewish majority, expulsion and exclusion were inevitable" (2001, 169). Separation is consistently put forward as the basic principle of a vision that advocates Jewish autonomy, "a kind of autonomy whose function is to separate the Palestinians from the Jews" (1998, 66). The definition of the state as a Jewish state rather than the state of its citizens "prevents any solution based on the principles of equality and partnership" (2001, 180). That such inequality remains the goal of what goes under the name of "peace process" (or other current "road-maps") is made clear when we "observe that in the Israeli public debate, the term 'peace' still does not mean primarily the fulfillment of Palestinian rights, including the rights of refugees, but rather the principle of separation, the same principle [Arendt] opposed in the 1940s" (2001, 171).[14] Today, in Israel "what is considered as a peace process," even one that should be revived, remains predicated on a concept that "preserves the exclusion of the Palestinian perspective from the discussion of Jewish identity," from the identity of the state (the means to such exclusion range from moving borders and erecting walls to population transfer by more or, well, still more violent means). It "enables one to ignore [the Palestinians'] political rights, and obviates the need to challenge the dominant historical narrative" (172), one that rewrites Jewish history as independent and autonomous, and diminishes the significance of a common history by relegating it to exceptional or even aberrant chapters.[15] In the final analysis, separation preserves (and aims to solidify) the history that would ineluctably associate *and* dissociate "Arab" and "Jew" as eternal enemies. Phrased another way, and more urgently perhaps, separation is what is already at work when "Tel-Aviv became the only city in the West to which the entrance of Arabs was forbidden. In many ways, then, we can regard the attitude behind the peace process as close to the radical right in Europe: the steps taken before and after the Oslo Accord are exactly those demanded by Le Pen and his followers in France" (1998, 67). What is missing from a debate with such shared parameters is "any considerable political position which could combine the discussion on Israeli-Jewish identity with the discussion on Palestinian rights" (75). What is missing is a "bi-national approach, namely one which does not separate the discussion on Israeli society from the Jewish-Palestinian conflict" (75). As Raz-Krakotzkin puts it elsewhere, "the concept of binationalism and the sense of responsibility on which Arendt insisted are even more relevant and important from the perspective of the present, when the Jewish State dominates the entire land, operating various systems of exclusion and dispossession with regard to the Arab inhabitants" (2001, 169). Binationalism "implies the realization that Palestinian history and Palestinian national identity are part of the discussion of Zionist history, essential parts of the context of responsibility. The definition of Palestinian rights and the definition of Jewish rights are one and the same. This is the context of responsibility that Zionism has created. . . . A binational perspective leads to . . . the definition of a common Jewish-Arab space."[16] In other words, binationalism directs us toward a thinking of the Jew, the Arab that would be named otherwise; otherwise, that is, than enmity.

Notes

1. Thus Kathleen Christison who, questioning the very appellation of the war of 1948 as Israel's "war of independence," nonetheless writes that the war "gave its independence" to the Jewish state (Christison 1999, 61). "Independence from whom," writes Joseph Massad, "remains unclear. After all, the British had already left voluntarily without being party to the war. The Arab armies had not been in occupation of any Palestinian land prior to the Zionist declaration" (Massad 2000a, 318).
2. The transition in the status (and the self-conception) of the Jews of Europe from a religious minority to an ethnic (or national) one has not gained the critical attention it deserves, but it has been documented and reflected upon by Hannah Arendt (1958) and, more recently, by Mitchell Hart (2000). The dichotomy between religious and ethnic, and more generally between religious and secular, should of course, be qualified, first and foremost in the historical linearity it maintains, but here is not the place to do so. Talal Asad (2003) has contributed most significantly to a rethinking of these last dichotomies.

3. The place of American Judaism in the history of ethnicization, partly manifest in the choice for nonhyphenation, has yet to be written. Pointers can be found in Hart 2000 and Massad 2003.

4. This has to do in part with the American scene, but also with the lack of account for the becoming-ethnic of Jews (see below, note 7). Invocations of an ethnic dimension in the "Middle East" and in the case of Israel and Palestine are, at any rate, rare in the West (less so, if still marginally, in Israel and Palestine), and are usually confined to highly specialized or activist circles. When they are made, all ideological shields are raised against them, and first of all the counter-accusation that one is thereby an anti-Semite and a racist, or, in even rarer cases (alas!), a self-hating Jew.

5. Oren Yiftachel (2000) fruitfully suggests analogies with Sri Lanka, Serbia, and South Africa. One may add, of course, India and Pakistan.

6. Massad has convincingly made the case in a number of publications. Most pertinently, during the implementation of the Oslo agreement, Massad (1999b) was pointing out the cruel ironies at work in these alleged resolutions. Nadia Abu El-Haj (2001) offers a different kind of analysis in which she demonstrates the existence of "spatial apartheid" in Israel and in occupied Palestine.

7. In an essential contribution to the issue at hand, Hart demonstrates that the nineteenth century witnessed the birth of a series of "Jewish sciences," among which social sciences (sociology and statistics, but also racial theory) held a prominent, if lesser known, place. These could be accurately described as the Jewish (mostly, but not only, Zionist) contribution to the rapidly evolving racial and racist discourses of the time—a long-lasting contribution. What took place with these scientific developments was a "redefinition of Jews and Judaism utilizing the language of social science." Typical of this Jewish endeavor is Alfred Nossig, according to whom "Jews must be redefined anthropologically as a *Volk* or *Stamm*, rather than as a religious community. . . . Nossig sought to demonstrate the essential unity of the Jewish *Stamm*" (Hart 2000, 34). Jewish social sciences (that is, the invention and adoption by Jewish scholars of a scientific discourse of auto-analysis) gave itself "two preeminent tasks." It would "illuminate the fact of the existence of a Jewish national or ethnic identity, and the 'worth' or 'value' of Jewry as a distinct and different collective entity." At the same time, it would "analyze and represent the causes for, and manifestations of, the dissolution of that identity—a process designated as 'abnormal' and 'diseased'—in the modern period" (43). The claim that Jews were diseased as a result of their diasporic existence became, of course, an essential argument for Zionism, which offered itself as the "cure." Others suggested more radical solutions, if still advocating the end of Jewish existence in Europe. Some begged to differ. Hart points out that at the turn of the century, "the denial by Zionism of the solely religious character of Jewry, and the attempt to redefine Jewry along national/racial lines, were anathema to the majority of Jews" (46). Although the term "race" has lost its currency in Jewish circles, one could hardly find any disagreement as to the basic terms that constitute Jewish identity today. Hart aptly depicts the beginnings of this modern development when he writes that "if, as Zionism claimed, Jews were united by more than a common faith, and yet lacked many of the attributes associated with nationhood—common territory, language, manners, customs— then on what basis could the Jews be said to constitute a *Volk?* Jewish racial unity and particularity provided scientific proof for Zionist claims that despite apparent differences between Jews around the world, they nonetheless consti-

tuted a people or a nation" (182). Within academic discourse, the *Wissenschaft des Judentums,* the more famous side of nineteenth-century "Jewish science" (which belonged mostly to what we would call the humanities), has undergone a radical (if not necessarily sufficient) critique. Yet, as Hart shows, there has been no debate, within Jewish studies or Jewish organizations, over the terms established by social scientists, only a massive occlusion (229ff.).

8. Lewis 1999, 34. As Amnon Raz-Krakotzkin points out, in her objection to the very notion of a Jewish state (which Yiftachel calls an "ethnocracy"), Arendt was already reading critically the history traced by Lewis. "Arendt pointed out that the main issue is not the separation of religion from the state, but rather the distinction between national identity and the state" (Raz-Krakotzkin 2001, 172).

9. Following Jacques Derrida's reflections on the concept of the enemy (1997), I have elaborated on this argument in my *The Jew, the Arab* (Anidjar 2003).

10. This program of separation is, as we will consider below, what Israeli left and right, along with Oslo and current "road-maps," have been advancing by way of a "solution."

11. Clearly, and without diminishing the importance of the significant, if few, scholars who have attended to it, what is occluded is much more than the history of colonialism. It also has to do with the history of the Jews, at least of those Jews who came to identify with Europe and with the West ("How the Jews Became White Folks," as Karen Brodkin [1998] puts it). This history too remains to be written, for it is not the "Jewish history" that is currently being taught. Surely, it could not be written without attending to a more general history of the enemy, a history, that is, of "Western Civilization."

12. Edward Said and Maxime Rodinson are prominent among these exceptions, but see also Shohat's groundbreaking study (1988), and see Massad's extensive work (1999a, 1999b, 2000a, 2000b, 2003), Chetrit 1999, and Alcalay 1993.

13. Arendt quoted in Raz-Krakotzkin 2001, 166.

14. Raz-Krakotzkin later contends that "even the two-state solution demands a binational position" (2001, 179).

15. Compare with Alcalay 1993. On the ruling, judeocentric conception of history that still passes for historiography, see Rodinson 1983, 1997.

16. Raz-Krakotzkin 2002, 321. Writing in a more somber tone, Massad 2000b reaches the same conclusion, orienting us toward a future that is already here. It is a "consequence of the triumph of the Zionist project," writes Massad, that "Palestinian Arab history and Zionist Jewish history have become inextricably linked. Events in Jewish history that Zionism appropriated became perforce connected to Palestinian history" (52). The state of Israel (and its allies) "have until today consistently refused to acknowledge the organic link between Zionism's successful history and the catastrophic history its success visited on the Palestinian people" (54).

Works Cited

Abu El-Haj, Nadia. 2001. *Facts on the Ground: Archaelogical Practice and Territorial Self-Fashioning in Israeli Society.* Chicago: University of Chicago Press.

Alcalay, Ammiel. 1993. *After Jews and Arabs: Remaking Levantine Culture.* Minneapolis: University of Minnesota Press.

Anidjar, Gil. 2003. *The Jew, the Arab: A History of the Enemy.* Stanford: Stanford University Press.

Arendt, Hannah. 1958. *The Origins of Totalitarianism.* New York: Meridian.

Asad, Talal. 2003. *Formations of the Secular: Christianity, Islam, Modernity.* Stanford: Stanford University Press.

Brodkin, Karen. 1998. *How Jews Became White Folks and What That Says about Race in America.* New Brunswick, N.J.: Rutgers University Press.

Chetrit, Sami Shalom. 1999. *The Ashkenazi Revolution Is Dead: Reflections on Israel from a Dark Angle* [in Hebrew]. Tel-Aviv: Kedem Publishing.

Christison, Kathleen. 1999. *Perceptions of Palestine: Their Influence on U.S. Middle East Policy.* Berkeley: University of California Press.

Derrida, Jacques. 1997. *Politics of Friendship.* Trans. George Collins. London: Verso.

Hart, Mitchell B. 2000. *Social Science and the Politics of Modern Jewish Identity.* Stanford: Stanford University Press.

Lewis, Bernard. 1999. *Semites and Anti-Semites.* New York: W.W. Norton.

Massad, Joseph. 1999a. "Repentant Terrorists, or Settler-Colonialism Revisited: The PLO-Israeli Agreement in Perspective." *Found Object* 3: 81–90.

Massad, Joseph. 1999b. "Return or Permanent Exile? Palestinian Refugees and the Ends of Oslo." *Critique* 14 (spring): 5–25.

Massad, Joseph. 2000a. "The Post-Colonial Colony: Time, Space, and Bodies in Palestine/Israel." In *The Pre-Occupation of Postcolonial Studies,* ed. Fawzia Afzal-Khan and Kalpana Seshadri-Crooks, 311–46. Durham: Duke University Press.

Massad, Joseph. 2000b. "Palestinians and Jewish History: Recognition or Submission?" *Journal of Palestine Studies* 30(1): 52–67.

Massad, Joseph. 2003. "The Ends of Zionism." *Interventions: The International Journal of Postcolonial Studies* 5: 440–48.

Raz-Krakotzkin. 1998. "A Peace without Arabs: The Discourse of Peace and the Limits of Israeli Consciousness." In *After Oslo: New Realities, Old Problems,* ed. G. Giacaman and D. J. Lonning, 59–76. London: Pluto Press.

Raz-Krakotzkin, Amnon. 2001. "Binationalism and Jewish Identity: Hannah Arendt and the Question of Palestine." In *Hannah Arendt in Jerusalem,* ed. Steven E. Aschheim, 165–80. Berkeley: University of California Press.

Raz-Krakotzkin, Amnon. 2002. "A National Colonial Theology—Religion, Orientalism and the Construction of the Secular in Zionist Discourse." *Tel Aviver Jahrbuch für deutsche Geschichte* 30: 312–26.

Rodinson, Maxime. 1983. *Cult, Ghetto, and State: The Persistence of the Jewish Question.* Trans. by Jon Rothschild. London: Al Saqi Books.

Rodinson, Maxime. 1997 [1981]. *Peuple juif ou problème juif?* Paris: La découverte.

Shohat, Ella. 1988. "Sephardim in Israel: Zionism from the Standpoint of its Jewish Victims." *Social Text* 19–20 (autumn): 1–35.

Yiftachel, Oren. 2000. "Ethnocracy and Its Discontents: Minorities, Protest and the Israeli Polity." *Critical Inquiry* 26: 725–56.

Chapter 12

Toward a Cherokee Theory of Violence

Laura E. Donaldson

Like most Americans, I have spent many moments since the terrorist attacks of September 11 trying to grasp both the acts themselves and the seemingly endless chain of depressing events following in their wake. Although many have rediscovered faith communities or a renewed social activism in their search for understanding, I have immersed myself in the lessons of my own Cherokee culture and history. This history teaches me to situate September 11 in the context of other tragedies that have occurred on American soil. For example, as many as ten thousand Cherokee people perished as a result of the forced march to Oklahoma known as the Trail of Tears—or, more accurately, the *nuna dat suny*, which literally translates as "they were crying in that place." Cherokee oral tradition is replete with stories acknowledging the trauma of what historians euphemistically call "Removal," and its physical, spiritual, and social wounds may never be completely healed. Other stories, and particularly those in the genre known as origin narratives, illuminate both September 11 and Removal by enabling the emergence of a distinctly Cherokee critical theory of violence.

One story tells of the time when animals, fishes, insects, plants, and humans lived with each other in peace and friendship (see Mooney 1982, 250–52). Eventually, however, humans began to crowd and crush their animal partners out of carelessness and contempt. Even worse, they invented weapons of mass destruction such as the blowgun and the spear, which allowed them to kill animals indiscriminately. Each animal nation then called a council and decided to invent diseases inflicting pain and death upon their human victimizers. Under the able leadership of their leader Little Deer, for example, the deer nation voted to send rheumatism to every hunter who killed one of them unless he respectfully asked forgiveness for his offense. The fish nation determined that they would afflict humans with nightmares about eating decayed food so they would lose their appetites. The birds, smaller animals, and insects each in their turn spoke about human cruelty and injustice. The birds condemned humans because "they burn our feet off"—meaning that hunters impaled them on sticks over the fire and singed off their feathers and tender feet. Along with the smaller animals and insects, the birds began to devise so many new diseases that if their inventiveness had not faltered, not one human would have survived. When the plants (who were friendly to humans) heard what had happened, they decided to help by furnishing a cure for each disease. Through this, they counteracted the harm wrought by the vengeful animals.

Although this story ostensibly concerns the origins of Cherokee medicine, it also thematizes the struggle to achieve a precarious balance among many forms of life with diverse needs. It addresses the responsibilities that we all must assume toward each other, and presents the complicated negotiations among animals, plants, humans, and the rest of creation. It also offers some insightful lessons about violence.

Hannah Arendt once remarked that violence does not depend on numbers or opinions, but rather on implements that amplify the strength of its perpetrators (Arendt 1970, 53). The Cherokee origin story of war between animals and humans vividly dramatizes this instrumental quality of violence: humans develop technologies of killing and animals retaliate with their own technologies of disease. Once this vicious cycle is set into motion, only further technological advances—the cures of the plants—can stop it. Or more succinctly, one can only counter violence with further violence. This represents, however, the most pessimistic interpretation of the tale. I find a much more constructive pedagogy in the way that the story does not attribute the propensity toward violence to a theology of depravity, but rather to the absence of a daily, sustainable, and life-affirming ethic. It is, in other words, a failure of responsibility rather than ontology. Further, as an origin story meant for humans, it confronts us with our violent capacity at the very beginning of our lives here on earth, and functions as a cautionary tale about the consequences of ignoring our interrelationships with animals, plants, and the earth itself. While the story's beginning certainly evokes an ancient time when animals and humans communicated freely with one another and lived in peace as partners, the ease of human transgression permits no romanticized view of this "golden age." Finally—and this is a much more fragmentary conceptualization—the story refuses its hearers the luxury of demonizing, suppressing, or repressing violence. Violence is not something that others do to us, but something we inflict upon others. The story consequently demands that we confront and internalize deeply the consequences of violence, and in this alone offers a profoundly important model of response.

Works Cited

Arendt, Hannah. 1970. *On Violence.* San Diego, New York, and London: Harcourt, Brace and Co.

Mooney, James. 1982. *Myths of the Cherokee and Sacred Formulas of the Cherokees: From 19th and 7th Annual Reports B.A.E.* Nashville, Tenn.: Charles and Randy Elder-Booksellers.

Chapter 13

Dangerous Crossings

Violence at the Borders

Lois Ann Lorentzen

Large numbers of the world's peoples participate in one of the great dramas of the early twenty-first century—massive displacement and migration. Escaping political persecution, wars, revolutions, economic devastation, environmental disasters, they move from rural to urban areas within their own countries and increasingly to western industrialized nations, especially to western Europe and the United States. Many come as professionals and skilled workers, although most live on the edge of survival and frequently support families back home. Worldwide, over 150 million migrants systematically endure abuse at the hands of governments and citizens in countries not their own. Before September 11, immigrants to the United States, especially those who were undocumented and/or of color, regularly faced violations of their First, Fourth, and Fifth Amendment rights. Thousands were jailed indefinitely, deported without due process, and lived without protections expected by most U.S. workers. In our post–September 11 era, collaboration among federal officials, Immigration and Naturalization Services (INS), and local police related to immigrant "law enforcement" is becoming institutionalized, and racial, ethnic, and religious profiling is conducted unapologetically.

This essay describes militarization and violence at the United States–Mexico border, the erosion of migrant rights following September 11, the role of the border metaphor in national identity construction, ways in which migration is gendered, and the Department of Homeland Security's dangerous conflation of home and nation.

Borders and Violence

Migrants and refugees cross international borders fleeing political persecution, terrorism, ethnic and racial strife, and unsustainable economic development. Root causes of involuntary migration often lie in global socioeconomic and political restructuring that maximizes export profits and investments at the expense of local communities. Protectionist policies of the West hurt cotton farmers in Africa, who can not compete against heavily subsidized cotton. Following the North American Free Trade Agreement (NAFTA), peasants in southern Mexico found their corn industry devastated by corn imports from United States agribusiness. NAFTA's neoliberal policies call for the deregulation of commodities including corn, resulting in less stable prices for this staple of the indigenous diet, especially in southern Mexico. Unable to survive on their own (once communally held) land, peasants from Oaxaca, Chiapas, Guerrero, and other Mexican states migrate north looking for work to ensure their families' survival. Liberation theologians refer to these socioeconomic and political structures as forms of "structural violence." The Latin American bishops warned in 1968, writing from Medellín, Colombia, that such structural violence results in a "temptation to violence." Although not promoting the violence of revolutionary movements, they clearly placed primary culpability on those who benefited from dominant economic structures.

The first violence experienced by the displaced occurs in countries of origin. This is the violence that Latin American feminists and feminist theologians such as Ivone Gebara call the violence of "*la vida cotidiana,*" daily life (Gebara 1999). Whether leaving the conflict in Colombia (which is now further escalating because of an infusion of U.S. arms and dollars), southern Mexico because of NAFTA policies, or El Salvador for economic and/or political reasons (again with clear U.S. complicity), migrants must cross a highly militarized border between the United States and Mexico.

The U.S. border has been militarized for some time. Before September 11, border communities already lived in a "deconstitutionalized zone" in which Border Patrol and other law enforcement agencies operated with impunity. In urban border areas such as Tijuana, walls with high-tech detection systems, including heat sensors, stadium lights, and retractable observation towers; all-terrain vehicles; and helicopters, etc., portray an image of a country at war. The San Diego/Tijuana boundary is arguably the world's most militarized divide between two friendly nations. Although we have become accustomed to a fortified border, today's boundary is radically different than that of the early 1990s, when the boundary fence had gaping holes and was relatively easy to cross. Operation Gatekeeper, initiated in 1994 along the California/Mexico border, increased fencing and walls from nineteen to over forty-five miles in length, and nearly tripled its number of border patrol agents. Operation Hold-the-Line in El Paso, Texas followed a similar trajectory. The INS enforcement budget tripled since FY 1993, making it the fastest-growing federal agency and the federal law enforcement group with the most agents authorized to carry guns (Andreas 2003, 3). In 1994, the U.S. Border Patrol initiated "Operation Blockade," intensifying its efforts at urban crossings, thus forcing migrants to cross in more dangerous terrains—deserts and rivers. Since 1994, over two thousand migrant deaths have been documented. In the last two years, two migrants died each day attempting to enter the United States. This is the "collateral damage" of militarization at work in the borderlands. Yet the press rarely reports on the state of siege created by INS border operations in border communities. It is a nonstory, and the attendant deaths are invisible to most U.S. citizens.

In spite of this highly militarized border to our south, following September 11, terrorism was blamed, in part, on a too-porous border. Terrorists and "illegal" immigrants threatened national security, and calls were made to "tighten" our borders. A verbal slippage occurred in which "illegals" became viewed as "terrorists" or potential terrorists. Joseph Nevins writes:

> State actors and politicians often construct migrants as a security problem. In so doing they define not only national territory but also membership in the nation. The construction of the center, the nation depends on the construction of the periphery from where the threat embodied by the unwanted migrant emerges. After September 11 in constructing the undesirable immigrant as a security threat, state actors give the immigrant the appearance of a destroyer of social harmony; the immigrant takes our jobs, commits crimes, threatens the social safety net, and undermines cultural cohesion. Implicit is that there would be more social harmony if migrants were not present (Nevins 2002, 175).

The irony is that militarization of the border created "precisely the kind of environment that is conducive to terrorists and criminals" (Flynn 2003, 111). As a "politically successful policy failure," the expansion of the INS and of the growth of high-profile programs such as Operation Gatekeeper and Operation Hold-the-Line did not decrease the flow of people or drugs into the United States (Andreas 2003, 4). The undocumented population in the United States has doubled since 1990, making the 1990s the decade with the highest level of immigration in U.S. history. Migrants use more dangerous routes through deserts and mountains, resulting in thousands of migrant deaths. Moreover, the increased danger has spawned more sophisticated migrant smuggling groups increasingly controlled by organized crime. Drug smuggling has also increased rather than decreased and now is likely to be mixed with legitimate cargo, making the customs service agent's task even more difficult. The case can be made that increased border patrol has led to *increased* criminalization as well as the increased militarization of border areas.

Collateral damage on the border has worsened. Border crossing deaths doubled in the year following September 11, 2001. The Enhanced Border Security and Visa Entry Reform, signed into law in May 2002, added three thousand immigration inspectors and investigators. President Bush's Border Security Initiative added another 2,200 new positions. The fiscal year 2003 budget saw a two-billion-dollar increase in border security funding with a 29 percent increase in the INS budget and the Coast Guard's largest ever budget increase. We can expect more border deaths (that will be under-reported and not counted as "war" deaths) and further erosion of migrant rights.

Representing the Border

The border as a "massive, militarized display of bounded national identity" reflects a system of physical, environmental, economic, and cultural violence (Davis 2002, x). The border, while material, also serves as a metaphor for how "we" (the nationalistic United States) perceive the world and behave within it. In this age of globalization, where boundaries supposedly become irrelevant, the U.S./Mexico border plays a larger role in U.S. imagination and identity construction than at any point in our history. At the same time that the United States allegedly opened its borders to Mexico through NAFTA, it attempted to secure the border from drugs and illegal migrants. If drugs and undocumented migrants (potential terrorists) provide a threat to national security, then Mexico (friend and NAFTA partner) becomes a threat. As Monica Serrano writes, "sharing a border with the U.S. now threatens Mexico with just such a redefinition of its sovereignly symbolic self from loyal adjunct to wild frontier" (Serrano 2003, 59).

The border serves as an ongoing place of national identity construction. Militarization and increased policing are attempts to hold boundary-related illegality at bay. This notion of the border as a crucial site for national identity construction seems to contradict the metaphor's use in academic border studies, popular since the 1980s, where the "image has served as a popular locus for discussion on the breakdown of monolithic structures . . . a place of politically exciting hybridity, intellectual creativity and moral possibility" (Castillo and Córdoba 2002, 3 and 34). When Pablo Vila and a group of ethnographers went to Ciudad Juárez-El Paso to see how the "border metaphor worked," they found that from the Mexican side the real geopolitical border loomed large and was rarely perceived as a hybrid multicultural space of erased boundaries (Vila 2003a, ix). Jessica Chapin writes, "While such claims (by border theorists) may accurately describe such pop cultural phenomena as the commercial success in the United States of the norteño group, Los Tigres del Norte, or the embrace of performance artist Guillermo Gomez-Peña by members of the academic and cultural left, they do little to elucidate the social and cultural realities of border residents such as Juana and Elena" (Chapin 2003, 20). In fact, "the river that runs between El Paso and Ciudad Juárez is manifestly not a cultural boundary or a racial one, yet corporate discourse repeatedly presents it as such. An epistemology of the border that foregrounds dissimilarity and disjuncture is complicit with the Border Patrol in maintaining the 'spatial incarceration' of Mexicans and Mexican culture in Mexico" (Chapin 2003, 15). The researchers found poverty, an actual physical border, and separation rather than erased boundaries and celebrations of hybridity.

National identity (security) is thus performed and constructed at the boundaries of the nation state. Drugs and terrorists come from without. Illegality and threats to security come from outside the national boundaries.

Migrants, who arrive in increasingly large numbers, represent the threat coming from "outside." The control of the U.S./Mexico border is not about territory per se. No one thinks national sovereignty or land is at stake. Control of territory becomes a way of performing identity—some belong on this land, others do not. When "millions of people from Third World countries are taking up residence in the United States . . . the U.S.-Mexico border plays a special role" as Vila writes, "to gain control over the identity construction process, to differentiate again between 'them' and 'us' during an era when 'they' reside among 'us'" (Vila 2000, 85).

The increased militarization of the border has failed in meeting its stated goals—curbing the flow of drugs and of undocumented migrants. As noted earlier, increased policing has had the paradoxical effect of increasing criminality. If boundary enforcing is about national identity construction, then border policing is as much about performance as about meeting concrete goals. The performance function of the state as embodied in border policing is seen in the Border Patrol Museum and Memorial Library in El Paso, Texas. The museum's two wings contain scenes using the "conventions of campfire scenes of a western, a snowmobile scene titled, 'The One That Got Away,' a display of 'Weapons Seized from Illegal Aliens' (primarily household knives), and plates with the names of agents who have died on duty" (Barrera 2003, 67). Nowhere does one find mention of the military surveillance technologies used by border patrol or of deaths of migrants. In his analysis of the Border Patrol Museum, Eduardo Barrera writes, "a common theme of all the artifacts on display and on sale is the threat that the immigrant, as a criminal . . . poses to American society . . . a situation of life and death, where two subjects are engaged in a conflict that can only be solved through reduction by annihilation or assimilation. The theme repeats in other displays that recreate scenes that use visual and textual metaphors of war, the frontier of westerns, and hunting" (Barrera 2003, 167). The life and death struggles of real migrants never appear in this collective imagination, with its appeal to war and national mythologies.

Gendered Crossings

The image most people hold of the border-crosser is of a young, single male. For many years this profile was accurate. A demographic shift has occurred, however, at both the border between Mexico and Guatemala, as well as between the United States and Mexico. More and more women are crossing, usually accompanied by children. Several reasons exist for this demographic shift: reunification with partners who have already migrated; the same economic and/or political reasons that push men to cross; and the recruitment of women (especially young women) by *maquilas* (factories owned by foreign companies). Studies by the Colegio de la Frontera Norte at both the northern and southern borders of Mexico show that women are routinely raped, robbed, and beaten at both borders. Women crossers can expect to be sexually assaulted by police, *coyotes* (smugglers who, for a high price, guide migrants across the border), gangs such as the infamous Mara Salvatrucha, or men in border towns. Nearly all commit these crimes with impunity. Women can also expect, if they go to work in *maquilas,* to earn less than men, to be sexually assaulted at work, and to work under substandard conditions (Tiano 1994). Thus, the violence of migration is also gendered.

The image of the border-crosser as young, single, and male is important metaphorically to perpetuate the idea of the immigrant as criminal and as the national security threat depicted in the Border Patrol Museum. The "protectors" of the Border Patrol Museum are also male. I visited Toys R Us to see how consumer culture represented gender during the current "war on terrorism." I found it striking that toy companies and the state utilize similar discursive and iconographic strategies to depict war, militarism, and the threat of terrorism (and implicit in the preceding, the danger posed by the stranger, the migrant). Toys R Us featured a toy called the "Army Forward Command Post" for children four years old and higher. The toy looks like a bombed-out version of Barbie's Dream House. This two-story house with pale yellow walls, checkerboard floors, and charming wood-framed windows has been destroyed. Bullet holes cover the walls, the windows are cracked, and a soldier in battle fatigues is inside the home. The soldier comes equipped with assault rifle, rocket launcher, and other military hardware. Where is Barbie? What does it mean that the soldier is inside the home?

In *Women and the War Story,* Miriam Cooke claims that when women contribute to what she calls the "war story," their stories contest the acceptance of a dyadically structured world and break down the easy oppositions—home vs. front, civilian vs. combatant, war vs. peace, victory vs. defeat—that have framed and ultimately promoted war. Ironically, Forward Command Post and the Department of Homeland Security make the same point. The Department of Homeland Security boldly conflates the discourse of the nation-state with that of "home." Yet feminists and antiviolence movements have always challenged the notion of safety at home, since that is where the majority of violence suffered by women occurs. And, as Andrea Smith writes, "Similarly, the notion that terrorism happens in other countries, makes it difficult to grasp that in the U.S., 'home' has never been a safe place for people of color" (Smith 2002).

Homeland security plays with the discourse of protection and thus of "saving women." Yet Forward Command Post graphically makes the point that "home" may not be the safest place. The soldier is inside the bombed house. Interpersonal and state violence exist simultaneously. As Minoo Moallem writes, this "metaphor of home is gendered and as a spatial metaphor it stands both for the inside which is protected from the outside, and a place of emotionality and affection. As a spatial and temporal metaphor it is related to discourses of protection in which men are protectors and women protected" (Moallem 2002). Yet, this home (Forward Command Post, the nation-state) is destroyed, and the soldier, as the embodiment of the gendered outside, is inside. Forward Command Post (Department of Homeland Security) clearly demonstrates what has always been the case and challenges the assumption that state violence protects. The soldier is in the house, in the domesticated bordered space, in the territorial homeland. Is anyone safe?

Responding to Border Violence

Since September 11, migrant and refugee rights groups have been establishing new alliances, both nationally and internationally, with racial justice and human rights organizations. In my city, San Francisco, the Interfaith Coalition for Migrant Rights works actively with a variety of religious traditions to combat human rights abuses against migrants. In 2002 it conducted the One Million Voices Campaign to lobby for the legalization of undocumented migrants. One million postcards were collected and on October 9–10, 2002, a group of migrants, activists, and human rights advocates delivered the million cards to the White House and lobbied congressional leaders.

Coalitions with labor unions have also been formed. For some migrant activists, labor unions are seen as the greatest hope for increased migrant rights. At the time of the writing of this essay, eighteen buses full of eight hundred immigrants are preparing to leave for the "Immigrant Workers Freedom Ride." Organized by labor unions, civil rights organizations, and migrant groups, the buses will stop in cities across the United States to bring attention to migrant rights. Taking their inspiration from the 1960s Freedom Rides, ride participants are pushing legalization of status for migrants working in the United States and civil rights protection for all migrant workers, including the undocumented. The Hotel Employees and Restaurant Employees International Union (which earlier convinced the A.F.L.-C.I.O. to reverse its anti-immigrant policy) came up with the idea for the immigrant freedom ride. Transnational organizing is also growing. Migrants often deal with three countries—the country of origin, country of transit, and the destination country. Thus, organizing in all three (or more) countries is appropriate.

Interestingly, outside the United States (at least in Mexico and Central America) the most vigorous monitoring of human rights abuses at the border and provision of direct services to people in transit often comes from religious groups. The Scalabrini Fathers are especially well known for their Casas del Migrante (migrant homes) in border areas, as well as for their important Center of Documentation for Migrant Rights.[1] The Interfaith Center for Migrant Rights, in collaboration with the Scalabrinis, conducts a well-attended *posada* at the border between Tijuana and San Diego. This cultural and religious production dramatizes the plight of migrants. Another interfaith group places large crosses on the border wall with the name, place of origin, and age of every person who has died attempting to cross. El Teatro Jornalero (Day Laborer Theater) conducts weekly theater workshops with migrant workers who line the streets of San Francisco. In workshops and plays migrant stories are told.[2] These and other artistic, religious, and cultural productions render these invisible lives visible. The images of La Virgen de la Frontera (the Virgin of the Border), the indigenous Juan Diego, and shrines to migrant saints such as Juan Soldado in Tijuana provide concrete religious symbols for border crossers.

Violence at the borders can only fail. The number of border-crossing deaths continues to grow. Migrants are increasingly criminalized. Political and intellectual projects that refuse to trade human suffering for illusory protection are desperately needed for true homeland security.

Notes

1. See the website: http://www.migrante.com.mx/.
2. Teatro Jornalero is a joint program of the Religion and Immigration Project (TRIP) and the Department of Fine and Performing Arts of the University of San Francisco.

Works Cited

Andreas, Peter. 2003. "A Tale of Two Borders: The U.S.-Canada and U.S. Mexico Lines after 9/11." In *The Rebordering of North America: Integration and Exclusion in a New Security Context,* ed. Peter Andreas and Thomas J. Bierstaker, 1–23. New York: Routledge.

Barrera, Eduardo. 2003. "Aliens in Heterotopia: An Intertextual Reading of the Border Patrol Museum." In *Ethnography at the Border,* ed. Pablo Vila, 166–82. Minneapolis: University of Minnesota Press.

Castillo, Debra A., and María Socorro Tabuence Córdoba. 2002. *Border Women: Writing from La Frontera.* Minneapolis: University of Minnesota Press.

Castillo, Guadalupe. 2002. "Collateral Damage: 9/11 and the U.S.-Mexico Border." *Network News: National Network for Immigrant and Refugee Rights.* Summer 2002: 5–6.

Chapin, Jessica. 2003. "Reflections from the Bridge." In *Ethnography at the Border,* ed. Pablo Vila, 1–23. Minneapolis: University of Minnesota Press.

Cooke, Miriam. 1997. *Women and the War Story.* Berkeley: University of California Press.

Davis, Mike. 2002. "Foreword." In *Operation Gatekeeper: The Rise of the "Illegal Alien" and the Making of the U.S.-Mexico Boundary,* by Joseph Nevins, ix-xv. New York: Routledge.

Flynn, Stephen E. 2003. "The False Conundrum: Continental Integration Versus Homeland Security." In *The Rebordering of North America: Integration and*

Exclusion in a New Security Context, ed. Peter Andreas and Thomas J. Bierstaker, 110–28. New York: Routledge.

Gebara, Ivone. 1999. *Longing for Running Water: Ecofeminism and Liberation.* Minneapolis: Fortress Press.

Moallem, Minoo. 2002. Paper prepared for Responding to Violence Conference. Barnard College. New York. October. http://www.barnard.edu/bcrw/respondingtoviolence/moallem.htm.

Naím, Moisés. 2001a. "Collateral Damage: Sorting through the Post-September 11 Intellectual Wreckage." *Foreign Policy,* no. 127 (November/December): 31–46.

Naím, Moisés. 2001b. "Reinventing War." *Foreign Policy,* no. 127 (November/December): 108–109.

Nevins, Joseph. 2002. *Operation Gatekeeper: The Rise of the "Illegal Alien" and the Making of the U.S.–Mexico Boundary.* New York: Routledge.

Serrano, Mónica. 2003. "Bordering on the Impossible: U.S. Mexico Security Relations after 9–11." *The Rebordering of North America: Integration and Exclusion in a New Security Context,"* ed. Peter Andreas and Thomas J. Bierstaker, 46–68. New York: Routledge.

Smith, Andrea. 2002. Paper prepared for Responding to Violence Conference. Barnard College. New York. October. http://www.barnard.edu/bcrw/respondingtoviolence/smith.htm

Tiano, Susan. 1994. *Patriarchy on the Line: Labor, Gender and Ideology in the Mexican Maquila Industry.* Philadelphia: Temple University Press.

Vila, Pablo. 2000. *Crossing Borders, Reinforcing Borders: Categories, Metaphors, and Narrative Identities on the U.S.-Mexico Border.* Austin: University of Texas Press.

Vila, Pablo. 2003a. "Introduction: Border Ethnographies." In *Ethnography at the Border,* ed. Pablo Vila, ix-xxxv. Minneapolis: University of Minnesota Press.

Vila, Pablo, ed. 2003b. *Ethnography at the Border.* Minneapolis: University of Minnesota Press.

Chapter 14

Domestic Terror[1]

Catherine Lutz and Jon Elliston

The crusty critic Paul Fussell observed that wars are always ironic, because things always end up so far from the glory-trailing myths that help start them. Irony, though, pales beside the fear and anger that now swirl around Fort Bragg, North Carolina, the source of many of the troops sent to Afghanistan. It was there that four soldiers recently confused their wives for the enemy and killed them. Marilyn Griffin was stabbed seventy times and her trailer set on fire, Teresa Nieves and Andrea Floyd were shot in the head, and Jennifer Wright was strangled. All four couples had children, several now orphaned as two of the men shot themselves after killing their wives.

The murders garnered wide attention because three of the soldiers served in special operations units that have fought in Afghanistan, and because the deaths clustered over a five-week period in June and July 2002. The killings have raised a host of questions—about the effect of war on the people who wage it, the spillover on civilians from training military personnel to kill, the role of military institutional values, and even the possible psychiatric side effects of an antimalarial drug the Army gives its soldiers. On the epidemic of violence against women throughout the United States and on the role of masculinity and misogyny in both military and civilian domestic violence, however, there has been a deafening silence.

Military officials have focused on "marital problems" and "family stress," and have fiercely contested the notion that domestic violence is a more severe problem in the military than in civilian populations, although the Pentagon has not invested much in finding out what the comparison would look like. One Army-funded study that was done, however, found that reports of "severe aggression" against spouses ran more than three times higher among Army families than among civilian ones in 1998.

The military nonetheless maintains that violence against spouses is no more prevalent in the armed forces, arguing that it uses different criteria than civilian authorities for identifying domestic violence, including severe verbal abuse. "People have been throwing some wild figures around," says Lieut. Col. James Cassella, a spokesman for the Defense Department. "My understanding is that it's kind of an apples and oranges comparison." But the military's method may actually underestimate the problem, since it long ignored violence against a legion of nonmarried partners, an especially important omission considering that one recent study found that single men represent nearly 60 percent of soldiers using a gun or knife in attacks on women. And there is no way to corroborate independently the figures the military releases on domestic violence cases that are handled through military judicial processes, since they are shielded, as civilian police records are not, from public view. Moreover, the cited studies did take into account the most important demographic differences—the apples and oranges—in military and civilian populations.

Mary Beth Loucks-Sorrell, interim director of the North Carolina Coalition Against Domestic Violence, a statewide umbrella group based in Durham, is convinced that women partnered with soldiers face disproportionate risks of domestic abuse, a conclusion reached through years of fielding reports from abused women (and occasionally men). Just since January, she said, North Carolina's 100 counties have seen at least forty men kill their partners, seven of them in Cumberland County, where Fort Bragg is located. Reports of abuse from military communities are not only more frequent but the level of violence they describe is more extreme and, according to domestic violence groups, getting worse over the past several years. Soldiers also terrorize their partners in unique ways, reminding the women of the sniper and bare-handed killing skills they acquire in training.

On hearing of the four murders, many people in the general public and media asked whether the soldiers might have suffered from postcombat trauma or simply, as the military suggested, from the stress of deployment and its disruption of family life. Some commentators on the Right went so far as to suggest that these killings are another kind of war casualty and give us one more reason for gratitude to U.S. soldiers. On the Left, the combat-stress explanation can draw on the notion of the soldier as a victim of class violence and as a reluctant imperial tool. In both these views, the soldier's home-front violence is the traumatic outcome of "what he saw" in combat rather than the much more significant trauma of what he did.

Stan Goff, a Special Forces veteran of Vietnam and Haiti, and now a democracy activist in Raleigh, scoffs at the "TV docudrama version of war" underlying this assumption. "Go to Afghanistan," he says, "where you are insulated from outside scrutiny, and all the taboos you learned as a child are suspended. You take life more and more with impunity, and discover that the universe doesn't collapse when you drop the hammer on a human being, and for some, there is a real sense of power. For others, for all maybe, it's PTSD (posttraumatic stress disorder) on the installment plan." The effect of this sense of impunity was evident when a Special Forces soldier, who was once arrested for domestic violence, told one of us that Memorial Day ceremonies always left him pondering why he would get medals for killing others in battle but would be arrested if he killed his wife.

A distracting sideshow to the murder investigations has been a United Press International report suggesting the soldiers might have suffered side effects of Lariam, a drug the Army gives prophylactically to all troops going to malarial areas. Prescribed to 22 million people since 1985, Lariam use is associated with vivid dreams, insomnia, and dizziness and is known to correlate with neuropsychiatric problems in a tiny percentage of cases, found in one large study to be 1 in 13,000. (In the wake of Pentagon stonewalling on the health effects of anthrax inoculation and depleted uranium weapons, Defense Department denial that Lariam is a problem might justifiably be taken with a grain of salt, but the epidemiological numbers suggest that skepticism is warranted about the drug's relationship to domestic violence.) Nonetheless, the Pentagon has sent an epidemiological team to Fort Bragg to investigate this and other potential roots of the murders.

In the Pentagon's approach to the problem and in virtually all media accounts, gender has been left hidden in plain sight. As in the 1990s schoolyard shootings, where a rhetoric of "kids killing kids" disguised the fact that boys were overwhelmingly the killers, here the soldiers are seen simply as an occupational group and the problem, at most, as one of an institutional culture where soldiers have difficulty "asking for help" from family service providers abundantly available on installations like Bragg.

Not only does the military remain by reputation the most "masculine" occupation available, but people in Fayetteville and in the armed forces generally consider Special Forces and Delta Force, where three of the four men worked, the Army's toughest units. Special operations units are some of the last in the military to exclude women, and they also specialize in unconventional warfare, which is combat that often follows neither the letter nor the spirit of the rules of war. As a sign in a Special Forces training area says: "Rule #1. There are no rules. Rule #2. Follow Rule #1." Such a macho, above-the-law culture provides not a small part of the recipe for domestic violence. Combine this with a double standard of sexuality, one in which, as many soldiers and their wives told us, some couples expect infidelity to take place on Special Forces deployments—where the men operate with unusual autonomy and are often surrounded by desperately poor women—whereas the infidelity of wives, reactive or not and real or imagined, can be punished with violence.

If there was a common thread that tied the murdered women's lives together, it was the one identified by Tanya Biank, a *Fayetteville Observer* reporter: All four of them had expressed a desire to leave their marriages, a situation that domestic violence workers have identified as the most dangerous time for women in abusive relationships. For that is when the control these men tend to insist on in their relationships appears about to dissolve. Christine Hansen is executive director of the Connecticut-based Miles Foundation, which has assisted more than 7,000 victims of military-related violence since 1996. Military personnel, she says, are controlled from above at work even more than most U.S. workers, and many come home looking to reassert control, often with violence. The anxieties about control, and consequently the violence, flare up most often before and after military deployments, Hansen says, as soldiers lose and then try to reinstate control.

As the war in Afghanistan began last October, for example, "We could literally tell what units were being deployed from where, based on the volume of calls we received from given bases. Then the same thing happened on the other end, when they came back."

After the wave of murders at Fort Bragg, the Senate set aside money for a new Pentagon investigation of military domestic violence—the latest in a long line of commissions established over the course of the many gendered scandals of the past ten years, from Tailhook to Aberdeen. Such investigations have neither stemmed the problem nor prompted the military to recognize the fundamental role of violent masculinity in crimes like the Fort Bragg killings. This would entail seeing the murders as a piece of the larger, epidemic problem of violent abuse by men within the military, including rape of female (and some male) soldiers and civilians, lesbian and gay bashing, and brutal hazing rituals, as Dorothy Mackey, director of Survivors Take Action Against Abuse by Military Personnel, a national network of counseling groups based in Ohio, points out.

Of the 1,213 reported domestic violence incidents known to military police and judged to merit disciplinary action and the 12,068 cases reported to family services, the military could report only 29 where the perpetrator was court-martialed or sent to a civilian court for prosecution. The military claims to have no data on the disciplinary outcome of all the family services cases and 81 percent of the police cases. This poor record-keeping and apparent reluctance to prosecute offenders can be explained by the military's institutional interests in burying the problem of domestic violence. One such interest is public relations. To recruit and retain a force of 1.4 million, including women and married men, remains a monumental task that would only be made harder by widespread knowledge of the extent of the violence. Second, there are financial motives. Many soldiers cost more than $100,000 each to recruit and train, money that goes down the drain if a soldier is discharged or imprisoned. Finally, there is the continuing, if waning, power of a belief, still widespread in the prevolunteer and mostly unmarried force, that "if the army had wanted you to have a wife, it would have issued you one." Protecting women from domestic violence in this environment falls even farther down the list of missions to be accomplished than it does in the civilian sector.

The difficulties women have in leaving their abusers are well known. Military wives have additional disincentives. The unemployment rate for military wives is extremely high—hovering around 20 percent for those living at Fort Bragg—and those who do find employment are often stuck in the minimum-wage retail jobs that are the main work available in the satellite economy around most large posts. If they report abuse, they risk not only retribution from their husbands, as do women in the civilian world, but loss of their total family income, healthcare and other benefits, and even their housing and neighbors if their husband is discharged. A relatively new Army program provides $900 a month plus healthcare for the few abused women whose husbands are removed from the force for domestic violence. Fort Bragg has no domestic violence shelter, though for many years was donating a paltry $10 a day to a local shelter when military wives fled there.

Women married to abusive soldiers have been calling the Fayetteville newspaper and domestic violence shelters around the country in sharply higher numbers since the Fort Bragg killings were reported. According to advocates, many callers are terrified, fearing they will be next because of their partners' ongoing violence and death threats. Women have spoken out about the frequent failure of commanders to take their calls for help seriously. And they have complained that they were often sent to military chaplains, some of whom advised them that suffering is a woman's lot or that their husbands were just "working off some excess energy." One counselor at Fort Bragg was quoted in the *Washington Post* describing how she tells women to prepare their partners returning from deployment for changes they have made in his absence, like cutting their hair short: "He might be thinking about running his hands through that long, luxuriant hair," she said. "Don't surprise your husband." After the murders, rather than implementing new measures to protect the thousands of women already in its police and family advocacy files, in late August the military began to screen soldiers leaving Afghanistan for mental health problems. While this may not be a bad idea in general, it presumes that combat stress alone is what leads to domestic abuse, and creates the illusion that something is being done about domestic violence without addressing its fundamental causes.

The cultural celebration of soldiers, which has grown more fervent since the war on terror began, has hampered attempts to address the problem. In the best of times, critical views of military practice are not well received; in the new climate of intimidation fostered by the Bush administration since September 11, 2001, they may be considered tantamount to treason. Christine Hansen, who has received death threats since her foundation appeared in news stories about the murders, notes that some civilian judges have been even more reluctant than before to convict soldiers of domestic violence, when doing so would trigger the Lautenberg amendment, a 1996 law that prohibits convicted abusers from owning firearms. The idea that the soldier makes an unrecompensable sacrifice creates a halo effect, so that the murderers are painted as victims of the horrors of combat, while scant attention is paid to the women they killed or the failures of the system to prevent those deaths. As Stan Goff told us, soldiers living in this climate can turn to their wives and say, "The culture's worshiping me. Why aren't you?"

In a widely disseminated Pentagon directive issued last November, Deputy Defense Secretary Paul Wolfowitz declared that "domestic violence is an offense against the institutional values of the military." But domestic violence, rape, and male supremacism itself are not anomalies or sideshows to war; instead, they lie near the center of how it is prosecuted and narrated. The millions of women throughout the world currently threatened by soldiers will look to their advocates and each other for their ultimate safety, and may have a unique appreciation for the ironies of focusing on more abstract terrors when they face such immediate dangers so close to home.

Notes

1. "Domestic Terror" by Catherine Lutz and Jon Elliston is reprinted with permission from the October 14, 2002, issue of *The Nation*. Portions of each week's *The Nation* magazine can be accessed at http://www.thenation.com. For subscription information, call 1–800-333–8536.

Chapter 15

Testifying to Violence

Gujarat as a State of Exception[1]

Anupama Rao

"It was"—that is the name of the will's gnashing of teeth and most secret melancholy. Powerless against what has been done, he [the will] is an angry spectator of all that is past. The will cannot will backwards; and that he cannot break time and time's covetousness, that is the will's loneliest melancholy. [. . .] Thus the will, the liberator, took to hurting; and on all who can suffer he wreaks revenge for his inability to go backwards. This, indeed this alone, is what revenge is—the will's ill will against time and its "it was."

—Nietzsche 1976, 251–52

Prem se kaho hum insaan hain [Say it with love, we are human beings].

Garv se kaho hum Hindu hain [Say it with pride, we are Hindus].[2]

In the past two decades, the decline of the Congress Party and the rise of Hindu nationalism in India indicate an emergent political order. The rapid liberalization of India's economy coupled with the growth of religious nationalism marks a distinct conjuncture posing challenges to the hitherto reigning ideologies of the developmental state. Hindu nationalism has been a political project of remaking the nation in the latest phase of the globalization of capital, attributing the failures of the developmental project to secularism, with the latter understood as a neocolonial hangover. To overcome it, Hindu nationalists have mobilized a rhetoric of strong but exclusivist nationalism while harnessing the partial, shifting forms of affiliation made available through globalizing markets and media (Rajagopal 2001). Hindu nationalists have rejected the tenets of constitutional secularism upon which the Indian constitution is based, insisting instead that India is a Hindu *rashtra*, a Hindu nation. Ironically, however, the ascendancy of a revitalized cultural nationalism has exacerbated the fragmentation of the polity along caste and regional lines, making it harder for Hindu nationalists to realize their aims.[3]

Although Hindu nationalism is culturally hegemonic, it remains politically unstable. The wave (*lehar,* in political campaign parlance) of Hindu enthusiasm that brought it to power is hardly matched by its political base, which requires more long-term effort and is uncertain of outcome as elections become increasingly competitive. The Bharatiya Janata Party (BJP, Indian People's Party) has allied with region-based parties, and this has increasingly meant that Hindu nationalists have formed alliances with parties whose political agenda undercut that of Hindu nationalists. The latter's visions of a top-down "Hindu" inclusion preserves traditional caste ordering, whereas the political assertion of lower castes and *dalits,* or ex-Untouchables, has often worked at cross-purposes with the aims of Hinduization.

The recent carnage in Gujarat, where over two thousand Muslims were killed in the city of Ahmedabad and its rural environs, gives little hope that the politics of caste might soon buffer Hindu nationalists' politics of hatred, however. Large numbers of *dalits* and tribals were involved in attacking Muslim property, though reports have maintained that they refrained from engaging in the acts of physical brutality perpetrated by caste Hindus.[4] Significant too is the broader political context within which the violence took place. Ethnic and religious violence is hardly unprecedented; it is publicly acknowledged that such violence is engineered by political parties for electoral advantage. What has distinguished the communal violence provoked by the current party of Hindu nationalism, the BJP, is that the political capital accumulated from this violence is at the level of the regional state and the national state, whereas with the Congress Party, every effort was made to restrict such political accumulation at the level of the village, the mohalla and ward, or the district (Rajagopal, forthcoming).[5] Thus the recent violence in Gujarat targeted at Muslims was extraordinary not only for its scale, even though more than two thousand were killed and many more raped and mutilated. Previous episodes of communal violence in Gujarat and elsewhere surpassed this figure, for instance. But for the first time, district, state, and national governments together supported Hindu militancy and insisted that, although local, the violence was meant to undermine national security and therefore called for a coordinated national response.

According to Weber, the modern state is understood to have the monopoly of the means of legitimate violence. Instead, the historical sociologist Philip Abrams has argued that one of the most common mistakes in studying the state has emerged from scholars who believe that the state functions as a single or individual historical actor. Rather, the representation of state as a coherent field of political action is itself an *effect* that produces the forms of legitimacy that states are assumed to possess (Abrams 1988). This is a powerful argument against realist conceptions of the state, which assume the definitions of the state as descriptive rather than productive of precisely those forms of power that the state is assumed to possess. Deconstructing the mythic power of the state in this manner is also significant for theorizing state violence. In the Gujarat carnage, for instance, the state undertook to privatize the means of violence, partially to present it as the force of a spontaneous popular outburst, even while it served to inaugurate (and legitimize) *new forms of state terror* explicitly directed against Muslims.

How do we understand this particular conjuncture in which, to follow Walter Benjamin's terminology, "law-making" violence is misrecognized as "law-preserving" violence? (Benjamin 1978). Or to put it more simply, how are we to understand when the inauguration of a new form of genocidal politics occurs through recourse to prevalent forms of legitimation such as through law courts and elections (Baxi 2002)?[6] In this essay, I will make some preliminary efforts to address this question, by exploring the ways in which the Gujarat state government's active legitimation of anti-Muslim violence took place in a "state-free political time" that succeeded in producing terror as the formative condition through which Muslims have come to experience themselves as "permanently endangered" communities living under a state of siege (Baxi 2002).

The Politics of Hindu Hatred

Godhra is the name of the town in the state of Gujarat where Muslims are alleged to have set the S-6 compartment of the Sabarmati Express alight on February 27, 2002, killing fifty-eight Hindu activists and their families, who were returning from a temple-building campaign in the northern Indian town of Ayodhya.[7] Journalistic reports have noted that the passengers on the train were angry and emotional, getting into arguments and fights with fellow passengers as well as Muslim vendors when the train stopped at Godhra. At least one Muslim vendor had been beaten up for refusing to say "*Jai Sri Ram*" or "Victory to Ram," the militant war cry of Hindu nationalists involved in the Ram Janmabhoomi movement. A young Muslim girl was thought to be abducted. As the train left the station, stones are reported to have been thrown at the train, apparently by Muslims on the platform. Soon after the train left Godhra station it burst into flames, killing men, women, and children.

The government forensic report released in early July contested the idea that the compartment was set on fire by miscreants who poured an inflammable liquid from outside through the train, because of the manner in which the S-6 compartment had caught on fire. Instead, the report suggested that there was evidence to either suggest a pattern of spontaneous combustion or the burning of the compartment from within the train.[8] To date, no evidence has been found linking alleged Muslim perpetrators belonging to any organized group who were involved in the burning of the train.

In the aftermath of the Godhra incident, orchestrated attacks by Hindu mobs on Muslims in the city of Ahmedabad and its rural environs left over 2,000 dead, and over 133,000 Muslims without shelter or relief from the state government.[9] Mobs of men and women shouting, "*Jai Sri Ram*," "Kill," "Slaughter," went on a rampage through the city of Ahmedabad, killing men, women, and children with the greatest brutality. Spears, knives, and *trishuls* (tridents) were used to perpetrate the violence, with all the intimacy and proximity that these instruments require to maim and kill.

An influential report by Human Rights Watch, *"We Have No Orders To Save You"* (2002), notes the extensive planning and coordination that had to have occurred prior to the incident, given the clinical precision with which Muslim shops and homes had been targeted, while nearby homes and shops belonging to Hindus had been left standing.[10] Eyewitness reports noted that the attacks on Muslims were coordinated by cell phones, that gasoline cylinders for cooking were not available anywhere in the city of Ahmedabad for three days before the riots.[11] Press reports brought to light a secret meeting called by chief minister Narendra Modi on the night of February 28, 2002, where senior members of the state government, along with high-ranking police officials, had been told to allow the anti-Muslim violence and rioting to continue. As millions watched their television sets in stunned horror, they saw the first televised pogrom in India, witnesses to the magnitude of violence broadcast in "real time."[12] It is also through such televisual witnessing that the country came to know about large-scale looting in middle- and upper-class neighborhoods, where affluent men and women were caught on tape driving to fancy malls and shopping areas, whence they carried away brand-name clothing and other items of conspicuous consumption. This was a startling juxtaposition of the extraordinary violence meted out to Muslims as sacrificial victims, alongside evidence of the material desires that a newly liberalizing economy had unleashed amongst the consuming classes.

"Godhra" has now become both the name and the explanation for the initial as well as the ensuing violence, invoking a political economy of cause and effect, of crime and punishment, provocation and just reprisal. It has also become an image standing for the violence, captured extraordinarily on television screens across the country and reproduced endlessly in newspapers and magazines: crowds standing outside the train, watching it burn while cameras rolled; Hindu mobs on the rampage destroying property, killing indiscriminately as horrified victims beg for mercy; and Narendra Modi's justification of the uncontrollable, elemental fury of Hindus. The repetitive structure of this invocation might suggest, however, not the processing of the events of Godhra as real, so much as the inability to do so, the effort to re-narrate it through a structure of repetition itself, thereby normalizing the atrocity through a kind of cultural narration, enacting a memory of the attack but in a way reproducing prevailing assumptions about violent Muslims and Hindus who only act in self-defense. In its sheer repetition, media realism acknowledges its inability to render the event transparent. What it does is to commemorate what it is unable to process and make meaningful, delineating instead the limits of its field of intelligibility.[13]

The Logic of Retalitation

Godhra was widely publicized by the Hindu right as *retaliatory violence* against Muslims, even though there was no connection between the victims of the burnt compartment and the indiscriminate targeting of all Muslims in the aftermath of the Godhra event. Narendra Modi as well as other members of the BJP, the party in power at the center, repeatedly argued that the scale of violence was a natural—almost elemental—reaction to the perceived damage inflicted on Hindu bodies, thereby removing this violence from the calculus of "just" or "measured" retaliation. The logic of retaliation, or even retribution for historic wrongs, characterizes the articulated logic of Hindu hatred of "the Muslim," based on a structure of punishment for a prior injury. The increasing levels of violence, however, that Hindu nationalists have unleashed in their bid for political and ideological control during the past two decades has meant that violence has increasingly obeyed the law of diminishing returns. The performance of violence requires the ever greater violation (and spectacular exhibition) of Muslim bodies, exceeding the actuarial logic in whose name it is summoned to do its work.

Ashok Singhal, president of the Vishwa Hindu Parishad (World Hindu Council) suggested on September 3, 2002, that Godhra was a successful "experiment" that would be repeated across India. Godhra had mobilized the Hindu crowd and "brought out 50 *lakh* [5 million] Hindus." There is mounting evidence that Godhra was awaited with intense anticipation and meticulous planning. On March 3, 2002, in a speech at the BJP's Congress held in Goa, Prime Minister A. B. Vajpayee retracted his earlier criticism of Narendra Modi and publicly laid blame for the carnage with Muslims, who, according to him, incited violence wherever they went. Thus, the enactment of violence against Muslims was itself a confirmation of their predisposition to violence that would be unleashed unless it was quelled by prophylactic violence by Hindus. The event manufactured images of Hindu hatred to justify the retaliation against Muslims, and Godhra became a symptom of the depth of Hindu hatred for Muslims as well as a portending sign of Hindu retaliation, of the attempts to produce a Hindu nation cleansed of Muslim presence.

Although the violent nature of Muslims is a staple of Hindutva rhetoric, and is constantly being warned against, it is in fact usually invisible, belonging to the past, made to emerge from Islamic texts or else requiring to be intuited, as for instance with the Bombay blasts of 1993. Indeed, it is usually thwarted by deft anticipatory violence by otherwise "tolerant" and "peaceful" Hindus, in most accounts. Typically, the enactment of violence against Muslims is itself treated as negative proof of the violent character of Muslims; the victims deserve their victimhood, which is why it has to be obsessively revisited upon them. The effects of violence in this case, the burnt carcasses and the severed body parts, are savage reminders of what Muslims would do to Hindus if they were able to, rather than a sign of Hindu hatred. In this logic, violence is a technology of visibility, making the invisible yet ever-present threat of Muslim perfidy visible, and the field of vision is one in which to see is to secure, to exclude danger and the unknown, and confirm knowledge already known (Feldman 2002). Thus the forces of mediation, the techniques of publicity, even as they served to bring a great deal of publicity to the carnage outside Gujarat, also confirmed the structures of excess through which retaliatory violence operates.

Sexual Violence

This logic of excess, evident in the spectacles of violence and humiliation, has become the representative modality through which the Gujarat pogrom has been addressed in the media even as it has served as a sign of Hindu will-to-power. This is nowhere more evident than in the centrality of sexual violence as a form of revenge. One of the most disturbing aspects of the violence against Muslims in Gujarat has been the targeting of women, as well as women's participation in the incitement to violence (Mukherjee 2002).[14] In this instance, sexual violence was offered up as a "solution" for the demographic riddle of Muslim overpopulation, itself a powerful stereotype of the Muslim family as composed of predatory, polygamous Muslim men with multiple wives. On August 12, 2002, Narendra Modi argued that the relief camps should be shut down because they were in effect "baby-making factories," intimate spaces where the sexual labor of making Muslim babies could counter the slow rate of Hindu growth, resulting in a Muslim population explosion supported by polygamous Muslim men.

This portrayal of the camps as spaces of intimacy is radically at odds with the accounts of destitution and misery in these camps. In fact, in an ironic fulfillment of the Hindutva slogan *"Musalman jao Pakistan ya qabristan"* (Muslims go to Pakistan or to the graveyard), even the living had to seek refuge in Muslim graveyards or *qabristans*. These graveyards became public places where many of the relief camps were erected, haunting reminders of the thin line between the living and the dead Muslim in Hindutva's logic. The graveyards became spaces where public relief and rehabilitation could be provided, as opposed to the so-called "public" spaces in Ahmedabad that had in effect been Hinduized in the process of the retaliatory violence after February 27. The Human Rights Watch report noted:

> Government aid, mainly food rations, did not reach the camps until at least one week after the onset of attacks. . . . Aid workers continue to report an acute shortage of food, cooking oil, sugar, medical supplies, clothes, and blankets in Ahmedabad. [. . .] By mid-April measles had broken out in the relief camps in Ahmedabad, raising fears of an epidemic. The overcrowded and unhygienic conditions in the camps—which include a shortage of toilets— have made it impossible to quarantine victims. According to a senior health ministry official in Delhi, "People are being forced to defecate in the open," a breeding ground for mosquitos and fleas. (Human Rights Watch 2002, 55–56)

Buried in Modi's statement, however, is a rationale for the brutal targeting of Muslim women and children during Godhra, as well as the accounts of Hindu women's support for sexualized violence. An increased Muslim population would mean that Muslims were no longer pliant political minorities, actuarial entities who *did not count*. The demographic anxieties animating violence against women congealed around babies, the magical products of women's sexual and reproductive labor, potential antinational, pro-Pakistani "foreign elements" in the heart of a Hindu homeland. Or so the Hindutva logic goes. And as international human rights activists have noted, the shaming of communities through the sexual violation of women has been a sustained repertoire of genocidal strategies.[15]

Independent fact-finding groups noted reports of fetuses being torn from womens' wombs and impaled on tridents, women and young girls being gang-raped, instruments such as glass bottles and Hindu symbols such as the *trishul* being shoved up their vaginas. The National commission for Women visited Gujarat five weeks after the killings began, and to feminists' consternation, absolved the state government of responsibility and did not identify the perpetrators of violence. A journalist noted that the commission's report "turns its back on the savagery against Muslim women. In this respect it compares poorly with the National Human Rights Commission and the National Commission for Minorities" (Basu 2002). Much in keeping with the denial of sexual violence as a central aspect of the pogrom, the Minister of Defence and one-time socialist George Fernandes, asked "What's new about rape?" to which M. J. Akbar, editor of the newspaper *The Telegraph*, and a Nehruvian secularist, responded: "Every womb is new about rape, George Fernandes. Every woman is new about rape. . . . Every scream is new about rape. . . . Every death is new about rape. . . . Every child who smelt burnt flesh is new about rape" (Akbar 2002).

The historian Tanika Sarkar has read the symbolic role of the Muslim woman as sexual property who can be looted and desecrated as trophies of conquest, much as Hindu histories of the precolonial past would have us believe Hindu women were treated by Muslim (i.e., Mughal) rulers between the sixteenth and eighteenth centuries (Sarkar 2002). Thus history's revenge lay in targeting women's sexual vulnerability, even as the contemporary fear of numbers, the anxiety about the Muslim population as a politically significant minority, overlay such histories of a psychic wound, of Hindu defeat. Hate literature circulated during the carnage noted:

> Narendra Modi you have fucked the mother of [Muslims]
> The volcano which was inactive for years has erupted
> It has burnt the arse of [Muslims] and made them dance nude
> We have untied the penises that were tied till now
> Without castor oil in the arse we have made them cry
> Wake up, Hindus there are still Muslims alive around you
> Learn from Panvad village where their mother was fucked
> She was fucked standing while she kept shouting
> She enjoyed the uncircumcised penis.
> . . . (qtd. in Nussbaum 2003)

The idea of revenge for historic wrongs is powerfully sexualized, and the violation of women is proclaimed as a sign of Hindu manliness while it is also addressed through the idiom of sadistic pleasure and enjoyment, "She enjoyed the uncircumscribed penis." The economies of sexual pleasure are conflated with the brutality of rape and collective violence, and Hindu masculinity is presented here through the capacity to resignify the intimacies of sexual possession as historic revenge. The cruel but uncontrollable passions of sexual possession were marked in the ways in which Muslim women were battered and violated, and then dismembered and burnt—thoroughly spent bodies discarded like refuse.

The cry of some attackers—"*saboot mat chodo*" (don't leave any evidence, don't leave a trace)—is important here, suggesting the acknowledgment of an existing juridical context, either as constraint or as norm, that made violence furtive, aware of its illegality. The evidence of sexual violence was abundant, but typically the only evidence connecting the perpetrators to it was the testimony of the victims. The refusal of the police to accept the accounts of survivors of the attacks prevented the registering of evidence, and the intimate violence of sexual humiliation, of sexed suffering, has remained largely unacknowledged by the state. Because masculine enjoyment was connected to the extinction of Muslim women, gendered visibility was a hazard to survival, evoked only in order to subject women to brutal violence and painful death.

In the Aftermath of Violence: Mourning, State Complicity, and Hindu Guilt

Upendra Baxi suggests that the Gujarat carnage manifests a particularly modern political mode, "state-free political time," in which violence occurs in a surreal non-place where the time of the state, of the police, and of discourses of law and order are effectively suspended. This view recalls Walter Benjamin's notion of the "state of emergency" that characterizes modern political power, as well as Giorgio Agamben's more recent expansion of this concept (Agamben 1998). Agamben, writing about the Nazi concentration camps, has argued that they functioned as spaces for the living dead, a liminal space between life and death where bare life has itself become an object of the most highly technologized forms of extinction. Agamben's suggestion that a politics of exception and excess grounds the exercise of sovereignty is useful as a political thought-experiment, but does not tell us as much as it might about the relationship between the exceptional and the everyday. The violence in Gujarat may have been state-free political time, but it was aimed at winning elections, and it accomplished this end. It articulated a relationship between a state government and its Hindu majority citizens that was one of identity and difference; the Hindu identity embraced by the state effectively rendered the lives of Muslim citizens available for sacrifice, as a confirmation and a celebration of this identity. Those who survived the sacrifice could neither speak against it nor be granted restitution. What did it mean then for those who still sought to fulfill their role as citizens, when the result of political expression was death and devastation?

In December 2002, Narendra Modi was re-elected by a landslide victory, even as many Muslim refugees left the state rather than return home to a state of continued terror and economic boycott. The state government, capitalizing on a politics of terror and hate, has succeeded, at least for now, in marking Gujarat as a successful experiment. Most significant is the documented extent of police involvement in supporting (and in some cases, perpetrating) violence against Muslims, even as the broader molecular transformation of Gujarati society reveals the participation of *dalits,* ex-Untouchables, and tribals in anti-Muslim violence, as well as a sustained refusal by Hindus in Ahmedabad to participate actively in relief efforts in the aftermath of the carnage.[16] As expressions of Hindu terror and arguments about historic revenge have come to be embedded within state logic, they have relied on an *unprecedented exhibition of Muslims' collective vulnerability as the grounds of their political recognition.*

In a profoundly moving tribute to Ahsan Jaffri, a Congressman and a former member of Parliament who was brutally murdered on the evening of February 28, 2002, his daughter Nishrin Hussain wrote, "Because he was burnt to death and we did not find his body, there is no closure for me in his death" (Hussain 2002). Jaffri was dragged outside his home in the Gulbarg Housing Society and butchered, as he pleaded with a Hindu mob to leave his home, where Muslims from the locality had taken shelter. Two hundred other Muslims were killed or burnt to death in Gulbarg Society. Jaffri's desperate phone calls to fellow party members in Ahmedabad as well as Delhi went unheeded and after he had been hacked to death in front of his home, a gasoline cylinder was detonated and thrown into the house. Nishrin's poignant protest at the inhumanity of Godhra rests on the impossibility of mourning her father, of dignifying his brutal death with the respect demanded for someone who tried to sacrifice himself to save the women and children who had taken shelter in his home. Nishrin's loss, like that of many others, is further compounded by the families' inability to find bodies that might be buried to commemorate their violent deaths.

If the impossibility of ritually mourning the dead is a continuation of the violence against Muslims, it is the issue of complicity and collective guilt that characterizes the response of sensitive Hindus. Relief camps opened by nongovernmental organizations and local Muslim charities have drawn many "secular Hindus" from across India (though few from Ahmedabad itself). They have come to volunteer, to show that not every Hindu hates Muslims, to bear witness. Over forty fact-finding reports have been generated about the incident. Their accounts of the camps, the continued violence against Muslims through attempts to "cleanse" neighborhoods, and new strategies for tolerating Muslims by asking them to remove all physical markers of their religious identity have been important in producing a zone of critical publicity where Godhra has been represented as a national shame. Many such accounts assume Hindu guilt—"I am ashamed to be called a

Hindu"—at the same time that they distance themselves from the politics of the Hindu right. For example: "I will not ask for forgiveness for I deserve none. I will not ask that you look at me, for I cannot look myself in the eye. I come to you Bhaijaan, to hang my head in shame."[17] Or there is Harsh Mander, who writes: "My heart is sickened, my soul wearied, my shoulders aching with the burden of guilt and shame" (Mander 2002).[18] The business-man Piyush Desai, who spoke about the money his family had received from a Muslim over a hundred years ago, to start their successful company, Gujarat Tea Processors and Packers Ltd., used the language of exchange, of giving and taking, when he asked "However can we repay such a debt?" (Nussbaum 2003).

The postcolonial state has now accumulated a number of such unpayable debts, from the massacre of Sikhs in 1984 after Indira Gandhi's death, to numerous episodes of state-sponsored violence against Muslims, or state condonement of upper-caste violence against *dalits*. The cumulative victims of these events run into the tens of thousands over the last two decades alone. Violence is hardly an invisible effect, or exceptional condition for establish-ing state legitimacy in India undertaken with collective consent. Spectacular displays of law-making violence have instead become the rule, showing the operation of a model of politics certainly at the margins of liberalism but nevertheless persisting as an electoral democracy. This offers a conundrum that will continue to exercise citizens, in India and elsewhere.

Notes

1. I would like to thank Ravi Rajendra for helping track down important citations for this paper.
2. Popular slogans heard at rallies and demonstrations.
3. The "new" politics of caste has been most visible in the aftermath of a 1989 decision by the central government to implement the Mandal Commission Report, which recommended a dramatic expansion of reservations, or affirma-tive action programs, for lower castes known as the Other Backward Classes. A constitutional dispensation under articles 15(4) and 16(4) identifies "backward classes" as eligible for reservations in government jobs, and in other arena of public life, respectively. Initially these safeguards had been directed to Sched-uled Castes and Scheduled Tribes—the governmental classification of untouch-able and tribal communities—who are defined in the Indian constitution as communities who have historically suffered extreme inequality. This constitu-tional mandate was expanded to address the disadvantages suffered by other castes.
4. See, e.g., Devy 2002.
5. Per Rajagopal (forthcoming), this point was first made by the trade unionist Ashim Roy, of Ahmedabad.
6. I am largely in agreement with Baxi's arguments against too easily comparing the Gujarat carnage as akin to the events of Nazi Germany, even though Baxi struggles to articulate what was inaugural about this pogrom.

7. Ayodhya was witness to the destruction of the Babri mosque on December 6, 1992. More recently, Hindu nationalists have revived the cry for building a temple on the site of the demolished mosque. Many of the passengers in S-6 were returning from the rally to build a temple in Ayodhya.

8. The BBC gave news of the forensic report on July 7, 2003. For reports see: http://www.ahmedabad.com/news/2k2/jul/6godhra.htm; http://www.rediff.com/news/2002/jul/04train.htm; http://www.hinduonnet.com/thehindu/2002/07/04/stories/2002070404781100.htm; http://www.atimes.com/atimes/South_Asia/DG27Df01.html; and http://news.bbc.co.uk/2/hi/south_asia/2087709.htm.

9. The figures for the displaced come from a *Times of India* report of July 22, 2002.

10. The report has noted a 1999 census that was carried out to generate detailed information about the location of Muslim homes and businesses.

11. The ninety-seven-year-old head of the Vishwa Hindu Parishad (World Hindu Council) in Gujarat, K. K. Shastri, casually revealed that the list of Muslim shops to be targeted for attack was prepared on the morning of February 28, just hours after the burning, because of the anger over Godhra.

12. Prem Shankar Jha, a columnist, wrote that the images of burnt bodies and charred bodies, beamed through the evening of February 27 and the morning after, "made it real."

13. For a reading of racialized spectatorship and enjoyment in the context of slavery, see Saidiya Hartman 1997. My argument about the character of media realism draws from Feldman 2002.

14. Shabnam Hashmi has confirmed that women, including those belonging to the upper middle class, were very much part of the looting that happened in Gujarat.

15. On the website OnlineVolunteers.org fact-finding reports about the violence against Muslim women are linked to similar reports on Bosnia, Kosovo, and Rwanda.

16. The complicity of diasporic South Asians, especially those living in Britain and the United States, has been carefully documented in "The Foreign Exchange of Hate." See http://www.sabrang.com/hnfund/sacw/.

17. See "To Bhaijaan with Shame," written by "an Indian Hindu Gujarati student," Satchit Balsari. See also "Responsibility and Revenge," by Mukul Dube, September 7, 2002, both on www.OnlineVolunteers.org/gujarat/news/articles (last accessed November 3, 2003). See also Chandra 2002.

18. Mander is a former officer of the elite Indian Administrative Service who resigned in protest over the government's handling of riots. Mander is the recipient of the 2002 M.A. Thomas National Human Rights Award, and currently serves as the Country Director for Action Aid, India.

Works Cited

Abrams, Philip. 1988. "Notes on the Difficulty of Studying the State." *Journal of Historical Sociology* 1(1): 58–89.

Agamben, Giorgio. 1998. *Homo Sacer: Sovereign Power and Bare Life.* Trans. Daniel Heller Roazen. Stanford: Stanford University Press.

Akbar, M.J. 2002. "What Is New about George?" *Asian Age* (Mumbai). May 5.

Bajpai, Rochana. 2002. "Minority Rights in the Indian Constituent Assembly Debates, 1946–1950." *Queen Elizabeth House Working Papers.* June. Available at: http://www.2.qeh.ox.ac.uk/pdf/qehwp/qehwps30.pdf.

Basu, Rasil. 2002. "Women in Shreds." *Asian Age* (Mumbai). May 26.

Baxi, Upendra. 2002. "Notes on Holocaustian Politics." In "Society Under Siege." *Seminar* 513. (May).

Benjamin, Walter. 1978. "Critique of Violence." In *Reflections: Essays, Aphorisms, Autobiographical Writings,* trans. Edmund Jephcott, ed. Peter Demetz, 277–300. New York: Harcourt Brace Jovanovich.

Chandra, Sudhir. 2002. "A Hindu's Protest." In "Society Under Siege." *Seminar* 513 (May).

Devy, Genesh. 2002. "Tribal Voice and Violence." In "Society Under Siege." *Seminar* 513 (May).

Feldman, Allen. 2002. "Ground Zero Point One: On the Cinematics of History." *Social Analysis* 46(1): 110–17.

Hartman, Saidiya. 1997. *Scenes of Subjection: Terror, Slavery, and Self-Making in Nineteenth-Century America.* New York: Oxford University Press.

Human Rights Watch 2002. *"We Have No Orders to Save You": State Participation and Complicity in Communal Violence in Gujarat.* HRW Reports 14.3 (April). Available at: http://www.hrw.org/reports/2002/india/gujarat.pdf.

Hussain, Nishrin. 2002. "Coping with Pain." *Outlook.* August 7.

Malekar, Anosh. 2002. "Modi's Experiments with Hate." *The Week.* August 4.

Mander, Harsh. 2002. "Cry, the Beloved Country: Reflections on the Gujarat Massacre." Unpublished report circulated over the Internet, March 21. See http://www.actionaidindia.org/cry.htm (last accessed November 3, 2003).

Mukherjee, Shruba. 2002. *"Gujarat ki prakruti* [Gujarat's nature]." *Deccan Herald.* May 26.

Mukherji, Debashish. 2002. "Muslims Approve of Dissolution." *The Week.* August 4.

Nietzsche, Friedrich. 1976. "On Redemption." In *Thus Spake Zarathustra,* in *The Portable Nietzsche,* ed. and trans. Walter Kaufman. New York: Penguin Books.

Nussbaum, Martha. 2003. "Genocide in Gujarat: The International Community Looks Away." *Dissent* (summer). See http://www.dissentmagazine.org/menutest/articles/su03/nussbaum.htm (last accessed November 3, 2003).

Pandey, Gyanendra. 1992. *The Construction of Communalism in North India.* Delhi: Oxford University Press.

Rajagopal, Arvind. Forthcoming. "Gujarat as an Experiment in Hindu National Realism." In the *Crisis of Secularism in India,* ed. Anuradha Needham and Rajeswari Sunder Rajan.

Rajagopal, Arvind. 2001. *Politics after Television: Religious Nationalism and the Reshaping of the Indian Public.* Cambridge: Cambridge University Press.

Sarkar, Tanika. 2002. "Semiotics of Terror." *Economic and Political Weekly.* July 13.

Chapter 16

Challenging What We Mean by Conflict Prevention: The Experience of East Timor

Gwi-Yeop Son

Introduction

Violent conflict is like a virus, its survival and sustenance depending upon its environment. Conflict breeds conflict and violence generates more violence; a recent World Bank study concluded that countries with a recent history of civil war face a 40 percent chance of further violent conflict (Collier 2000, 6).

Academics continue to study the rapidly increasing number of conflicts around the world ostensibly to identify the ingredients for building sustainable peace and thereby to prevent future conflict. Development practitioners benefit from this work but are increasingly questioning the validity of some of these studies, in particular those that seek to promote a "cookbook" approach to conflict prevention.

The emergence of violent conflict is above all circumstantial and more often than not generated by seemingly disconnected factors. Some may be "homegrown" (or internal) but many are "international" in nature (or external) and therefore beyond the sphere of control of a particular country. Not surprisingly it is extremely difficult to weigh the relative importance of these factors, and by implication, therefore, to try to eliminate the causes of conflict in advance seems unrealistic.

This essay briefly examines the emergence and re-emergence of violent conflict in East Timor over the past twenty-five years. It identifies and discusses contributing factors and considers whether the conflict was avoidable or inevitable. It offers some thoughts on the essential ingredients for creating a post-conflict environment conducive to sustainable peace, yet questions the value of the notion of conflict prevention. A number of areas for further research are proposed where academics and development practitioners can work constructively together in the future.

East Timor: A Conflict-Torn Country

East Timor became independent in May 2002 and is the world's youngest nation. Its people have lived through 400 years of colonial occupation with a tenacity that helps to explain why East Timor was successful in achieving independence while others fail. Recent Timorese history for most of us begins in 1975 with the withdrawal of Portugal as the colonial power, sparking twenty-five years of violent conflict, which, for the purposes of this essay, divides into four phases.

Civil War

More than 2,000 civilians were killed during the 1975 civil war, which ended with Indonesian occupation on December 8. The available historical information can be summarized in a relatively straightforward way. In 1974, a left-wing coup in Portugal (the Revolucao do Cravos) sparked the decolonization of Portuguese territories. In East Timor the governor announced general elections and called for the establishment of political parties. Three major parties were formed: the nationalist Timorese Social-Democratic Association (ASDT), which later became the Revolutionary Front for an Independent East Timor (Fretilin); the conservative Timorese Democratic Union (UDT), which sought "progressive autonomy" and proposed self-determination with links to Portugal; and the smaller Timorese Popular Democratic Association (APODETI), which supported the integration of East Timor into Indonesia under certain conditions.

General elections were held in March 1975.[1] Then, on August 11, UDT launched a coup in an attempt to seize power from the Portuguese and prevent the ascendancy of Fretilin. Clashes between the two main East Timorese parties escalated into violence resulting in more than 2,000 deaths (UNDP 2002, 72). On November 28, Fretilin declared the República Democrática de Timor Leste (RDTL-Democratic Republic of East Timor), recognized by a handful of countries only, mainly former Portuguese colonies. Two days later, UDT and APODETI leaders signed the Balibo Declaration inviting the Indonesians to "liberate" East Timor.

During the elections, Fretilin had campaigned on a platform that "stressed the need for land reform which meant re-distributing the large holdings, [belonging] to both private hands and the Portuguese state companies" and even the Catholic church (Aditjondro 1998, 132). Fretilin's membership was largely composed of intellectuals who had studied abroad (and were much influenced by socialist ideology), and students who could easily reach out to the grassroots level. The issue of land reform was appealing to the mainly landless population, from which Fretilin derived its greatest support, despite UDT's close network of landlords and ability to influence rural communities.

Some say that UDT misunderstood Fretilin's ideology, believing it to be synonymous with rapidly expanding communism in Southeast Asia. UDT leader Joao Carrascalao[2] claims that the spirit behind its opposition to Fretilin was the need for "unity, independence, and non-communists for Timor" (Gusmão 2000, 23). This interpretation, however, is difficult to equate with East Timor's tightly knit culture and society, where information flows freely and rapidly between groups. A second view is that UDT and APODETI leaders, most of whom were connected to the landowning class, used the "threat" of communism as a means of expressing personal concerns over the political and socioeconomic implications of Fretilin's overwhelming victory. Therefore the coup was a means of protecting self-interest and maintaining the status quo.

A third view is that the war was induced externally. With the implicit support of the western democracies, Indonesia had manipulated a chaotic situation in Timor by cajoling, bribing, and threatening UDT and APODETI leaders, thereby triggering a breakdown of relations with Fretilin. James Dunn points out that Indonesian generals had convinced UDT leaders that "Fretilin was about to launch a coup with the help of the North Vietnamese agents and seize power" (Dunn 1998, 211). But again the interwoven nature of East Timorese society, with its multiple alliances and family ties criss-crossing all layers of society, makes it hard to believe that UDT could have been so easily misled.

But there were undoubtedly other external factors. The West's fear of East Timor being transformed into another "Cuba" was real at that time.[3] The United States had just failed to prevent the spread of communism in Indochina. Naturally the containment of communism in the archipelago would have been a key foreign policy objective, important enough, it seems, for President Ford and Henry Kissenger to meet President Suharto in Jakarta on December 6. Indonesia's invasion of East Timor took place only sixteen hours after this meeting (Nairin 2001, 163).

Australia was eager to settle the issue of oil and gas revenues from the Timor Sea and evidently felt that it had more to gain from negotiating with the government of Indonesia than with a small and newly established country. In return for Australia's recognition of East Timor as a province of Indonesia, it expected to obtain a larger share of the pie (Martin 2001, 20). How much Australia's encouragement played a role in Indonesia's invasion of East Timor is difficult to weigh; but it must have been important enough for Indonesia to view Australia as its strongest ally for the next twenty-five years.

Lastly, there were strong incentives in play for achieving greater Indonesian "consolidation" within the Indonesian Archipelago. In fact, everyone had something to gain from consolidation (not only Indonesia)—everyone except the East Timorese.

There are elements of both greed and grievance in understanding the civil war of 1975, but what emerges most clearly is the complexity of factors involved and the difficulties in discerning their relative importance, even with the benefit of hindsight. Internal factors may have ignited the violence, but external determinants provided a conducive environment for the violence to spread and ultimately for Indonesian occupation. If civil war had been preventable at any stage, there were few with an interest in doing so.

Resisting Occupation

During the twenty-five years of occupation that followed, violent conflict persisted between the Indonesian military and East Timorese resistance fighters. An estimated two hundred thousand East Timorese lives were lost, an appalling cost bearing in mind an indigenous population of less than one million. Falantil (the pro-independence guerilla army) was supported by an organized and broad-based clandestine movement that provided logistical support, liaised with international organizations, and raised the awareness of tourists and visiting dignitaries (Salla 1998, 37–38).

Conditions were harsh. Constantly on the move, there was seldom much food, proper medication, shelter, or clothing. According to one student activist, the fighters living in the jungle "appeared to be suffering from malnutrition; but all of them were very high-spirited and were determined to continue to fight" (Pinto and Jardine 1997, 197). The casualties were also far greater than on the Indonesian side, and yet the impact on Indonesia was not insignificant. From December 1975 to August 1976, for example, five hundred Indonesian soldiers were killed and two thousand seriously wounded (Aditjondro 1998, 126).

But if East Timorese resistance was violent, many argue that the tactics employed by the occupying forces were unnecessarily brutal, which helped to sustain the conflict. Royal Netherlands Institute researcher and specialist on Indonesia Gerry van Klinken notes that had Indonesia made more efforts to improve the lives of the Timorese after the invasion, the resistance would have gradually decayed (G. van Klinken 2001, 212–13). Instead the "eye for an eye" policy applied by Falantil resulted in an ever-deepening cycle of violence. Ultimately this increased the visibility of Indonesia's activities and recruited many international NGOs and civil rights activists to the East Timorese cause.

It was this dynamic that internationalized the conflict. By the late 1980s, a range of external factors combined to raise the political stakes for continuing Indonesian occupation (Suter 1997; Tanter et al. 2001). The cold war had come to an end and with it the West's fear of communism. Iraq's invasion of Kuwait, and resulting military intervention with a clear UN mandate, drew inevitable parallels with East Timor and uncomfortable questions for some. Then, a year later, with worldwide reporting of the 1991 Santa Cruz massacre,[4] the conflict shifted decisively into a public relations phase, despite Indonesia's best efforts to promote the East Timor question as a matter of national sovereignty.

By the mid-1990s, with the award of the Nobel Peace Prize to two prominent East Timorese (Bishop Ximenes Belo and José Ramos Horta), East Timor was winning the public relations battle. Most significantly East Timor's successes in getting its case across with the UN and elsewhere had helped to change Australia's position on Indonesian occupation (Martin 2001, 22). Moreover, Indonesia itself was changing. The 1997–98 Asian economic crises had forced President Mohamed Suharto's resignation. Subsequently, his successor Bacharuddin Jusuf Habibie's unwillingness to maintain the burden of an "expensive province" became an open debate, and in January 1999 he offered East Timor wide-ranging autonomy. Agreement on a "popular consultation" was finally reached in May 1999 under the auspices of the UN Secretary-General, and a referendum on independence was duly held in August.

In brief, a phase of the conflict based on genuine grievance had ebbed and flowed for a decade or more. External factors (geopolitical and otherwise), however, were not sufficiently well aligned at that time to convert this effort into real gains for the East Timorese. By the mid-1990s the situation had changed, and we begin to see the conflict building into peaks of violence as the occupying forces felt the pressure of increased international scrutiny. Perhaps more enlightened civilian administration during the initial years of occupation could have isolated the resistance movement and eroded its popular appeal. But by now external determinants (including the increasing role of the international media) had driven the conflict well beyond the control of Jakarta-based politicians and bureaucrats, let alone the military-backed administration in Dili.

After the Referendum

There are as many "informed views" as unanswered questions when it comes to understanding the violence that followed the 1999 independence referendum. Here are some of the facts: On August 30, 1999, the people of East Timor voted overwhelmingly—78.5 percent—in favor of independence from Indonesia. Pro-integration militia then embarked on a systematic program of looting and killing across the province. One-third of the population[5] was forced to resettle in refugee camps in West Timor and neighboring islands. Another third sought refuge in the hills and forests. Between one thousand and two thousand people were reported killed, and 90 percent of the infrastructure was destroyed. The severity of the reprisals called for international action, and on September 15, 1999, the UN Security Council authorized a multinational force under Australian command to restore peace and security. This force started deploying on September 19, and a large-scale humanitarian and peace-keeping operation was subsequently established.

How and why were the pro-integration militia allowed to terrorize their own people with such brutality? Many would point the finger at the Government of Indonesia for failing to meet the terms and conditions of the May 5 Agreements, which gave the Indonesian military responsibility for security arrangements during the referendum.[6] Few would contest that the pro-integration militia, most of whom were young East Timorese, were instruments of the Indonesian military (H. van Klinken 2001, 92). Jeffrey

Robinson, a historian and eyewitness to the events, later wrote: "The . . . armed pro-Indonesian militia gangs . . . roamed with impunity throughout the territory, engaging in acts of violence and terror against ordinary people. These militia groups were armed, trained and fully backed by the Indonesian armed forces, the TNI, and in many cases TNI soldiers were themselves militia members" (Robinson 2001, 57; see Martin 2001, 71).

Richard Tanter, specialist in Indonesian military politics and the role of intelligence organizations, reports on the expansion of Indonesian military activity and the establishment of militia groups prior to the referendum: "In late 1998 and early 1999, the number of militia groups, and the pace and scale of terrorist militia activities supported by the Indonesian military, increased considerably. . . . Large numbers of weapons were provided from sources within the Indonesian military (TNI), and militia members were offered payment to participate. Young men who did not accept an invitation to join were often subject to violent intimidation" (Tanter 2001, 191).

Tanter further points out that reprisals were sequentially planned and executed to prevent the referendum from taking place; when this failed, to ensure that a vote in support of autonomy rather than full independence was returned; and when this also failed, to foment civil war in an attempt to nullify the results of the vote (Tanter 2001, 192). According to one UN staff member at the time, an Indonesian police chief had confided that he had been told not to interfere with militia activities and that he otherwise could have easily put an end to the violence (H. van Klinken 2001, 101).

Some blame the United Nations for not having questioned the terms of the May 5 Agreements. Nicola Dahrendorf, who worked on security issues in East Timor both before and after the referendum, argues that the May 5 Agreements could have been amended before being signed.[7] But Ian Martin, Special Representative of the Secretary General in East Timor at the time, argues that it would have been impossible for Indonesia to give up responsibility for security (Martin 2001, 80–84). President Habibie's fragile political future depended very much on garnering internal support, particularly that of the military, a powerful and overwhelmingly nationalist force in Indonesian politics. To question the May 5 Agreements could have led to a suspension of the process by Habibie. He puts the difficulty of the UN's position in the following way: "To proceed with the consultation in the midst of violence could not only put the East Timorese and the UN's own staff at risk but also set the scene for the UN to sanction an outcome that was the result of intimidation. Yet to suspend the process risked handing victory to those who were bent on preventing the vote from taking place and losing what many East Timorese, including Gusmao, believed might prove the unique window of opportunity for them to determine their own future" (Martin 2001, 50).

The Security Council is held accountable by some for failing to send in peacekeepers quickly enough. The Secretary-General had been providing regular briefings to the Security Council during and after the referendum, and in August tried to get early deployment of peace-keepers sanctioned. A final decision was made, however, not to send in any military or police until after the vote (Martin 2001, 85). Jamsheed Marker, the Secretary-General's representative on East Timor in 1998, recalls that even he was pressured by both Australian and U.S. governments not to disrupt the May 5 Agreement (Martin 2001, 33), and Indonesian historian John Roosa observes that in the weeks before the ballot, " . . . the Clinton administration refused to discuss with Australia and other countries the formation of [an international force]" (Chomsky 2001, 128). When later a military force was sent in, the United States provided minimal support and in fact requested the UN to reduce the size of the peacekeeping force (Chomsky 2001, 129).

Other voices held out in support of Indonesia at the time. ASEAN member-states were inclined to believe that Indonesia was doing its best to contain the violence and that its security role should not be removed without prior consent (Martin 2001, 120). There was little appetite at this time for any initiative that might undermine Indonesian political and economic stability in view of Habibie's precarious hold on power, and particularly in the wake of the Asian economic crisis. China, Russia, and several G-7 members also argued that international assistance, including military and police, should "only be provided at the invitation of Indonesia" (Martin 2001, 120).

What is clear above all is that the violence of September 1999 was not prevented even though it was anticipated and its more obvious contributing factors were known. A number of less obvious external influencing factors have since emerged and are debated in much of the literature on East Timor. Had the May 5 Agreements reflected the need for a solid international peace-keeping during the referendum, then East Timor's transition to independence would not have been so bloody. But to understand why this did not happen is to begin to reflect on the chaotic interplay of factors affecting the emergence of violent conflict and, indeed, to carefully consider the meaning of "conflict prevention."

Since Independence

For the first time, East Timor has a chance to write a chapter in its own history. In August 2001 Constituent Assembly elections were held peacefully under the auspices of the UN. When the result showed that Fretilin, the main political party, had won an overwhelming majority,[8] the peace continued to hold. This successful transition can be attributed to efforts to achieve social and political reconciliation[9] as well as to the existence of several functioning elements of the state, namely:

- a large peace-keeping force and subsequent establishment of the East Timor Defence Force;
- an internationally backed Police Service with more than 1300 police officers deployed to 13 districts;
- humanitarian and reconstruction activities; and

- establishment of a civilian administration including basic judicial and legal systems.

Yet the risk of further violent conflict remains, and there will undoubtedly continue to be incidents such as the one that occurred in December 2002. Eighteen people were shot (three fatally) and eighty incarcerated following a night of arson and looting, much of which targeted the prime minister's property as well as foreign businesses. The government attributed the violence to hard-line nationalist elements (Toohey and Kerin 2002), while the media cited lack of employment opportunities, rising fuel prices, and the appointment of police officers with links to the previous regime (Toohey and Kerin 2002; *Publico* 2002; Reuters 2002; Associated Press 2002; LUSA 2002; DPA 2002). Whatever the causes, such events are a particular concern in a country where half the population has grown up with violence and sees it as a legitimate means of achieving political goals.

Externally there is a continued threat from former militia groups still active in West Timor, while internally a process of reconciliation is required both with Indonesians who continue to live in East Timor, as well as East Timorese implicated in atrocities carried out by the former regime. Truth and Reconciliation Commissions, modeled on the South African example, have been established, though the process will be long and extremely costly for a country with virtually no economy and a per capita GDP ranking alongside the poorest countries in Africa.

Language continues to be a source of tension, with only 5 percent of the population speaking Portuguese, East Timor's official language. Those who do speak Portuguese come principally from the political and economic elites currently holding most of the decision-making posts. Moreover, the administration requires that public sector employees learn to speak Portuguese, and there is a suspicion that those who do receive preferential treatment. Other potential threats to peace and security include: lack of progress on land reform, limited capacity to establish genuine rule of law, ineffective usage of Timor Sea oil and gas royalties, and the composition and management of the East Timor Defense Force.

Undoubtedly the controlling factor is the pace of economic development, which is failing to match the expectations of the majority in terms of employment opportunities and a rise in living standards. With an economy very much dependent on future oil and gas, there is a risk of elite capture of that resource, undermining the government's ability to provide vital services to the poor. East Timor will need to make efforts to use its natural resources in a very explicit way for the provision of basic services to the people. It will also be important to pursue policies of diversification of the economy away from dependence on primary commodities and associated rent-seeking behavior.

This is where the international community has an important role to play and must maintain its presence (both in terms of development aid and peace-keeping) until the state can itself begin to broker competing interests. The inexperience of the existing leadership and the immaturity of its political systems means that mistakes will be made. With East Timor's history of violent conflict and with more than half of its people knowing little else, the stakes are extremely high.

Lessons Learned and Moving Forward

East Timor's recent past teaches us that the causes of violent conflict are complex, multilevel, and often invisible at the time, needing to be pieced together with the benefit of history and hindsight. Like a disease, and in chaotic fashion, violent conflict both transforms and is transformed by its environment. Initial causes (or triggers) very quickly combine with other contextual factors, some publicly acknowledged and others not. All of this makes it very difficult to generate credible analyses of the causes of conflict as a means of predicting or preventing future ones.

There are no circuit-breakers. At best, intervention (such as military intervention) can provide "time" to attempt to address underlying issues. Such intervention must seek to transform the environment that is sustaining that conflict, rather than to attempt to address the "perceived" causes. This calls for rapid establishment of accountable governance with the capacity to deliver change and (at least a perception of) greater equity. In the context of East Timor this means:

- establishing participatory and transparent administration;
- building sound legal and judicial frameworks promoting the rule of law and balance of power;
- fostering sociopolitical reconciliation while respecting human rights; and
- promoting economic growth and employment generation through foreign investment and reconstruction.

Development practitioners and academics need to continue to work together in ways that will help to deepen understanding of the nature of violent conflict and its complex forces. Further research would be beneficial in the following areas: undertaking case studies that track the emergence and re-emergence of intrastate conflicts; understanding the role of the international community in peace building; and managing the transition between emergency relief and the re-establishment of government.

Notes

1. Some claim that an Indonesian covert destabilization operation beginning in October 1974 prevented East Timor from completing the elections.

2. Joao Carrascalao, after the 1999 referendum, reorganized UDT as one of the parties running for the Constituent Assembly elections in 2001. His party gained only one seat in the Constituent Assembly, representing a very small minority party.
3. Although Fretilin had no links with the Soviet Union or China, their communist-socialist ideology intimidated both Indonesia and the Western countries, particularly the United States. The invasion was therefore blessed by the United States, Australia, and other western countries because of the fear of spreading communism.
4. This most publicized violence resulted in the death of two hundred people at a cemetery in the capital (Dili) during a funeral procession of a young man who had protested against the cancellation of a Portuguese Parliamentary delegation.
5. Different books and papers note different numbers as the precise number is unknown. It is, however, estimated that at least 200,000 people were displaced into West Timor. Total population of East Timor is estimated to be somewhere between 800,000 and 1 million.
6. Agreements signed by the governments of Indonesia and Portugal, and the UN allowing the people of East Timor to vote for autonomy or full independence.
7. Includes Nicole Dharendorf, who worked at the UN Secretariat at the time and later as the National Security Advisor with UNTAET in Dili, East Timor.
8. Contexts and circumstances were quite similar between 1975 and 2002 elections. Both times, the elections were held under the auspices of others—Portuguese and the UN and one party, Fretilin, won overwhelmingly. Additionally, internal disagreements among parties were prevalent in both periods.
9. Truth Commissions were established as an important form of social catharsis and a means of striking a balance between amnesty and prosecution of those who had committed atrocities.

Works Cited

Aditjondro, George. 1998. "The Environment in East Timor." In *East Timor: Occupation and Resistance,* ed. Torben Retbøll and International Work Group for Indigenous Affairs, 123–40. IWGIA Document 89. Copenhagen: IWGIA.

The Age (Melbourne, Australia). 2002. "Outside elements linked to Dili riots." December 6.

Agence France-Press. 2002. "US concerned over Timor violence." December 5. Online at: http://iiasnt.leidenuniv.nl:8080/DR/2002/12/DR_2002_12_10/14, accessed December 5, 2003.

Associated Press. 2002. "Police In East Timor Arrest 80 People Following Riots." December 5. Online at: http://iiasnt.leidenuniv.nl:8080/DR/2002/12/DR_2002_12_10/12, accessed December 5, 2003.

Brett, E. A. 2002. *Liberal Theory, Uneven Development, and Institutional Reform: Responding to the Crisis in Weak States.* London School of Economics and Political Science, Development Studies Institute (DESTIN), Crisis States Programme, Working Paper 12. Available at: http://www.crisisstates.com/download/wp/WP12TB.pdf.

Chomsky, Noam. 2001. "East Timor, the United States, and International Responsibility: 'Green Light' for War Crimes." In *Bitter Flowers, Sweet Flowers:*

East Timor, Indonesia, and the World Community, ed. Richard Tanter, Mark Selden, and Stephen Shalom, 127–47. Lanham, MD: Rowman and Littlefield. 2001.

Collier, Paul. 2000. *Economic Causes of Civil Conflict and their Implications for Policy.* Development Research Group of the World Bank. Available at: http://www.worldbank.org/research/conflict/papers/civilconflict.pdf.

DPA (Jakarta). 2002. "Indonesian citizens seek shelter in riot-torn East Timor." December 4. Online at: http://iiasnt.leidenuniv.nl:8080/DR/2002/12/DR_2002_12_10/1, accessed December 5, 2003.

Dunn, James. 1998. "An International Betrayal." In *East Timor: Occupation and Resistance,* ed. Torben Retbøll and International Work Group for Indigenous Affairs, 208–13. IWGIA Document 89. Copenhagen: IWGIA.

The Economist. 2003. "East Timor: Freedom's Disappointments." March 20. Online at: http://iiasnt.leidenuniv.nl:8080/DR/2003/03/DR_2003_03_26/5, accessed December 5, 2003.

Gusmão, Xanana. 2000. *To Resist Is to Win: The Autobiography of Xanana Gusmão,* ed. Sarah Niner, trans. Perestrelo Botelheiro and Ana Noronha. Ringwood, Australia: Aurora Books/David Lovell Publishing.

Khan, Mushtaq H. 2002. *State Failure in Developing Countries and Strategies of Institutional Reform.* World Bank ABCDE Conference, Oslo, June 24–26. Available at: http://wbln0018.worldbank.org/eurvp/web.nsf/Pages/Paper+by+Mushtaq+Khan/$File/KHAN+STATE+FAILURE.PDF.

Klinken, Gerry van. 2001. "Big States and Little Independence Movements." In *Bitter Flowers, Sweet Flowers: East Timor, Indonesia, and the World Community,* ed. Richard Tanter, Mark Selden, and Stephen Shalom, 209–25. Lanham, MD: Rowman and Littlefield. 2001.

Klinken, Helene van. 2001. "Taking the Risk, Paying the Price: East Timorese Vote in Ermera." In *Bitter Flowers, Sweet Flowers: East Timor, Indonesia, and the World Community,* ed. Richard Tanter, Mark Selden, and Stephen Shalom, 91–107. Lanham, MD: Rowman and Littlefield. 2001.

Latto, Benedict. 2002. *Governance and Conflict Management: Implications for Donor Intervention.* London School of Economics and Political Science, Development Studies Institute (DESTIN), Crisis States Programme, Working Paper 9. Available at: http://www.simians.co.uk/drc/working/WP9BL.pdf.

LUSA. 2002. "Gusmao asks UN for continued use of Portuguese peacekeepers in Dili." December 5. Online at: http://iiasnt.leidenuniv.nl:8080/DR/2002/12/DR_2002_12_10/19, accessed December 5, 2003.

Magalhães, A. Barbedo de. 1998. "Portugal and East Timor." In *East Timor: Occupation and Resistance,* ed. Torben Retbøll and International Work Group for Indigenous Affairs, 229–37. IWGIA Document 89. Copenhagen: IWGIA.

Martin, Ian. 2001. *Self-Determination in East Timor: The United Nations, the Ballot, and International Intervention.* Boulder, Colo.: Lynne Rienner.

Nairin, Allan. 2001. "US Support for the Indonesian Military: Congressional Testimony." In *Bitter Flowers, Sweet Flowers: East Timor, Indonesia, and the World Community,* ed. Richard Tanter, Mark Selden, and Stephen Shalom, 163–72. Lanham, MD: Rowman and Littlefield. 2001.

Pinto, Constancio, and Matthew Jardine. 1997. *East Timor's Unfinished Struggle: Inside the Timorese Resistance.* Boston: South End Press.

Publico. 2002. "Slowness of UN Led to Portugal's Full Control of Contingent." December 5.

Retbøll, Torben, and International Work Group for Indigenous Affairs, eds. 1998. *East Timor: Occupation and Resistance*. IWGIA Document 89. Copenhagen: IWGIA.

Reuters. 2002. "Australia condemns East Timor violence." December 5. Online at: http://iiasnt.leidenuniv.nl:8080/DR/2002/12/DR_2002_12_10/9, accessed December 5, 2003.

Robinson, Geoffrey. 2001. "With UNAMET in East Timor: An Historian's Personal View." In *Bitter Flowers, Sweet Flowers: East Timor, Indonesia, and the World Community,* ed. Richard Tanter, Mark Selden, and Stephen Shalom, 55–72. Lanham, MD: Rowman and Littlefield. 2001.

Salla, Michael Emin. 1998. "A Visit to East Timor." In *East Timor: Occupation and Resistance,* ed. Torben Retbøll and International Work Group for Indigenous Affairs, 32–40. IWGIA Document 89. Copenhagen: IWGIA.

Suter, Keith. 1997. *East Timor, West Papua/Irian and Indonesia*. Minority Rights Group International Report 97/4. London: Minority Rights Group.

Tanter, Richard. 2001. "East Timor and the Crisis of the Indonesian Intelligence State." In *Bitter Flowers, Sweet Flowers: East Timor, Indonesia, and the World Community,* ed. Richard Tanter, Mark Selden, and Stephen Shalom, 189–207. Lanham, MD: Rowman and Littlefield. 2001.

Tanter, Richard, Mark Selden, and Stephen Shalom, eds. 2001. *Bitter Flowers, Sweet Flowers: East Timor, Indonesia, and the World Community*. Lanham, MD: Rowman and Littlefield.

Toohey, Paul, and John Kerin. 2002. "Timor PM orders inquiry into riots." *Herald Sun*. December 6.

UNDP. 1999a. *Governance Foundations for Post-Conflict Situations: UNDP's Experience*. Available at: http://magnet.undp.org/Docs/crisis/monograph/monograph.htm.

UNDP. 1999b. *Promoting Conflict Prevention and Conflict Resolution through Effective Governance: A Conceptual Survey and Literature Review*. Available at: http://magnet.undp.org/Docs/crisis/mapexercise.htm.

UNDP. 2002. *East Timor Human Development Report: Ukun Rasik A'an/The Way Ahead*. Available at: http://www.undp.east-timor.org/documentsreports/nhdr/nhdr_full.pdf.

Part IV

Antiviolence Ethics and Strategies: Coalitions, Theatres, Interdependencies

Chapter 17

Sisterhood after Terrorism

Filipino Ecumenical Women and the U.S. Wars[1]

Kathryn Poethig

In August 2002, I joined an international women's peace mission to Basilan Island off Mindanao, the stronghold of the Abu Sayyaf, a Muslim extremist group notorious for kidnapping foreign tourists. The International Women's Peace Mission and Forum was organized by the Filipino Ecumenical Women's Forum (EWF) and aimed at "drawing local and international attention to the atrocities and ill effects of deepening U.S. military involvement in the Philippines and to pose a challenge of faith and sisterhood to Christian women all over the world, but especially to the Filipino ecumenical women" (Ecumenical Women's Forum, no date). Arrangements for our "fact finding mission" were left to the Mindanao Christian People's Alliance, whose director is the only Muslim member of EWF. When she said she could not guarantee the safety of the twenty-five women (particularly the Americans) because of heightened violence, the mission was rerouted to central Luzon to reflect on the effects of U.S. militarism a decade after the United States had evacuated its two bases, Clark Airbase and Subic Naval Base. Since central Luzon is also the birthplace of the New People's Army, the armed forces of the Communist Party of the Philippines (CPP), we turned from the concerns and demands of Muslim insurgents to the analysis of rural poverty by peasants sympathetic to the CPP's vision of national democracy.

The particular rhetoric of leftist Filipino Christian women sympathetic to both Muslim and Communist insurgencies at home offers a unique Asian Christian critique of the U.S. war on international terrorism. The Ecumenical Women's Forum, a gathering of Protestant, Roman Catholic, and a few Muslim women, offers the most critical religious women's voice in the current antiwar mood in the Philippines. Though there had been ecumenical women's gatherings since the mid-1990s, the EWF formally emerged in 2002 as the U.S. war on terrorism drew increasing hostility worldwide. Because of this convergence, EWF's statements have consistently linked the wars at home to the war abroad. In this essay, I will analyze the intersection of two frameworks used in the EWF critique—unjust war and just peace— and the contribution of women to peacemaking. By doing so, I indicate that the current critique of U.S. war on terrorism is imbricated with earlier critiques at the same time as it expands the borders of analysis.

The EWF links two powerful Protestant and Catholic women's organizations.[2] It has drawn together a "sisterhood" from as varied local religious groups as the United Church of Christ in the Philippines, the Philippine Independent Church, Baptists, and Roman Catholic orders such as the Carmelites, Good Shepherd, and Maryknoll. Drawing on an international Protestant ecumenical "sisterhood" that was evident during the Peace Mission, EWF leaders have connections with progressive Christian Conference of Asia in Hong Kong and the women's desk of the World Council of Churches in Geneva. While it organizes annual "fact finding missions," EWF's key event is the celebration of International Women's Day on March 8. In addition, it prepares and distributes thematic liturgies, Bible studies, and theological essays that are feminist and leftist in orientation. Indeed, EWF's statements suggest that the organization shares the Marxist alignment of the National Democratic Front of the Philippines (NDFP), the united front fighting for national and social liberation under the leadership of the CPP, with the New People's Army as its armed force.[3]

Wars and Rumors of Peace

The starting point for this discourse on just peace and unjust wars is an analysis of the Philippine colonial relationship to America, a case in which Philippine sovereignty and territorial integrity are continually threatened by U.S. imperialist intervention. This neocolonial status informs the Filipino leftist discourse of violence and peace. A brief recap of U.S. presence and influence in the Philippines is thus necessary. After four hundred years of colonization, Spain ceded the Philippines to the United States in 1898 at the close of the Spanish-American War. As the Philippine revolution against Spain was in full swing, it was not an easy transition. To establish its sovereignty, the United States turned on the Filipinos, and a bloody American-Filipino war continued until 1913. The United States attempted to create the Philippines in its likeness before it granted the colony independence in 1946 (see Karnow 1989). In addition to a U.S.-modeled political system, the United States contributed an educational system taught in English, Protestant churches, a proclivity toward Hollywood, and twenty-three military bases. In addition, the Americans granted themselves a favorable business environment and laws to continue this legacy (Constantino and Constantino 1978). Suarez points out that the hard-line militarist and anticommunist policies of the Philippine government are the result of "Filipino schooling in the ideological tradition of colonial politics" (1999, 43). America's bulky military presence in the Philippines from independence through the cold war was justified as protection for its former colony's democracy and as a staging ground to flush out the "Communist menace" in Asia (the bases were critical during the Vietnam War). Communist insurgency began soon after the United States granted full independence to the Philippines in 1946. The armed wing of the Communist Party was the HUKs, a guerilla movement that fought against Japanese occupation during World War II. Squashed by the U.S.-funded anti-Communist campaign, the Communist Party revived under new leadership in the 1960s and renamed its armed unit the New People's Army (NPA). It gained many adherents during the harsh Marcos dictatorship (1972–86) and the Aquino administration (1986–91), which registered worse human rights violations than Marcos. Particularly galling for Filipino nationalists was the continued existence of two large U.S. bases. When the U.S.-Republic of the Philippines Military Bases Agreement came up for renewal in 1991, the Philippine Senate voted against it, a remarkable rout. In 1999, the Visiting Forces Agreement admitted U.S. troops back on Philippine territory. It is this agreement that allowed the Bush administration to send U.S. military into Mindanao.

The U.S. also left behind a more fully colonized Muslim territory in the South. The southernmost islands of the Philippines known as Mindanao had never been successfully hispanicized by Spain. Its Muslim "Moro" population, named after their association with the Moors, was more successfully integrated into Philippine governance in the fifty years of U.S. occupation, though not necessarily to their advantage. Resettlement programs brought land-hungry Filipino Christians to the south, and U.S. "pensionado" programs sent promising Muslims to the United States to study while incorporating others into government positions. In addition, American corporations set up extensive plantations. The continued disenfranchisement of the Muslim minority in the south erupted in insurgency in the 1970s, first with the Moro National Liberation Front (MNLF) and later with its splinter group, the Moro Islamic Liberation Front (MILF).[4]

Peace talks between the government and these insurgent groups, the Communist New People's Army and the Muslim MNLF/MILF, have dominated the language of peacemaking for the last fifteen years. The Communist leaders argue that their ultimate goal of a "just and lasting peace" is impeded by Philippine neocolonialism, the exploitative conditions of semifeudalism, and bureaucratic capitalism (see Sison 1991).[5] The route to CPP's particular version of peace is armed struggle. Jose Sison, the CPP's chief political consultant, has pursued peace talks that have been curtailed since the U.S. war on terrorism. Muslims in the southern Philippines are fighting for a "Bangsamoro" (literally Moro nation) free from "imperial Manila's" economic, political and military hegemony. They claim that they lost their political sovereignty, ancestral land, and economic resources under Philippine neocolonial control (Kamlian 1999, 21). In both peace negotiations, the government's rendition of peace is primarily disarmament as well as addressing social and economic concerns (this primarily with MILF).

In his 2002 State of the Union address, President George W. Bush declared the Philippines a "second front" in the U.S. war on terrorism, inaugurated by joint military exercises called Balikatan 02–1, which means "shoulder to shoulder." The primary reason for these exercises was the suppression of Islamic international terrorist networks such as the Abu Sayyaf, Muslim extremist terrorists (some would say bandits) who were holding Filipino and American hostages on Basilan Island. By February, more than a thousand American troops had arrived. The U.S. war on terrorism was immediately entangled with the peace processes between the Philippine government on the one hand and NPA and MILF on the other. In August the United States listed the CPP-NPA as a foreign terrorist organization because of their anti-American stance and killings of Americans. This cut short the existing peace process, tentative though it was. Though there were threats to label the MILF terrorist, the United States instead inserted itself into the peace process, offering aid, diplomatic assistance, and the support of the U.S. Institute of Peace.

"And She Said NO!": Peacemaking as Resistance

From the beginning, EWF materials have expressed a longing for genuine peace and have called religious women to work for it.[6] EWF's primary route to peace, however, is not predicated on the nurturing, conciliatory proclivities of women that have featured prominently in women and peace studies (Reardon 1985, Brock-Utne 1985). Filipino Christian feminists choose resistance to make peace. This resistance follows from the militant positionality of Filipino feminist liberation theologians who helped to develop a Filipino theology of struggle under the Marcos dictatorship (Battung et al. 1988; de la Torre 1986; Fernandez 1998). Like Latin American liberation theologies, it claimed a Marxist Christianity and asserted "God's preferential option for the poor." Philippine feminist theology added patriarchy to this critical theology (Mananzan 1987).

EWF burst onto the national scene with its annual campaign, "And She Said NO!" expressing outrage at the arrival of America's war on Philippine shores. The campaign, which focused on violence against women, emphasized women's violations in military conflict. Like the biblical figure whom EWF members call "our sister Queen Vashti," who refused to display her beauty at Persian King Ahasuerus' directive, ecumenical women were called upon to "voice out a resounding NO! to U.S. wars of aggression and the Balikatan! In the midst of the horrendous effects of war and the social ills that the presence of U.S. military troops brings, we are continuing our unwavering tradition to resistance to all forms of violence."[7] The "And She Said NO!" campaign thus charged Filipino women with agency against victimization. The impetus of this agency is nationalism. Naming Filipino women who died for Philippine independence, EWF proclaims, "it is our solemn pledge never to betray them." This pledge to preserve "hard won sovereignty" is repeated in the "'And She Said NO!' Primer" (Ecumenical Women's Forum 2002a). Offering a history of the present, the authors of the primer note that during the Filipino-American war, the United States sent 126,000 troops "to crush down the revolutionaries and smash their hopes for national liberation." Now, the U.S. war on terrorism has opened up an opportunity to use the Philippines as its "second front" in Asia as a strategic location to monitor Muslim countries. The authors divine that, "the souls of innocent victims and Filipino revolutionaries will not rest until the present and next generation resolutely pledge never to allow this thing to happen again. Thus there is continued resistance to U.S. intervention in our land" (Ecumenical Women's Forum 2002a, 4). Such statements offer ample evidence that EWF advocates a faith-based revolutionary nationalist resistance. The theme, "And She Said NO!" was lifted from an eponymous biblical reflection on activist women during the martial law era (Graham 1990). Graham writes that Vashti is one of the few biblical women to confront the existing "patriarchal dominance system" and offers her as a model for activist Asian women. The writers of EWF make a canny connection between Persian imperial expectations of Vashti's obeisance and American imperial(ist) assumptions that the Philippines could be "used as justification for military expansionism in support of America's economic globalization agenda" (Ecumenical Women's Forum 2002c). The EWF thus calls Filipino women to be revolutionary Vashtis and does not refer to her successor, the Jewish Queen Esther. The lack of a closer reading of this biblical passage in EWF materials is curious, for in the biblical story, it is Esther, as a member of the marginalized Jewish community under Persia, who saves her people from extermination.

EWF leaders are troubled by the patriarchal and "macho" mannerisms of both the Philippine and U.S. administrations. They are particularly critical of their president, Gloria Arroyo-Macapagal, whom they characterize as a "self-proclaimed mother of the nation." Instead, she is a "certified lackey of globalization" who favors big business and "assaults the people with militarism" (Ecumenical Women's Forum 2002d). The evidence of this is the renewed presence of U.S. troops in Mindanao. It would appear, then, that a motherly leader would be an ardent anticapitalist and defender of national autonomy, and would be particularly wary of the state military apparatus.

Peace Based on Justice and Unjust Wars

In a country where 40 percent of the population falls below the poverty line, earning less than \$300 a year, Filipino theologians argue that peace must be based on "the people's agenda," a phrase that turns up in such EWF statements as "Women of Faith, Carry Forward the People's Agenda!" which calls "Christians who long for peace based on justice . . . to voice out a resounding NO! to the further degradation of poor Filipino women and men" (Women's Ecumenical Forum 2002d).

Given this concern for the poor—who are "the people"—a peace based on justice according to EWF is: "adequate provisions for daily life, respect for dignity of human beings regardless of race, class, gender and age, and the integrity of the entire creation" (Ecumenical Women's Forum 2003). Peace is thus the absence of structural violence (unequal life choices based on unequal power) and is often referred to as positive peace. Beyond a reference to peace as the elimination of violence against women, there is not much gendered analysis of peace. Negative peace is the absence of direct organized violence, most often war. Thus, given the wars at home, EWF further defines peace as "bringing to the table the negotiations for the achievement of peace. Peace is not terrorizing the countryside with military show of force by deploying more troops, increasing prices of basic life commodities. . . . Peace is not ignoring the people's cry for life and dignity, as if all is at peace when there is really unpeace" (Ecumenical Women's Forum 2002b).

EWF's references to local wars are less developed than its attention to U.S. wars. Its initial concept paper expresses concern for the "violence against women wrought by the war of aggression in Mindanao" (Ecumenical Women's Forum 2002b). Whose "war of aggression" is this—Muslims, the Philippine government, or the U.S. military? Given the common reference to U.S. "wars of aggression," one must assume that insurgents do not conduct this kind of war, thus implicating the Philippine government (and by association, the United States) as the source of the Mindanao conflict. In none of the EWF statements, then, are the insurgents castigated, except perhaps in a reference to wars in "other parts of the country" where people flee to escape the crossfire. EWF does not reflect on the NPA's "people's protracted war" as a *war*. This is undoubtedly related to a sympathy to the NDFP-CPP's social vision. When the EWF leadership argues that peace is thwarted when the government labels "political forces for national freedom and sovereignty" as "international terrorists," they reveal their hand (Ecumenical Women's Forum 2003). Certainly there are arguments against designating the NPA a terrorist organization. It does not follow, however, that the Philippine government would recognize the NPA, who have declared themselves enemies of the state as vanguards for "national freedom and sovereignty." These pro-CPP sympathies will reveal further friction in EWF's definition of war, which I will address further on.

In the realm of intervention, it does not augur well for Philippine sovereignty that its civil wars are waged by America's old and new enemies—Communists and Muslims. Given the status of the Philippines as a "second front" for the U.S. war on terrorism, a definition of peace requires attention to U.S. military presence in the Philippines. Thus, an earlier definition is revised to read: "Peace is not terrorizing the countryside with military show of force by deploying more troops, including foreign troops, under the guise of joint military exercises. Peace is not waging a war on terror to counter terror" (Ecumenical Women's Forum 2003). The progressive critique of the Visiting Forces Agreement was based on its contravention of the 1987 Philippine constitution, which considers the presence of foreign military on Philippine soil as a violation of national sovereignty. In a theological reflection on "Seeking Faith Based on Justice," Sister Leonila Bermisa states that American intransigence is "ripping apart the heart and soul of our nation" (Bermisa 2002, 1). She offers the metaphor of the Trojan Horse, in whose hollowed belly Greek warriors hid, waiting to attack once the Trojans had wheeled the horse inside their battlements. Thus Greek cunning subjugated their enemies. She adds a caveat to the story, the warning of Cassandra, the Trojan princess cursed by Apollo to foretell what none will believe. This is a warning to us, notes Bermisa, to listen for the truth. For the U.S. troops arrive with the latest matériel, eliciting admiration and gratitude for their gifts, but what are the conditions for this aid? "We got rid of the U.S. Bases which were encroachments on our land. Shall we enter into another agreement that will erode an already fragile relationship and enter once again in a master-slave relationship?" (Bermisa 2002, 4). This war, argues Bermisa, is a continuation of the Philippine neocolonial relationship with America. While the United States offers to assist the Philippines on the domestic front, it is ultimately the war abroad that uses the war at home for its own interests.

In early 2003 EWF's theme turned from intervention to invasion. "Women Say: Never Again to Unjust Wars!" condemned the U.S. war in Iraq and the Philippine Armed Forces' new offensive against the MILF. Predicated on earlier foreboding, EWF declared that the Philippines was now a "staging ground for U.S. wars of aggression against Afghanistan, Iraq and other countries which have dared challenge the new Empire" (Ecumenical Women's Forum 2003). As waves of protests against the U.S. invasion of Iraq washed over Asia in mid-February 2003,[8] six thousand Filipinos marched to the U.S. embassy in Manila. Affirming their unity with peace-loving women to resist the U.S.-led war, the ecumenical network of women held peace vigils throughout Manila to pray for an alternative to war. This in itself was a remarkable moment for the many Protestants who had never prayed in the pews of Catholic churches nor lit candles for peace together with Roman Catholics.

While the meaning of "unjust wars" is never explicit, EWF references to wars of aggression in the service of Empire, the immorality of the U.S. war on Iraq as unnecessary destruction and arrogant in the extreme, and the particular violations of U.S. intervention in the Philippines give its reference weight. The U.S. war on terrorism is thus one more American war of aggression, this time seeking to expand its economic and military Empire in a borderless hunt for terrorists. Just peace thus requires "freedom from foreign intervention." In order to change the conditions that make such aggression possible, there must be "resistance to the global hegemony of Empire" (Ecumenical Women's Forum 2003).

Given the complex layers of hostilities and alliances, leftist Christians are challenged to find a theological language for peace. The Hebrew shalom is useful as it is rendered a peace with justice, particularly for Protestants (Gomez 2000; National Council of Churches of the Philippines 1995, Ecumenical Bishops' Forum 2003). Archie Ligo, a Roman Catholic and speaker at an EWF event, suggests that "for the prophets of Israel, the opposite of peace is not war but social injustice" (Ligo 2002, 2). Thus the exploitation that leads to (insurrectionary) war can only be resolved through the end of violent conflict and the revolutionary reversal of existing social conditions. Bermisa agrees, but presses further the necessity of personal metamorphosis. She argues that love calls Christians to break out of the culture of violence and hatred, and that peace is the fruit of the moral transformation of humankind. In a brilliant recoup of the Balikatan metaphor, Bermisa shifts its meaning—shoulder to shoulder—from its military reference to a vision of a transformed community (Bermisa 2002, 5).

The Routes to Peace: Nonviolence or Just War

Catholic lawyer and peace advocate Soliman Santos offers a framework for peacemaking that characterizes tensions between peacemaking and violence in the Philippine struggle (2002).[9] He suggests that peace can be divided into substantive, processual, and personal peace. Substantive peace is just peace. Processual peace refers to the routes toward substantial peace such as peace negotiations, cease-fires, and peace zones. Finally, personal peace is the transformation of values through prayer, fasting, worship, and Bible study. Santos identifies the obstacles to peace as four kinds of violence: repressive, structural, revolutionary, and personal (Santos 2002, 4). Structural violence and repressive violence are state-sanctioned violence aimed at maintaining this unjust order. Revolutionary violence, unlike state violence, attempts to change the social order.[10] Among Filipino theologians of struggle, revolutionary violence is permissible when it is conducted with a sense of justice and resolution of government abuse. Personal violence is the opposite of personal peace.

Santos notes that there is tension in processual peace in the Philippine context, where peace advocates either press for nonviolence or express sympathies for revolutionary violence. Indeed, neither Roman Catholics nor Protestant denominations (except peace churches such as the Mennonites) have publicly promoted nonviolence in the Philippine conflicts.[11] Kroger (2002) notes that while the Filipino Catholic Bishops turned to nonviolence at the end of the Marcos era, they favor the traditional Catholic theology of just war. This was reflected in their position on military intervention and the Abu Sayyaf (Quevedo 2001).[12] Thus the criteria for just war are complicated by the military force represented. The bishops use classical theory of just war to support state military, and EWF—and only by inference—suggests that just wars are resistance to "foreign intervention and . . . the global hegemony of Empire." Insofar as U.S. wars of aggression are unjust, by contrast wars combating aggression are just and the "protracted people's war" is a means to peace. It is reasonable to assume that the EWF would consider the revolutionary armed struggle more "just" than the current military activities of the Philippine Armed Forces. This is the unresolved tension to which Santos refers.

Conclusion

This essay reviews a Filipino ecumenical women's discourse of just peace and unjust war developed in the first two years of the George W. Bush administration's global war on terrorism. The Philippine critique of the U.S. war on terrorism offers a unique lens to consider how political orientation informs the meanings of justice, peace, and war. The EWF reflects this in powerful ways. While their sympathies with the NDFP are never explicit, their rhetoric is coded to reflect this alliance (i.e., people's agenda, wars of aggression, hegemony of Empire). Given this positionality and its support through a theology of struggle, the peace agenda calls for *struggle*. In pursuit of a culture of peace, women are called to resist all forms of violence against women, but particularly foreign military intervention. Thus EWF offers a feminist praxis of resistance to imperial power: Women must say No! to militarization and all forms of exploitation. They must act not because they are mothers, but because they are nationalists, revolutionaries, antiglobalizationist, and concerned about the people's agenda.

This does not mean that EWF is not concerned about pursuing genuine peace. Indeed, all its efforts are guided by this hope and vision. Though the organization was formed to celebrate International Women's Day, and thus the global interests of women, its version of peace reflects much broader gender interests. While EWF uses "peace" to signify the absence of violence against women, they also mean the absence of structural violence in which such violence is implicated and a condition of shalom that embraces economic justice, harmonious relationships, and a secure state of being. Their emergence at the point of renewed U.S. intervention in the Philippines galvanizes a critique of U.S. imperialism that knits local wars to a wide web of unjust aggressions. Thus, just peace must address local injustice brought on both by globalization (U.S. "Empire") and by unjust wars on both national and international fronts (U.S. wars of aggression). These fronts are intermingled, the national front reassembled to serve an American hydra of fronts that span the globe. Domestic peace requires global peace, meaning the absence of U.S. domination.

Returning to the "No!", it is clear, however, that not all military efforts are to be rejected. For the EWF, negative peace is complicated by a range of wars; some wars lead to peace while others do not. Thus the U.S. invasion of Iraq is indisputably an unjust war. One can infer from EWF materials that just wars combat unjust wars and other obstacles to a just peace. In Filipino historical experience, the U.S. war on terrorism is one more war in a sequence of unjust wars of aggression. There are many routes to substantial peace that religious Filipino women travel. While the EWF is not a pacifist organization, it is a vigorous advocate for just peace amid the protracted conflicts in the Philippines.

Notes

1. I would like to acknowledge funding from St. Lawrence University in 2001 and Fulbright Teaching/Research fellowship 2003 for field research conducted for this essay.

2. The Ecumenical Women's Forum brought together the Women's Desk of the National Council of Churches of the Philippines (henceforth NCCP) representing ten denominations. NCCP leadership has been sympathetic to the national democratic vision of the Communist Party of the Philippines since the 1980s (Suarez 1999). Also included in the EWF are a number of women's activist groups and centers related to church bodies. Among the Roman Catholics, the Association of Major Religious Superiors of the Philippines (AMRSP) representing the leaders of all women's orders in the Philippines can be compared to the Catholic Bishops Conference of the Philippines (CBCP) in significance. Its Women Gender Commission is the representative body of the EWF.

3. This is commonly referred to as CPP-NPA-NDFP.

4. For a background on contemporary Muslim insurgency, see Gaerlan and Stankovitch 1999; Kamlian 1999; McKenna 1998; Vitug and Gloria 2000.

5. The peace negotiations between the CPP-NPA-NDFP and Philippine government are supported by the Philippine Peace Center.

6. This call was timely as, from its founding in 2002, the EWF had embraced the values and goals of the World Council of Churches' Decade to Overcome Violence. See World Council of Churches' Decade to Overcome Violence website: http://www.wcc-coe.org/wcc/dov/index-e.html.

7. Ecumenical Women's Forum 2002b. The biblical reference for this theme cited by organizers is Esther 1:12.

8. Anti-U.S. demonstrations swept eleven Asian countries between February 14 and 16, the largest in Tokyo with 25,000 people. See http://greenleftorg.au/back/2003/527/527p21b.htm.

9. New frameworks for peacemaking have been developed since the early 1990s, through such groups as Coalition for Peace, the National Peace Conference, and the Gaston Z. Ortigas Peace Institute, which situate themselves as civil society actors. These groups tend to promote peaceful political dialogue and negotiation over armed struggle. But these routes are contested by the Philippine Peace Center of the NDFP and others in Mindanao.

10. Gutierrez 1999 offers a more useful framework for the violence in Mindanao. These "entrepreneurs of violence" successfully employ five kinds of violence to meet their ends. The first is random, spontaneous violence of native-settler conflicts, such as frontier violence. The second type of violence is syndicated violence often managed by a warlord or leader of a vigilante group. The most notorious of these would be the Christian Ilagas (who cut off the ears of their victims) and Muslim Barracudas or Blackshirts. The third type of violence emerging in Mindanao results from the first two and is revolutionary or political violence of MNLF and MILF, which has political objectives and protocols that "humanize" the war. Fourth, there is vigilante violence supported by the state. The fifth, he argues, is new and the most complex; it represents forms of "local political competition" where there is both weak state and revolutionary presence. This began with Moro-Moro violence, but evolved into turf wars over moneymaking rackets including kidnapping. The Abu Sayyaf represents this fifth form of violence in Mindanao.

11. Fr. Daniel Kroger 2002 notes that there has been Roman Catholic support for active nonviolence, such as the training sessions in nonviolence that preceded the first People's Power event that brought down Marcos (and later Estrada), but it has not been codified in a theology or widespread practice.

12. The women religious of the Association of the Major Religious Superiors of the Philippines (AMRSP), on the other hand, offered a more nuanced and national-

ist response to the same issue, with a stronger call for alternatives to militarism (Kroger 2002, 174).

Works Cited

Battung, Sr. Mary Rosario, Liberato Bautista, Ma. Sophia Lizares-Bodegon, and Alice G. Guillermo, eds. 1988. *Religion and Society: Towards a Theology of Struggle, Book I.* Manila: Forum for Interdisciplinary Endeavors and Studies.

Bermisa, Sr. Leonila V. MM. 2002. "Seeking Faith Based on Justice." Ecumenical Women's Forum. Philippines. February 14. Photocopy.

Brock-Utne, Birgit. 1985. *Educating for Peace.* New York: Pergamon Press.

Constantino, Renato, and Letizia Constantino. 1978. *The Philippines: The Continuing Past.* Quezon City, Philippines: Foundation for Nationalist Studies.

de la Torre, Edicio. 1986. *Touching Ground, Taking Root. Theological and Political Reflections on the Philippine Struggle.* Philippines: Socio-Pastoral Institute.

Ecumenical Bishops' Forum. 2003. "Declaration." Quezon City, Philippines. March 21. Available at: http://ifi.ph/ebf.htm, or http://www.defendsison.be/archive/pages/0303/030321EBF.html.

Ecumenical Women's Forum. No date. "'Women's Voices to Overcome Violence': International Women's Forum." Philippines. Photocopy.

Ecumenical Women's Forum. 2002a. "And She Said No! Primer." Philippines. February. Photocopy.

Ecumenical Women's Forum. 2002b. "Concept Paper: Ecumenical Women's Forum 2002." Philippines. February. Photocopy.

Ecumenical Women's Forum. 2002c. "Unity Statement." Philippines. February 27. Photocopy.

Ecumenical Women's Forum. 2002d. "Women of Faith, Carry Forward the People's Agenda!" Philippines. July 20. Photocopy.

Ecumenical Women's Forum. 2003. "Statement." Philippines. February 14. Photocopy.

Fernandez, Eleazer. 1998. *Toward a Theology of Struggle in the Philippine Context.* Maryknoll, New York: Orbis Press.

Gaerlan, Kristina and Mara Stankovitch, eds. 1999. *Rebels, Warlords, and Ulama: A Reader on Muslim Separatism and the War in Southern Philippines.* Quezon City, Philippines: Institute for Popular Democracy.

Gomez, Hilario M. Jr. 2000. *The Moro Rebellion and the Search for Peace. A Study on Christian-Muslim Relations in the Philippines.* Zamboanga City, Philippines: Silsilah Publications.

Graham, Helen. 1990. ". . . And She Said No!" In *And She Said No! Human Rights, Women's Identities and Struggles,* ed. Liberto Bautista and Elizabeth Rifareal, 34–37. Quezon City, Philippines: Program Unit on Human Rights, National Council of Churches of the Philippines.

Gutierrez, Eric. 1999. "New Faces of Violence in Mindanao" In *Rebels, Warlords, and Ulama: A Reader on Muslim Separatism and the War in Southern Philippines,* ed. Kristina Gaerlan and Mara Stankowitz, 351–62. Quezon City, Philippines: Silsilah Publications.

Kamlian, Jamail. 1999. *Bangsamoro Society and Culture. A Book of Readings on Peace and Development in Southern Philippines.* Philippines: Iligan Center for Peace Education and Research, MSU-Iligan Institute of Technology.

Karnow, Stanley. 1989. *In Our Image: America's Empire in the Philippines*. New York: Random House,

Kroger, Daniel. O.F.M. 2002. *Disarming Peter: Retrieving a Christian Ethic of Nonviolence in the Philippine Context*. Manila, Philippines: De La Salle University Press, Inc.

Ligo, Archie. 2002. "'And she said NO!' (Esther 1:1–20). Rehabilitating 'No' in Peace and Women's Discourse." Paper presented at EWF International Women's Day Celebration, Manila, Philippines, March 19.

Mananzan, Mary John, ed. 1987. *Essays on Women*. Manila: St. Scholastica's College.

McKenna, Thomas M. 1998. *Muslim Rulers and Rebels: Everyday Politics and Armed Separatism in the Southern Philippines*. Berkeley: University of California Press.

National Council of Churches of the Philippines. 1995. "Policy Paper on Peace." In *A Public Faith, A Social Witness, Policy Papers and Study Documents of the National Council of Churches in the Philippines*, vol. 2. Quezon City, Philippines: National Council of Churches of the Philippines.

Quevedo, Orlando. 2001. "Message of the National Pastoral Consultation on Church Renewal." *Landas: Journal of Loyola School of Theology* 14: 257–63.

Reardon, Betty. 1985. *Sexism and the War System*. New York: Columbia University Press.

Santos, Soliman M. Jr. 2002. *Peace Advocate*. Manila, Philippines: De La Salle University Press.

Sison, Jose Maria. 1991. *A People's Struggle for a Just Peace*. Utrecht, Netherlands: International Network for Philippine Studies.

Suarez, Oscar. 1999. *Protestantism and Authoritarian Politics. The Politics of Repression and the Future Ecumenical Witness in the Philippines*. Manila, Philippines: New Day Publisher.

Vitug, Maritez Danguilan, and Glenda M. Gloria. 2000. *Under the Crescent Moon: Rebellion in Mindanao*. Quezon City, Philippines: Ateneo Center for Social Policy and Public Affairs and Institute for Popular Democracy.

Chapter 18

The Female Body as Site of Attack

Will the "Real" Muslim Woman's Body Please Reveal Itself?

Fawzia Afzal-Khan

I do believe, as an artist and cultural activist, that the kind of role that artistic work can perform to mount resistance against dominant paradigms of violence in our times as well as to institute healing through constructing and reconstructing cultural memories will be inspirational for new thought and action. Indeed, I have myself been involved since 9/11 in a number of artistic ventures that have brought together artists, intellectuals, and cultural activists from New York and other regions in a collective spirit of defiance and resistance to the Bush administration's "War on Terror." I am, among other things, engaged in developing a project for a theatre arts company to which I belong (Compagnie Faim de Siècle—and we are indeed, "hungry for a 'new' century"!) that could provide an opportunity for people to reflect on the historical significance of what happened on 9/11, why it happened, and how it is linked with issues we all experience on a variety of domestic and international fronts, and to think hard about where we are headed as a civilization. I provide below some parts of a paper I wrote and delivered in July 2002 at an international theatre conference in Amsterdam. The arts in general and the theatre arts in particular can provide us with tools we can use to question, challenge, and hopefully resist the seemingly all-powerful juggernaut of violence—whether it be violence at the level of the state or the community, or the violence more powerful individuals commit routinely by silencing the voices of the less powerful.

There are a few issues I focus on in this paper that are relevant to a discussion of violence (particularly linked to 9/11) and artistic responses to it. Most important is the issue of violence against women, and how the notion of "Muslim womanhood" as a collectively "victimized" category has been circulated effectively to perpetuate both discursive violence in the United States (and the West in general) against Islam, as well as to sanction the "War on Terror." Needless to say, violence against women in different parts of the Islamic world and within Muslim societies everywhere has also escalated in the name of a "return" to an imaginary theocratic past, posited as an identitarian necessity to ward off the evils of a Satanic West bent on destroying the "ummah" (believers). The question for me, as a performing artist, is, How can we create, through art, spaces for complicated identities to exist and challenge all such over-simplifications, which are forms of violence in themselves? How, and in the name of what, does one negotiate the balance between collective and individual identity, between a memory of trauma and a healing for the future?

In this paper, I will attempt to show, through my own enacting of multiple identities and voyages as a performing theorist/theorizing performer, both the impossibility of, and desire to, reduce the complex negotiations involved in performing my identity as a "Muslim woman" to a set of simplistic but compelling binaries. These binaries keep getting re-enacted in the world of performance and the performance of the world, thus contributing to the creation of a particular kind of cultural memory; they demand our very serious attention at this critical juncture of human history. Perhaps the most compelling of these binaries is the one that structures the question implicit in my "western" audience's eye/I's: Are my "I/eyes" those of a "Muslim (*read:* secularized) feminist," who is on the side of "(western) civilization," or are they veils that perform my identity as a figure of "Oppressed Muslim Womanhood," one that flips curiously into another trope, that of "Hijab-toting Terrorist Lover," an image simultaneously evoking horror and titillation, encapsulating the terror/erotic possibilities of a body veiled from the all-seeing I/eye of the spectator's camera?

While such binaristic identitarian categories of "Muslim woman" have shot to prominence following the melodramatic events of 9/11, we would do well to remember their mobilization in the colonialist dramas of the past, which are once again taking center stage now. I am thinking particularly of Malek Alloula's marvelous pictorial compilation of Algerian postcards from the early part of the last century, which showed photographs of "authentic" Algerian women, gauzy garments drawn aside to reveal ripe tits glimpsed but out of reach of the white man's desire because they are behind bars, the bars symbolizing the women's oppressive societies (1995). When Alloula informs us that these photographs were staged, constructed for the benefit of the photographer, who paid the models to pose in this way for him, we realize the phantasmic purpose such performative acts fulfill for the colonialist edifice, a structure that is ultimately based on illusions that can only be sustained by a reiterative fetishizing of the "Other." Yet, while grateful to Alloula for pointing out the colonialist drama being played out on the postcards, we become aware of his complicity in the nationalist drama of postcolonial independence in which young male heroes, angered at the metaphoric rape of "their" women by the white man's penetrating "I/eye," became once again the guardians of feminine virtue while women's bodies became the sites of nationalist struggle, the stages upon which the patriotic fervor of the newly liberated (male) can be performed.

The cultural memories set in motion by both the colonialist and anticolonialist performances I have just described—those inscribed in the fashioning of the postcards, and in Alloula's gesture of returning them to the sender—have once again been mobilized in the wake of 9/11 in ways that are circumscribed or overdetermined by these overlapping yet divergent "takes" on the past. In this context, it becomes important to raise the question of how our cultural pasts have been perceived, explored, and debated by the theatre (whose theatre?) and how today's theatrical events can construct cultural memories in the present and for the future (by whom, for whom?). How might cultural memories and performances fuse with each other in the experiences and perceptions of the participants in a theatrical event and possibly create healing effects?

The preceding questions have acquired for me a special resonance in the wake of 9/11, given the framework of my own experiential cultural history and "identity" as a "Muslim" woman. I would like to attend to them by way of pointing to a few of the performative circumstances in which I found myself post-9/11, some more obviously theatrical than others, but all involving the negotiation and enforcement, the construction and deconstruction, the acceptance and rejection of personal and cultural history and identity by both myself and other "performers," other "spect-actors."

The first of these "events" involves a journey I undertook across Italy and into the Balkans, starting in Venice by car and crossing into Croatia and Slovenia, skirting Serbia, and passing finally into Bosnia-Herzegovina to perform in the Mess Festival of Theatre held in October 2001 in Sarajevo. Occurring almost exactly a month after my journey to perform the same multimedia piece had to be aborted because of the closure of airports following the "terrorist" attacks on the World Trade Center and Pentagon— the day, incidentally, that I was to travel to Canada to join my company—it was first of all an opportunity to perform a gesture of solidarity with Muslims who had been left to rot by Europe and its NATO ally, the United States, victims of a war of genocide the likes of which the world has not seen since the extermination of the Jews by the Nazis; second, it was a chance to observe firsthand the effects of such a devastating war of "ethnic cleansing" on the inhabitants of a multiethnic culture and city; and third, it was an occasion to see if, in the example of Sarajevo, I could learn anything at all to help me navigate the waters of cultural memory for myself following 9/11, in which I was perforce assigned to play the role of "Muslim woman."

Perhaps it was the third imperative that provided me the richest material for thought following my trip. Certainly, the notion that I would be performing an action of "solidarity" with the Bosnian Muslim victims of Serbian aggression by my very presence, by my willingness to enter Bosnian territory in the company of three white men and one Latino American man, was immediately put to rest by the suspicion aroused by my presence in this motley crew as we tried to negotiate an entry into Bosnia in the middle of the night. The border guards were not impressed by our "multiethnic" façade— we were all holders of U.S. passports, all from different U.S. cities, had flown on the eve (unbeknownst to us at this time) of an attack on the U.S. embassy in Sarajevo, had entered Bosnia after having driven 1,000 miles from Venice in a rented car that, as we now found out, was not authorized to be driven

past the border of Bosnia. My performance as a Muslim "sister" to these
men, sharing in some cultural "essence" of a "shared past" made no sense to
them—nor to me, really, upon rational reflection. In fact, my travel compan-
ions bonded with the non-Muslim men when one of them whipped out a
poster advertising the Mess Festival, emblematized by a pair of shiny red
voluptuous female lips! They finally let us go—some four hours after they
detained us; and the identities that had been negotiated, constructed, and
deconstructed had made me see the folly of working with any kind of
essentialist notions of memory/identity at all. We had played roles for the
guards, the roles of pleading, powerless American theater workers, chauvin-
istic men against the sole woman in their midst, who was told to shut up and
stay out of sight in the car, so that things could be "worked out" man to man,
as it were. For the guards, to hold power over naïve and powerless American
men must have been a novel and satisfying experience, the implicit threat
against "their" woman (it seemed to matter not a whit that "their" woman
was in fact, a Pakistani-born U.S. citizen, and a Muslim to boot)—rich in
postcolonial, post-war, and post-9/11 irony.

A conception of the transforming, connective/cooperative potential of
memory (suggested by John Dewey, for instance), however, was borne out
by reactions of some of the audience members to the images and action we
tried to enact on stage during our performance of Heiner Muller's *Abandoned Shores (Rivages à l'Abandon)*, performed at the Skandirje Audito-
rium in Sarajevo on October 14, 2001. We performed at night, in a hall with
no heat and no lights, a bombed-out shell of a hall that at one point in its
history had been a mosque. The performance evoked in two of our audience
members, Barbara Soros and Salma Hassan, both working in Sarajevo in
some sort of "humanitarian" capacity, cultural memories of western imperialism, rape, and violence against women. The story of Medea and Jason was
juxtaposed against the screaming Sufi chants issuing from the lips of a
"Muslim" woman. I performed the role of a culturally "Other" Medea to
the white western Medea whose body goes up in flames behind an orange
screen. I sing my Sufi chants, and she screams of Jason's betrayal, of being
raped, violated, and cast aside. The juxtositioning of the visual and sonic
elements evoked two different cultural memories—one that was more
accessible to Barbara the westerner, the other, evoked by the woman singing
in an Islamic Sufi tradition, that left her both puzzled but also in awe. The
play conjured an untranslatable gulf but also a moment of solidarity, of
listening to the "Other" woman, speaking a universal language, a female
language, of oppression and resistance, love and sorrow, anger and peace
across cultural and historical divides. Salma commented simply on the
beauty of a Sufi chant in a space that had once been a mosque and was now a
theatrical monument to the ravages of war. Outside, on its walls, there was a
big peace sign drawn by some graffiti artist, with a big question mark asking
"Why?" next to it. To Salma, our performance suggested the answer.

Were we, in our exchanges that night following the performance, engaging in what Addams (2002 [1918]) and Dewey (1958 [1929]) would have

recognized as cooperative communication, a mutually respectful reminiscing of the "past" of our different cultural trajectories that nevertheless resulted in a shared vision—for a collective endeavor to transform the world's future? Late into the night, our excited exchanges led to the discussion of plans earlier envisioned by Barbara and mentioned to Salma, and now to me, about a world congress of women activists from around the globe to come up with alternative visions for the planet—alternatives to the cycle of death and destruction set in motion, according to Soros, by the rape of Lucretia, upon which the idea of western democracy rests.[1]

Such an admission of a fundamental flaw in the idea of western civilization, one that implicates the West in the unending horrors unfolding in the so-called non-West—specifically, now, the antithesis of the West, the Islamic world—must clearly be part of the project of a postcolonial theory and praxis of performativity. But so too must it be a project that aims to fracture the notion of the unity of identity and that obliterates the authenticity of an Islamic subject, "the" Muslim woman.

Playing with Muslim Women in New York, Post–9/11

My second point concerns the discursive violence that gets committed when the "Other" (in this case "Muslim women") are talked at/about, rather than with; that is, the perennial problem of "who speaks?"

The spate of performative activity around the image of "Muslim women" that has been unleashed in the wake of 9/11 has been remarkable, to say the least. What, pray, do these performances signify: by whom, for whom, where?

The biggest splash was made by Tony Kushner's play disjointedly titled *Homebody/Kabul*. Despite lukewarm reviews emphasizing this lack of cohesion, the play has done phenomenally well, running to packed houses at a minimum of $65 a ticket. When I tried to get tickets in September 2002, I was informed that it was sold out till mid-May. Clearly, the New York theatre-going audiences are hungry and appreciative of the images of Kabul being dished up by Kushner, one of their "own" after all—in contradistinction to the lack of interest in a one-woman play that had a brief run last December in an off-off-Broadway production entitled simply *An Afghan Woman*, directed and acted by Bina Sharif, a Pakistani immigrant to the United States. Without getting into questions of comparative aesthetic values, production budgets, access to audiences, and so on, it seems fairly obvious from various reviews of *Homebody/Kabul* that part of what has been mobilized by Kushner is the old colonialist phantasm. Consider critic Daniel Lazarre's astute observation that, "Kushner's vision is ultimately a clichéd one in which Afghans are either poetic wise men or crazed religious fanatics, yet always inscrutable, while Westerners are either angry or drugged out, yet always hungry and dissatisfied and longing for more. The result is to reduce Kabul to little more than a backdrop for the West's long-running spiritual malaise" (2002: 48).

It is a similar obsession that drives the current interest in labeling, identifying the Muslim woman's malaise as a crisis of the Veil: Witness the titles of books and articles we have been barraged with lately: "Behind the Veil," "Beneath the Veil," "Beyond the Veil"; so many veils, veils everywhere, and not one for me to wear!

Thus, even a play like *I, Unseen,* written by an American woman playwright named Marika Mashburn out of "sympathy" for the plight of Afghan women, produces ambivalent results. On the one hand, Mashburn was careful to use sources of information provided by Afghan women themselves, such as the website of the Revolutionary Association of the Women of Afghanistan (RAWA), which allows for a critique of U.S. involvement in the region and its role in creating the Taliban. On the other hand, her play nevertheless ends up in the awkward position of endorsing western (American) women's need to speak on behalf of Afghan women who, victimized by the veil, cannot in the final analysis speak for themselves. Isn't this a form of violence? I saw the concluding powerful scene enacted in a student production at my university, done as a staged reading and directed and produced by two of my women's studies students with whom I had shared the script. The scene shows the American woman researcher, who has just returned from a six-month stay in Kabul trying to ascertain the extent of the Taliban government's repression against its female citizens, in a Senate hearing reporting her findings and urging the members to get the U.S. government to intervene" to "save" these women, and in this plea, she is slowly joined by every other member of the cast, who rises up from his/her chair (they are all seated in a semi-circle for the duration of the one-act), joining the chorus, "We must speak for those who cannot speak for themselves."

In January of 2002, the Immigrants' Theatre Project and the Lower East Side Tenement Museum, in collaboration with the Kazbah Project, presented the Sixth Immigrant Theatre Festival, entitled "Unexpected Journeys," focusing on plays by women "who have been influenced or grown up in Muslim cultures" (Sixth Immigrant Theatre Project, 2002). During this festival, I saw two one-act mainstage productions. The first was a play entitled *Cracking Mud Is Pinching Me,* by Haya Husseini, a Jordanian-Palestinian now living in Australia. The second was *Bermuda Triangle,* by Egyptian playwright Nora Amin. The first was directed by Marcy Arlin, founder of the Immigrants' Theatre Project (a Brooklyn-based professional theater company, founded in 1988), and the second was directed by Lucinda Kidder, who is earning her MFA from the University of Massachusetts and who also, as part of the festival, coordinated a Saturday afternoon panel discussion at the New Dramatists' Theatre entitled "Theatre as a Method for Re-Examining Women's Roles in Muslim Cultures."

What were my impressions of these performative circumstances?

The first play, *Cracking Mud,* was rather interesting, I thought, especially in terms of the three main female characters, who represent three generations of women in one family, the youngest one having decided to wear the hijab, the "traditional" head-covering, while her mother runs around in shorts, much to her daughter's chagrin! The grandmother could be seen to represent the "tradition" to which the granddaughter wished to return through the adoption of the veil. Yet, as the play unfolds, we see that the grandmother's character defies any easy categorization. Her reveries of the past, her ironic musings on the present, the dream-like state that envelops her, and the surreal quality of the action, which does not proceed on any linear model, shows "tradition" to be a vast and contradictory landscape, extending into an endless labyrinth of elements: life, death, desire, dreaming, covering/discovering, loving, dancing, all memorialized by that heavily salted, deeply sunk, miserably misunderstood sea—the Dead Sea, which is where the three women are headed for a vacation. In such a landscape of ideas, the question to which Husseini says she began writing the play in response, "why were younger generation Arabs becoming more traditional than their parents?" becomes a moot point, because we see the question as a deeply flawed one, simplistic and one-dimensional in its appeal to a static notion of identity, whereas the pushes and pulls of life and history are complex and multidimensional.

It was a shame then to have such a provocative play followed by one in which all of the stereotypes of the oppressed Muslim woman, beaten into submission by husband, lover, and pimp coalesce around the reified image of her donning the head-scarf, the veil, the hijab, as a sign of power she reclaims at the end against the male "gaze" that has sought to reduce her in every relationship with a man. Thus, while ostensibly the play follows a trajectory of liberation for the heroine, and the choice of the principal actor to don a head-scarf was meant, as Husseini said to me in a conversation, to signal that the veil is not always a signifier of oppression, I felt depressed at the thought of life's possibilities for this Muslim woman reduced to the representation of such banal gestures that have been thrust upon us with such symbolic force by the mullah and his antithesis alike (symbolic force is also a form of violence). To veil or not to veil—is that now the question for our times I find myself asking dispiritedly?

Meanwhile, at the panel discussion organized by Lucinda Kidder later that week at the New Dramatists' Theatre, I was mortified to see that not one of the panelists—on a panel devoted to asking questions about women's roles in Muslim cultures as depicted through theatre—was a woman from a Muslim culture! Lest I be accused of resorting to essentialism when I have been arguing against the adoption of facile identitarianism, let me say unequivocally that I am *not* advancing an identitarian argument here. Rather, I wish to call attention to the power asymmetry that exists and that makes it crucial for those wishing to "help" in this moment of critical world history by showing "solidarity" with those labeled "Muslim"—whether that term then gets affixed to "woman" or "terrorist," "victim" or "funda-mentalist"—to ensure that the variety of voices out there labeled "Muslim" are heard from, not just spoken for, and about. In other words—let us stop this form of discursive violence perpetuated once again by western feminists against their "Others"! For it is these "Other" voices in all of their variety and complexity that can eventually move us away from the limited and limiting binaristic roles we are being forced to perform these days in a neverending cycle of violence.

I think that we need to focus now on breaking through the violence perpetuated by the orientalist prison-house of phantasmatic veils that covers over the world of Islam rather covering anything of substance. Perhaps it is time for western academics, intellectuals, theatre workers, and activists to stop pursuing their own obsessions and really take that leap of faith into the world of an/other, a Muslim woman of substance, a Muslim woman who demands that one read history contrapuntally, that one remember justly, and in so remembering create a just and peaceful vision for the future. I am referring here to Scheherezade, of the *Arabian Nights*, whose figure I now invoke as metaphor in a playscript I am working on to be produced in France next year by Compagnie Faim de Siècle.[2] Scheherezade's voice is, for me, the voice of a woman of passionate intellect and reason, a woman whose fight for life is not personal but collective, the voice of a woman who wants to see justice, not murder, meted out to other oppressed women like herself, a woman unafraid to voice her dissent with the powerful when that power becomes abusive and unjust.

Scheherazade's is the voice of a Muslim feminist. Assigned that label by those of us still caught in a play not yet of our making, as a totem to help us to perform our solidarities and our resistances, she has mastered the art of performing identity fluidly. In fact, it is the performance of that complexity that saves her life. It is time to invite Scheherazade to perform once again, so that the world, watching her, can save itself. Her performance is a model of solidarity-building that could serve as the bridge between the memory of a binaristic model of cultural identity and a more progressive future of intercultural affiliations/performances and memories.

Notes

1. Barbara Soros, in "Revolution of the Heart: Women Revisioning Democracy," argues: "If we look to the evolution of western democracy . . . we can see it is fitting that the first Roman Republic was ignited by the rape of the exquisite and chaste Lucrece [Lucretia], wife of the boastful Colatine, by the young emperor of Tarquine, who intruded upon her sleep and forced his advances." Soros goes on to remind us that when Lucretia appealed to the men of the Roman Forum for justice after being raped, there is only an uncomfortable silence, which leads Lucretia to plunge a knife (a symbol of phallic power) into her heart. As her blood spills, and Colantine and her father argue over her fallen body, Junius Brutus, withdrawing the knife from her heart, says, "The Tarquines must go, we must drive out the monarchy." Thus, the first western representative government begins with a story in which we can observe the symbolic seeds

of contemporary democratic societies, "mirroring as it does some of the more unfortunate, prevailing social principles: violence, betrayal, deceit, the objectification and disrespect of those who are denied the full enjoyment of human rights, be they women or minorities" (Soros no date, 1).

2. "Scheherezade Goes West" was recently published. See Afzal-Kahn 2004.

Works Cited

Addams, Jane. 2002 [1918]. *The Long Road of Woman's Memory*. Urbana: University of Illinois Press.

Afzal-Kahn, Fawzia. 2004. "Scheherezade Goes West." *TDR: The Drama Review* 48.2 (T 182): 11–23.

Alloula, Malek. 1995. *The Colonial Harem*. Minneapolis: University of Minnesota Press.

Dewey, John. 1958 [1929]. *Experience and Nature*. Chicago: Open Court.

Duncombe, Charles. 2003. "Muller at City Garage, Los Angeles." In *Muller in America*, ed. Dan Friedman, 111–121. New York: Castillo Cultural Center.

Lazarre, Daniel. 2002. "Review of Kushner's *Homebody/Kabul*." *Westchester Spotlight*, February. 48.

Mernissi, Fatima. 2001. *Scheherazade Goes West: Different Cultures, Different Harems*. New York: Washington Square Press.

Sixth Immigrant Theatre Project. 2002. "Unexpected Journeys." Program. New York: Immigrants' Theatre Project/Lower East Side Tenement Museum in collaboration with the Kazbah Project.

Soros, Barbara. Unpublished manuscript. No date. "Revolution of the Heart: Women Revisioning Democracy."

Chapter 19

Responses to Violence

Healing vs. Punishment

Helena Cobban

When we want to think about violence, talk about violence, or—crucially—
think of ways to escape from cycles of violence, I think it is important to
make clear the ontology on which our work draws. To think of violence is,
after all, to think of a specific kind of human-enacted phenomenon, so we
need to articulate our understanding of the nature of the human condition.
Personally, I resonate much more to a kind of Buddhist view that the essence
of being human is *to be in productive relationship with other humans* than to
the classic Enlightenment view of "man" as a self-sufficient, self-organizing
monad. I love the gentle derision that Seyla Benhabib and other feminist
philosophers have directed against the various versions of the Enlightenment
view expressed by Hobbes, Rousseau, and other pillars of the Enlightenment.

Actually, since I work mainly in cross-cultural settings and on global/
international issues, I am very aware that it is the Hobbesian/Enlightenment
ontology that is, in world-historical terms, decidedly a minority view. What
I have described above as a "Buddhist" view of the human condition is
shared by many, probably most, other cultures throughout human history.
For example, the African view of *ubuntu,* as described by Archbishop Tutu
and others, relies on an exactly similar foundation; and nearly all the
nonwestern cultures I have encountered around the world adhere to an
ontology that is far more communitarian than the highly individualistic
ontology of Enlightenment "man."

This has direct implications, I think, for the way we respond to the
violence from which our own communities suffer. If we say that the essence
of being human is to be in productive relationship with other humans, then
we can give an "explanation" of violence that says that violence stems from
people's disconnection or alienation from an appropriate recognition of the
fundamental facts of: (1) their ontological connection with other humans,
(2) human equality, and (3) the reciprocity of relationships that stems from
this. Projects to end violence can then be directed toward strengthening the
ability of perpetrating individuals to arrive at such a state of interhuman
recognition and to draw on this new awareness in such a way that their
behavior changes and they start to experience the actual benefits of trans-

forming the nature of their relationships with other people into more productive ones.

This focus on effecting a long-term change in the *mentality* of the perpetrating individual rather than on simply curbing his/her *behavior* in some way has long antecedents in the history of penal reform in Western nations: The whole concept of the "penitentiary" was based on one (to my mind, fairly unsatisfactory) version of it. The United States, however, has taken some gigantic strides in recent decades away even from that mildly reformist view of incarceration and other court-ordered punishments. Now, the aim of incarceration is nearly always incapacitation pure and simple; the idea of effecting long-term change in the prisoners' mindsets—and indeed, the idea that prisoners might even have minds worth engaging—long ago fell by the wayside. Reintroducing into U.S. discourse the idea of focusing on the mindsets of perpetrating individuals has been left to advocates of "restorative justice," a newer school of thought and practice that often consciously draws on nonwestern approaches to inform its view of the nature of violence.

This was, in essence, the view of the nature of human violence that informed Archbishop Tutu's work with his country's Truth and Reconciliation Commission. It is also the view that informed the pioneering campaign led by Mahatma Gandhi for over a quarter-century against the deeply rooted edifice of structural violence known as the British Raj in India. One of the core goals that Gandhi and his followers pursued in their *satyagraha* campaigns was to increase the awareness of people, on both sides of the ruler/ruled dividing line, of the humanity that they shared in common with people on the "other" side.

I have been blessed in my own life to have had the opportunity to cross over many different kinds of boundaries. I've also been blessed to have experienced or witnessed at close quarters on numerous occasions the kinds of transformation toward which *satyagraha* campaigns work. In the early 1990s, I directed a program that brought together dozens of Israelis, Palestinians, and Arab state nationals to work together on joint projects that would both (1) register some actual and valued achievements, and (2) enable the participants, through working together, to change their view of people on the other side of the national divide. I was able to help bring that diverse group together precisely because I had previously made a point of establishing relationships of trust with people throughout the Middle East. (I worked there as a "foreign" correspondent for various news outlets, back in the 1970s.)

One of the earliest meetings of our group was held in Rome. Beforehand, my colleagues and I had been discreetly in touch with the Italian authorities and had asked them to provide an extra layer of physical security around our meetings. On the first day, some of the *carabinieri* assigned to guard us were knocking around a little noisily in the corridor outside our meeting room, and some of the right-wing Israeli participants became visibly nervous. Later, they told us that they had been very scared about meeting with

Palestinians. (They had never before sat and worked with Palestinians as equals.) And when they heard the noises in the corridor, they feared that some guerrilla group was about to burst in and kidnap them. Luckily, though, they stayed with the group and built whole webs of new relationships. Soon after, we were all able to laugh about the *carabinieri* episode together. That experience was transformative for many of the people involved, including me. In a city and setting where I felt quite safe, those individuals, whom previously I'd thought of as extremely powerful supermentype figures, were actually very jittery!

Later, in a subgroup of that project, I brought together Israelis, Palestinians, and Arab state nationals who were all seasoned activists with human rights organizations. For these individuals, commitment to the universality of human values and to human equality was already a given. But because of the many "national security" considerations involved, the Israeli activists had never previously met with the Arab-state activists. At the first meeting of this group, participants were still a little wary. But I found the second meeting, a year later, profoundly transformative. The location was a former headquarters for the Spanish Inquisition in the rugged Spanish interior. The time was the spring of 1993, 501 years after the Spanish *reconquista* chased the Muslims and Jews out of Andalusia, and started submitting the remnants of both groups to the horrors of the Inquisition. We were all—including our Spanish hosts—profoundly aware of those facts and their resonance with the work at hand. One of the joint projects decided upon, indeed, was precisely to find ways to network throughout the Middle East in a campaign against torture.

And then, in summer 2002, I was in Rwanda. I was staying in an evangelical mission in a shantytown in the capital, Kigali, while I did some research. While I was there, the mission was hosting a two-week workshop on faith-based community development work for grassroots church activists from throughout the country. Three times a day, the forty participants in the workshop would gather for worship, and the whole neighborhood would ring with their lovely African harmonies before they returned to their desks, break-out groups, and flip-charts. These participants included numerous survivors of the 1994 genocide—along with the wives or other close family members of people accused of having participated in it. That genocide had a killing rate more than five times the daily killing rate during the height of the European Holocaust. Only one in five of the Tutsis then present in the country was able to survive it. But here were some of those survivors working and worshipping together alongside close relatives of their people's persecutors! The mission where I was staying, moreover, was far from being the only place in the country where such deep-seated relationship healing was going on.

I have also experienced the transformative power of the *satyagraha* approach closer to home. Participating in a city-level campaign against the frequent use of the death penalty by my state, Virginia, I joined a delegation of four or five people from our campaign that was assigned the task of "lobbying" on the issue with the local delegate in the state legislature. This delegate, Paul Harris, was well known as an extremely right-wing, pro–death penalty Republican. We decided not to try to score rhetorical points or even to try to "win" in our discussion with Harris. Instead, our approach was to try to build a long-term relationship of trust and dialogue with him that would provide him with a friendly forum in which he could safely express and develop his views on capital punishment. I think we had some success. After just our second meeting with him, he then went out and became the only Republican on the state legislature's Courts of Justice Committee who voted for a moratorium on the death penalty, pending presentation of a promised advisory report. (Since then, our campaign has seen some setbacks, and Harris moved to Washington, D.C., to work in John Ashcroft's Justice Department. Perhaps we should be more persistent in continuing to work on our relationship with him.)

What does all this have to do with ontology? In my own case, my capacity for social engagement of the sort that seeks to help people to escape from cyclical or other iterative forms of violence has been deeply informed by my increasingly strong view that the essence of being human is to be in productive relationship with other humans. This view has, moreover, helped inform my further conclusion that the best, most effective responses to episodes of violence are those that focus on *healing*—and in particular, healing the relationships that were severed by the violence, and whose continued severance can only prolong the enacting of further violence—rather than on *judging* and *punishing,* two linked activities that, I believe, only tend to perpetuate existing divisions between "us" and "them."

Frequently, the rhetoric of judging and punishing can itself become very hate-filled and violent. Moreover, this rhetoric is certainly often used to try to justify the enactment of a lot of further violence. This is the case with the rhetoric around the death penalty, for example, or when President Bush, speaking of Osama Bin Laden, says things like, "We shall bring him to justice—or we shall *bring justice to him.*" What kind of vision of "justice" was the president drawing on there? In the context of the very heavy bombing of Afghanistan and then of the war that Bush launched against Iraq in pursuit of his anti-"terror" campaign, one can only conclude that the kind of justice he had in mind was a very vengeful and violent kind indeed.

If a commitment to a healing-based response precludes any easy recourse to the idea of punishment as we know it, what then can we say about the need for "justice"? I asked this question in 2001 of Rejoyce Mubadafhasi, a minister in the present South African government who, as an activist against the long, drawn-out form of structural violence called apartheid, had been at the receiving end of many forms of the regime's violence, including considerable physical violence. Mubadafhasi's view was that enacting any kind of fairly calibrated "justice" after the kinds of massive violations that the apartheid system inflicted is an impossible task for *humans* to undertake. "Healing must happen inside us," she told me. "It's as simple as this: If we can't have reconciliation, we'll never rebuild the country. It's no good keeping grudges. God will deal with them [the perpetrators of apartheid] in the end!"

In the present era, I guess we need to ask sincerely if reconciliation could even be imagined to be possible with hate-driven perpetrators of extremely violent acts like the organizers of the September 11 attacks. But people like Ms. Mubadafhasi and the genocide survivors I met in Rwanda pose an enormous challenge to us in this regard. For our present circumstances as Americans are still, taken as a whole, considerably more comfortable and secure than those in which the black South Africans or the Rwandan genocide survivors had to make their respective choices about how to respond to the violence inflicted on them. Our circumstances are more also much comfortable and secure than those in which, for example, the peoples of Burma or Tibet currently live. But significant leaders within all those other "victim" communities have found it possible, even in the direst of circumstances, to continue to pursue a clear goal of building a cooperative and equality-based reconciliation with their people's present or former persecutors. So surely we Americans can choose to be at least as calm, generous-spirited, and farsighted in our response to violence as some of those other deeply victimized peoples.

Chapter 20

Our Enemies, Ourselves

Why Antiviolence Movements Must Replace the Dualism of "Us and Them" with an Ethic of Interdependence

Kay Whitlock

Justice, peace, and nonviolence—like injustice, war, and violence—arise within an ever-fluid fabric of relationship among peoples and nations, and in relation to the earth itself. Those relationships, whether involving individuals, families, religious groups, communities, cultures, or nation-states, may be governed by an ethic of interdependence, which encourages respect, generosity, compassion, and just relationship across differences, or an ethic of dominance and supremacy, which produces disregard, coercion, abuse, separation, exploitation, and exclusion.

The contrast between ethical choices seems so great, and therefore the choice seems so simple. But that perceived simplicity is a siren song, deceptive and misleading, luring us directly into the spiritual quagmire of dualistic thinking, in which the world is divided into "either/or," into the virtuous and worthy "us" and the lesser, unworthy "them." We who work in movements for peace, human rights, social justice, and economic security are often quick to embrace such dualism, denouncing those who use obviously violent means to subordinate others and staking our own claim to the high moral ground of righteousness.

Yet a worldview based on the need for enemies and dependent upon the social construction of "us and them" is a distorting, fear-based perspective that threatens to corrupt the good intentions of progressive social justice advocates and antiviolence activists. Although it is painful to admit, many of us who fight for justice sometimes participate in the abuse or exploitation of others or permit, without protest, the violation of the human, civil, and constitutional rights of groups other than our own, thereby compounding rather than interrupting cycles of violence.

To mount effective responses to violence, particularly in the post–September 11 era, we must be willing to challenge not only others whose actions we perceive as violent, but also ourselves, in whom violence also resides and seeks expression—often in subtle, disguised, and unexamined forms. We must ask difficult questions about the rhetoric we use, the ways in which we frame issues, and the interrelated impacts of the strategic choices we make. Above all, in seeking to end violence, activists and scholars working for social change must guard against the all-too-real possibility of becoming mirror images of that against which we struggle.

This essay briefly explores four major spiritual and political challenges faced by those in the United States who seek to confront and respond effectively to interpersonal and state violence. I suggest that these challenges are at once our greatest obstacles and the source of possibility for imaginative conceptual and strategic breakthroughs. The dynamic interrelationships of race, class, gender, and gender identity and sexuality, and how power relationships are structured according to these factors, are central to this exploration.

Recognizing Our Own Complicity in Perpetuating Violence and Reinforcing Structural Inequities

Violence is never a problem located only in the "Other." We, too, the workers for peace and justice, must face our own complicity, however unintentional, in violence that targets vulnerable or less powerful groups. This includes complicity in "public" or "visible" forms of violence, such as war, and more "invisible" forms of violence. By "invisible," I mean violence that is so ordinary, so deeply engrained in the daily working of our social, political, economic, and religious institutions that it is considered normative. It is as common as air and is seldom viewed by dominant groups as violence at all.

In the United States, "invisible" violence renders certain peoples expendable, particularly people of color (U.S.-born, immigrants, and refugees), indigenous peoples, poor people, women, queer people (those who self-identify as lesbian, gay, bisexual, and transgender [LGBT], and two-spirit and intersex), people with disabilities, and youth. It does its wounding quietly, sometimes under the guise of care and concern, and often bureaucratically, shielded from critical public scrutiny by custom and convenience. Because its function is to reinforce and maintain existing patterns of dominance and subordination, it is hardly surprising that "invisible" violence targets those who exist at the fault lines in our society, those cracks in the civic and spiritual terrain that separate "us" from "them."

Examples of "invisible violence" include racial profiling, the mass incarceration of people of color, secret detentions of immigrants, felony disenfranchisement, and institutional tolerance of physical and sexual harassment and assault. "Invisible" violence also includes coercive restrictions of reproductive rights, legislative assaults on the rights and recognition of queer people, the criminalization of youth, and the resegregation of public schools. It includes impoverishment, economic exploitation, and the widening, hardening gap between the rich and the poor. It includes theft of land and ecological devastation in pursuit of profit. It includes the misappropriation, commodification, and destruction of indigenous cultures.

Many of us active in movements for peace, social justice, and economic security examine such a litany of wrongs from a distance. "Yes," we say to ourselves, "we know about these things and we oppose the oppressive people and governments who permit these wrongs to continue." Yet while our rhetoric rings loud with proclamations of solidarity, our actions are not always consistent with our words. It is not at all unusual for many of us, especially those of us who are white and have at least some degree of economic privilege, to protest some forms of violence while making strategic choices that actually support the continuation of and reinforce other forms of "invisible" violence. After all, dualistic thinking encourages even antiviolence workers to imagine that retribution *is* justice and creates safety. It encourages us to believe that "our" safety depends absolutely upon the exclusion, control, containment, and physical domination of the despised and feared "Others."

For example, many white activists and white-dominated organizations in the domestic violence movement began to rely increasingly upon law enforcement strategies, including harsher punishments for abusers ("them") in order to create greater safety (for "us"). They proposed policies and won political victories that actually expanded the scope and authority of the criminal justice system in the United States. In doing so, many major advocacy groups failed to recognize and challenge the systemic racial, class, and gender biases of law enforcement agencies. They failed to take into account the massive abuses of human rights routinely directed against women of color by immigration and criminal justice authorities in crafting their policy agendas, abuses that were a mirror image of the violence advocates sought to end (Silliman and Bhattacharjee 2002; Bhattacharjee 2001).

Similarly, seeking safety for their own identity-based constituents (including LGBT people, people of color, Jews, Muslims, people with disabilities, and women), major civil rights and advocacy organizations have responded to hate violence with penalty enhancement bills. At the same time, they have sidestepped inconvenient questions about the massive systemic violence and corruption and widespread violations of human rights within that system. Much of that systemic violence, of course, is directed against most of the same groups that hate violence legislation seeks to protect (Whitlock 2001).

A number of predominantly white organizations working on issues ranging from reproductive rights and family planning to championing the environment have uncritically accepted arguments for "population control" and tolerated coercive reproductive policies without inquiring into the history of twentieth-century population control ideology. But that history brings us directly into collision with various recycled forms of a eugenics movement that has always been racist at its core. Eugenics ideology has, in its various incarnations, appealed to liberal birth control reformers as well as to colonial bureaucrats seeking to contain and "assimilate" indigenous populations, Nazis, anti-immigration and nativist organizations, and various governments seeking to control fertility of particular populations for political and economic purposes. The concept of population control is appealing to so many precisely because it promises a way to create more safety and security for some peoples ("us") by reducing the numbers of those ("them") whose reproduction is perceived to threaten "our" status, "our" claim to resources and land, and so on (see Hartmann 1995).

Many faith communities, serving both predominately white and people of color constituencies, have carried the banner for peace or particular social justice struggles while shunning LGBT people, naming "them" as less spiritually worthy, and, therefore, expendable. Not only does such religious triage provide cultural permission for hate violence and other systemic forms of discrimination, but these exclusionary practices within many faith communities are taking chilling new forms in policy arenas. Anti-LGBT faith activists work for amendments to the U.S. and state constitutions that not only define marriage as exclusively heterosexual, but also would deconstruct domestic partner policies in public and private work places by not permitting unmarried couples, gay or bisexual, the "legal incidents of marriage." Proponents suggest that the sanctity of "our" relationships and religious commitments will be destroyed if "they" are permitted equal civil rights in marriage as in other arenas of civic life. At the same time, many pro-marriage LGBT activists often do not recognize that their failure to address the larger issue of "marriage politics" (e.g., proposed coercive "marriage promotion" politics directed at impoverished single mothers, many of whom would be at risk of domestic violence should they be forced to marry) and uncritical support for marriage as the only appropriate state funnel for many basic economic benefits, rights, and forms of legal recognition may produce unintended harmful consequences for others.

How is it that in our own desire to obtain justice and create safety and security for our own constituents, so many of us committed to antiviolence work become so willing to accept certain kinds of structural violence directed by the state against less valued "Others"? When will we begin to comprehend that, in terms of political policy, the very real and legitimate need people have for safety in their personal, civic, and spiritual lives generally transmutes into yet another form of retributive violence? At what point will we recognize that, in accepting this particular calculus, we agree, at least tacitly, that some peoples are expendable?

The long struggle for human rights, peace, social justice, and economic security is not comprised of a set of parallel but disconnected issues and struggles. Rather, it can be likened to a powerful, life-giving river, flowing across obstructive and socially constructed borders and boundaries, fed by many different streams and tributaries, each of which affects and influences the whole. Our fates are intertwined, for better or worse.

But to embrace this understanding fully would profoundly change the way many groups do their work, and it is here that the hesitancy, and sometimes hostility, is most likely to arise. The commitment to "justice for all" voiced by so many progressive groups is often vague, more rhetorical than actual. And movements for progressive social change are foundering upon that vagueness.

It is my experience that many peace and justice groups shy away from this dynamic concept of interdependence with a defensive triage of "issues," prioritizing "ours" at the expense of "theirs." Many of us say that we cannot remain effective (or funded) if we dilute "our message" by "adding on" a rhetorical laundry list of "other issues." But this is a lifeless and defensive posture, dominated by a vision of competition, fear, and scarcity. Many groups, struggling for survival, appear to have internalized the belief, so ascendant in contemporary political life, that there is in fact a scarcity of human and civil rights, constitutional protections, and economic goods. And this scarcity is perceived to be so severe that each group must save itself by getting all it can while remaining indifferent to, or at least detached from, the needs of others.

We have created movements and organizations focused on single issues, and we organize campaigns around those issues. As a result, many organizations and movements move in parallel but essentially disconnected ways, often making strategic choices that may adversely affect others who have not been involved in framing the issues or making the decisions. We compete for the foundation funding, donor dollars, and media attention that help sustain institutions, but do not do the hard work of building new, more just relationships by organizing across issues and constituencies.

I suggest that building trustworthy and just relationships across differences, a discipline requiring ongoing attention, is not merely a tactical component of the work. It *is* the work, and it is the only foundation upon which lasting peace, rooted in justice, will be built.

An essential step in building new relationships is to examine through engaged dialogue across constituencies what terms such as *peace, justice,* and *safety* actually mean to different peoples with different histories and status. As we listen closely to one another, risking critical examination of the multiple, interrelated impacts of the ways in which we frame issues and make strategic choices, we will begin to perceive the world in a much more interdependent way. We will begin to discern in practical ways how this links to that, how this particular choice might influence many other groups, how our own good intentions might sometimes produce unintended harmful consequences.

Because the ethos and dynamics of white supremacy saturate political and economic life in the United States, it is particularly important that intentional efforts to deconstruct those dynamics as they manifest in our own organizations be a central part of this work. Only in this way can we begin to form a new vision of what those terms could and should mean in a society that refuses to declare anyone expendable.

Rejecting Violence by Institutional Proxy: The Challenge of Unmasking the Flim-Flam Artist

The rhetoric of antiviolence, peace, and justice organizations is replete with such familiar and ennobling terms as *peace, justice, disarmament, demilitarization, justice, equality, safety, nonviolence, resistance, reconciliation,* and *creating change.* These terms are often used in a careless and facile way, as if they hold the same meaning for every person and all peoples across time. But they do not. At the center of different and often conflicting experiences of the meaning of these words lie those pesky and persistent dynamics of racial, cultural, gendered, sexual, and economic power and privilege.

Scholars note the importance of identifying the "authorized speaking voice" in social, political, economic, cultural, and religious arenas. In practical, activist terms, this means we must ask who participates in framing issues and making strategic choices. Whose voice is considered authoritative and worthy of attention within our own groups and by mainstream institutions, including government and the media? Whose voices are demeaned, discredited, or ignored? Whose experiences are addressed in the framing of issues and in the making of strategic decisions? Whose are left out?

Too often, the authorized speaking voice for antiviolence groups and peace and justice organizations, as for many mainstream institutions, is white, Western, and in possession of some degree of social and economic privilege. Unspoken assumptions about how the world is, and how it should be, are embedded in that voice. These assumptions both permeate and shape the very nature and scope of public discourse.

It is illustrative to return briefly to the issue of the reliance (I would suggest the more accurate term is over-reliance) of the domestic violence and LGBT antiviolence movements upon law enforcement authorities and the criminal justice system to create justice and safety for women, children, and queers. We must ask whether the promise of these strategic choices has been fulfilled.

From the point of view of a person who has just been beaten senseless, and a community made a frequent target of hate violence, expanding the scope of the criminal justice system and permitting courts to sentence convicted offenders more harshly undoubtedly appears to be useful. Hate violence brutalizes individuals and entire communities; it must be taken seriously by our society. Its victims must be supported, and offenders must be held accountable. But do penalty enhancement laws really send the message, promised by its supporters, that "this kind of violence will not be tolerated?" To answer this, we must begin peeling away the layers of violence, asking additional questions.

Who is placed at risk when our strategic choices ignore the deep-seated structural violence of law enforcement and the criminal justice system? How are youth, people of color, women, queers, and people with disabilities treated within that system? Who is most likely to get sent to prison, in terms of race and class, given similar offenses? Who is most likely to avoid prison? What is the actual nature of this justice that is being dispensed? Are victims really helped over the long run? What happens to people within that system, once they are removed from our sight?

In the United States today, as I write this in the year 2003, the people who are most likely to be arrested for offenses, tried, convicted, and sentenced harshly are people of color and poor people. That is not speculation; it is fact. And it is fact because of the racial and class biases that permeate the criminal justice system at every level. In the aftermath of September 11, 2001, those biases have only intensified. Once prison doors clang shut, human rights violations and violence that is indistinguishable from torture are commonplace.

Does it matter to "us" what happens to "them"? Should it? Or do "they" deserve whatever they get? Does the violence done by the offenders justify our own violent response in return, even if our response is by institutional proxy? Can we really wash our hands of this violence by proxy, or does it cling to us, spiritually corrupting the virtuous "us" as surely as it has corrupted others whom we hold in low regard?

The predominant voice in U.S. society, echoed in many antiviolence movements, insists that justice is a zero-sum game, in which the humanity and rights of victims and offenders must forever be antithetical and in opposition. Justice is essentially defined as the eternal construction and punishment. But that defining voice is the voice of the con artist, the flim-flam man, the Great and Mighty Oz who fronts for a fraud hiding behind a curtain.

The more messy and complicated truth is that most of us are sometimes victims of violence in one context, perpetrators of violence in other contexts.

Many scholars, activists, and feminist theologians have called attention to powerful and organic links between "privatized" forms of violence done to individuals—hate violence, rape, physical assault, theft of private property—and state-sponsored violence. But even antiviolence movements have often been reluctant to recognize these interrelationships, these "dangerous inter-sections."[1]

Effective responses to violence in the United States and perpetrated by the U.S. government depend upon ensuring that the voices of those who are poor and marginalized are centrally involved in framing issues and making strategic decisions. For example, in November 2002, the Audre Lorde Project convened, and the American Friends Service Committee co-sponsored, a historic first national strategy meeting for LGBT organizations opposing war on Iraq and the U.S. government's widening "war on terrorism."[2] Each invited organization was permitted to send a maximum of two representatives, at least one of whom had to be a person of color. If an organization could only send one representative, that person had to be a person of color. This was an extremely simple, practical way of ensuring that the voices and leadership of people of color would be centralized not only at the meeting, but in subsequent communication and the collaborative work that came about as a result of the meeting.

Because the violent ethos of vengeance, retribution, and white supremacy dominates discussion about safety, national security, and justice in the United States, it is vitally important that progressive activists frame our issues and work strategically in ways that expose and help to deconstruct that ethos.

The Necessity of Replacing the Dualism of "Us and Them" with an Ethic of Interdependence

The lethal spiritual alchemy of "us and them" transmutes George W. Bush, Osama bin Laden, and Ariel Sharon into grimly ironic mirror-image reflections of one another, each possessed of a triumphalist narrative of good versus evil that justifies violence on a massive scale. The reduction of complex interrelationships to a dangerously simplistic worldview that requires expendable enemies and "inferior" people whom we can exploit, degrade, and exclude with impunity is at the heart of all forms of violence and injustice.

By giving us an easy, uncomplicated narrative and granting us cultural permission to deny the essential humanity of the "Other," this dualism shields us from recognizing and accepting responsibility for the harmful consequences, intended and unintended, of our actions.

Antiviolence activists regularly denounce politicians and religious leaders on the far right for resorting to the fear-saturated politics of polarization, but we too reduce complex, multilayered tensions and conflicts to something less messy, less complicated, less . . . real. We too often organize on the basis of enemy formation while demonizing the feared or despised "Other."

But whether expressed in the rhetoric of the right or the left, the dynamics of hatred and dehumanization are a toxic and powerful glue that forever binds us in reactive and violent relationship to those whom we hate, fear, and hold in contemptuous regard.

When we work this way, we force many people to choose, usually on the basis of fear and resentment, between polarized and false extremes. You're with us or against us. If you are for the right of the Jewish population to live in peace, you must be against the Palestinians. If you support Palestinian rights and recognition, you must be anti-Semitic. The possibility for authentic and nuanced dialogue vanishes within such a rigidly binary framework.

But the politic of polarization is seductive because it offers vicarious power to those who have themselves felt disenfranchised and who have a chance to strike back at their perceived enemies with tactics of bullying and intimidation. At its most seductive, the politic of polarization seeks not to end violence and coercion, but only to shift control of its administration from "them" to "us." That is a political and spiritual corruption we should never accept.

Work for peace and justice is most alive when we admit that we do not have all the answers but are willing to engage one another in new ways in order to find new answers. It is most hopeful when we become willing to risk new and unfamiliar relationships in order to explore the possibilities for breaking through conflicted histories and ancient animosities. I believe this requires a willingness to work to end violence without taking sides.

Yes, I can hear the furious denunciations directed against me as I write those trembling words: *without taking sides.* I hasten to note that by "without taking sides," I mean "without the hypocritical employment of a double standard." I mean to work in ways that affirm the humanity, dignity, and rights of our own constituents without sacrificing those of others.

To refuse to take sides does not mean passively accepting oppression, or accepting everything others say and do without judgment. But we can challenge that which we experience as violent and unjust without degrading, humiliating, or silencing others. We can express strong viewpoints and confront one another in principled ways without trying to eradicate one another. Our futures depend upon it.

At the same time, we must begin building engaged relationships across constituencies and issues in ways that go far deeper than conventional coalition relationships and political marriages of convenience formed in times of crisis. We must re-examine campaign- and single-issue-based ways of working, emphasizing instead the importance of relationship-building across constituencies. (A caveat: many of us, especially those of us who are white, male, and heterosexual, possess degrees of privilege and entitlement that are not easily transcended in our work.)

Not coincidentally, an emphasis on cross-constituency relationship-building can help us make visible the many forms of violence without succumbing to paralyzing states of numbness and denial. That paralysis results from distancing ourselves from the magnitude of pain and suffering and from refusing to feel. When we are face to face with those who are deeply wounded and suffering, there is opportunity to grieve together. Permitting ourselves to feel our grief and despair deeply, letting our hearts break, is necessary for moving through numbness and denial. Because we have already encountered one another, we can reach out in the hard and hurting times with compassionate, healing, and life-giving responses. This transforms us, individually and collectively, opening the way for also experiencing joy in one another's good company.

It seems critically important to bring more than our minds to this task. We will not create this just and beloved community simply by going to more meetings and issuing more press releases. We must bring our hearts and spiritual imagination as well. James Baldwin once observed that, "The purpose of art is to lay bare the questions which have been hidden by the answers." The profound importance of theatre, dance, music, poetry and spoken word artistry, painting, sculpture, radical cheerleading, and other forms of performance and art in helping us break through states of numbness and denial cannot be overstated. Cultural expression has the ability to cut through abstraction and intellectualization with the presentation of direct experience. It becomes possible to remember, witness, comprehend, and memorialize, which is to say, it becomes possible, at least for a time, to connect more immediately with our own humanity, and with the humanity of others.

Complicating the Story and Expanding the Framework for Antiviolence Work in the United States

I find it impossible to discuss effective responses to violence against LGBT people, people of color, women, or any other group without serious consideration of the central role of militarism and the U.S. government in administering violence and fostering an overall climate of violence domestically and throughout the world. Similarly, I cannot imagine that it is even remotely possible to reduce and prevent violence without considering how to create and support thoughtful, comprehensive processes of demilitarization.

Militarism must be understood not only as a complex system that deploys armed forces in geopolitical conflict and for other strategic ends, but as one that is instrumental in shaping the economic priorities of civil society. It exerts a profound cultural influence that both legitimizes and escalates many forms of violence. The scholar and activist Cynthia Enloe rightly notes that the militarization of a society "affects not just the executives and factory workers who make fighter planes, land mines, and intercontinental missiles, but also the employees of food companies, toy companies, clothing companies, film studies, stock brokerages, and advertising companies" (Enloe 2000, 2).

In the post–cold war era, the United States is the only global superpower. It seeks not to end violence, but to assert a global monopoly on the right to administer and authorize violence (White House 2002). (While the United States is by no means the only state perpetrator of mass violence, the sheer magnitude of its power and influence demands the attention of those of us who do not want this violence done in our name.) The authorized discourse about terrorism and the U.S. "war on terrorism" does not seek to illuminate the ways in which both governmental and nongovernmental actors employ terror to achieve strategic ends. Rather, it seeks to justify violence on the part of the U.S. government, violence that is directed at home and abroad in an almost stunning variety of ways.

Just as the U.S. military-industrial complex has mushroomed over the past several decades, and war profiteering by such corporations as Halliburton, Bechtel, and others is accelerating, so, too has there been an accompanying expansion of U.S. law enforcement and the rise of an increasingly privatized prison-industrial complex. The expansion of human and ecological suffering has become a growth industry whose stocks are publicly traded.

The yawning financial needs of both of these public-private systems direct the resources of civil society away from human need into prisons, policing, and militarization. Both reinforce the message that safety and security are created only through the administration of state violence, which is most often directed against poor people and people of color, including immigrants, refugees, and indigenous peoples. Both administer death, use torture, and are responsible for massive abuses of human rights in the United States and throughout the world. Both produce enormous profits for suppliers and subcontractors while exploiting low-waged work forces. Both depend upon the social construction of enemies, the primacy of fear and hatred as the motivation for public policy, and the continued existence of social and economic inequities. We fashion our political battles and policies around war: the "war on drugs," the "war on crime," the "war on illegal immigration," "culture wars," and the "war on terrorism." War has, in fact, become a central organizing concept for U.S. political and economic life.

The scholar and activist Mab Segrest suggests that this is the result of decades of intentional political work and propaganda. "[The Right] has constantly rerouted conversations about class and power, race and power, gender and power, and sexuality and power into narratives of 'reverse discrimination' or 'special rights,' or 'right to life;' or conversations about colonialism or neocolonialism into support for 'freedom fighters' and 'free markets'" (Segrest 2002, 223). All of these narratives emphasize the dualism of "us and them."

What is actually occurring is the systemic destruction of the notion of "the common good." Critical assessment of the impacts of these perpetual wars demonstrates that no one is made safe by the relentless march of empire, the exaltation of military might, the expansion of human and ecological misery and exploitation that comes with colonial occupation, or the false promises of the Department of Homeland Security, that obscenely named law enforcement apparatus that authorizes roundups and secret detentions of immigrants. To the contrary. We are all placed in greater jeopardy as the violence of the state becomes the model for every other form of human relationship.

When the long shadow of state violence spreads over every aspect of our lives, it is almost impossible to imagine what authentic justice arising from an ethic of nonviolence, just relationship, and interdependence might look like.

Conclusion

I end where I began, with the suggestion that justice, peace, and nonviolence are the result of just relationships in all areas of our lives. They can never be bought with force of arms, death chambers, prisons, and triage of human worthiness. Nor can they be established and maintained if we deny our own responsibility for the perpetuation of violence. Those who continually project responsibility for war and other, more "invisible" forms of violence onto others whom they name as enemy, while denying any role for themselves, persist in a lethal delusion.

How we choose to accept the bad news that we too are complicit in the perpetuation of violence will determine the success of our resistance to the kinds of violence that targets people of color, poor people, women, queers, and whoever else is named "Other." Rejection of the dualism of "us and them" is a creative, courageous, and necessary first step, but it is not easy and cannot be taken in the abstract. We will have to risk entirely new relationships in which familiar power relationships are turned upside down because they produce no lasting, systemic change. When we step outside "acceptable" boundaries, we can expect to be singled out for harsh criticism. No matter. Discomfort in such a situation actually means that the situation is full of life, because there is something new with which to engage.

The highly regarded theatrical director Anne Bogart has written, "Everything we do alters who we are. A great play offers the finest resistance to the theatre artist because it asks big questions and addresses critical human issues. Why choose a small play with minor themes? Why choose material you feel you can handle? Why not choose a play that is just beyond your reach? The reach is what changes you and gives your work energy and vitality" (Bogart 2001, 151).

This is useful advice for antiviolence activists, as well.

Notes

1. See, for example, Silliman and King 1999. This anthology is an excellent mode for analysis of the impacts of short-sighted policies supported by often well-meaning mainstream politicians and organizations.
2. The Audre Lorde Project (ALP) is a lesbian, gay, bisexual, two-spirit, and transgender people of color center for community organizing, focusing on the New York City area. Through mobilization, education, and capacity building, ALP works for community wellness and progressive social and economic justice. The American Friends Service Committee (AFSC) is a Quaker organization that includes people of various faiths who are committed to social justice, economic security, peace, demilitarization, and humanitarian service. Its work with grassroots communities throughout the United States and internationally is based on the Religious Society of Friends (Quaker) belief in the worth of every person and all peoples, and faith in the power of love to overcome violence and injustice.

Works Cited

Bhattacharjee, Anannya. 2001. *Whose Safety? Women of Color and the Violence of Law Enforcement.* A Justice Visions Working Paper, American Friends Service

Committee and the Committee on Women, Population, and the Environment. Philadelphia: American Friends Service Committee.

Bogart, Anne. 2001. *A Director Prepares: Seven Essays on Art and Theatre.* London: Routledge.

Enloe, Cynthia. 2000. *Maneuvers: The International Politics of Militarizing Women's Lives.* Berkeley: University of California Press.

Hartmann, Betsy. 1995. *Reproductive Rights and Wrongs: The Global Politics of Population Control.* Rev. ed. Boston: South End Press.

Segrest, Mab. 2002. *Born to Belonging: Writings on Spirit and Justice.* New Brunswick: Rutgers University Press.

Silliman, Jael, and Anannya Bhattacharjee, eds. 2002. *Policing the National Body: Race, Gender, and Criminalization.* Boston: South End Press.

Silliman, Jael, and Ynestra King, eds. 1999. *Dangerous Intersections: Feminist Perspectives on Population, Environment, and Development. A Project of the Committee on Women, Population, and the Environment.* Boston: South End Press.

White House. 2002. *The National Security Strategy of the United States of America.* Washington, D.C.: The White House. September. Available at: www.white house.gov/nsc/nss.html.

Whitlock, Katherine. 2001. *In a Time of Broken Bones: A Call to Dialogue on Hate Violence and the Limitations of Hate Crimes Legislation.* A Justice Visions Working Paper, American Friends Service Committee. Philadelphia: American Friends Service Committee.

Recommended Bibliography

Compiled by Elizabeth A. Castelli

Note: This bibliography is suggestive rather than exhaustive, including only a small sampling of available scholarship and other writing on issues of war, violence, and structures of coercion from a feminist perspective. The material collected here comprises theoretical works, policy reports and initiatives, historical case studies, and work in arenas related to matters of violence (especially religion, gender, and ethnicity). The bibliographies at the end of each essay in the volume can provide more guidance for further reading.

Policy Reports

Amnesty International. 1997. *The International Criminal Court: Making the Right Choices.* Part 1. Available at: http://web.amnesty.org/ai.nsf/index/ior400011997.

Amnesty International. 2000. *Hidden Scandal, Secret Shame—Torture and Ill-Treatment of Children.* London: Amnesty International Publications.

Amnesty International. 2001a. *Broken Bodies, Shattered Minds: Torture and Ill-Treatment of Women.* London: Amnesty International Publications.

Amnesty International. 2001b. *Crimes of Hate, Conspiracy of Silence: Torture and Ill-Treatment Based on Sexual Identity.* Available at: http://web.amnesry.org/library/index/engact400162001.

Amnesty International. 2001c. *Stopping the Torture Trade.* London: Amnesty International Publications.

Csete, Joanne. 2002. *The War within the War: Sexual Violence against Women and Girls in Eastern Congo.* New York: Human Rights Watch.

Femmes Africa Solidarité. 2001. "African Women on Peace and Solidarity Mission to DRC." Available at: http://www.allafrica.com/stories/200201070692.html.

Fitzgerald, Mary Anne. 2002. *Throwing the Stick Forward: The Impact of War on Southern Sudanese Women.* Nairobi: UNIFEM and UNICEF.

International Federation for Human Rights. 2002. *No to American Exceptionalism: Under Cover of the War against Terrorism, a Destructive U.S. Offensive against the ICC.* No. 345/2 (December). Available at: http://www.fidh.org/justice/rapport/2002/cpi345n8a.pdf.

Nainar, Vahida, and Pam Spees. 2000. *The International Criminal Court: The Beijing Platform in Action.* New York: Women's Caucus for Gender Justice.

United Nations Committee on the Elimination of Discrimination against Women (CEDAW). No date. Mission Statement. Available at: http://www.un.org/womenwatch/daw/cedaw/committee.

Women's Caucus for Gender Justice. 1999–2000. "Advocacy Papers Submitted to the Preparatory Commission for the International Criminal Court." New York: Women's Caucus for Gender Justice. Available at: http://www.iccwomen.org/icc/pcindex.htm.

Special Issues of Journals

Gender and History 16 (November 2004): *Violence, Vulnerability, and Embodiment.* Edited by Shani D'Cruze and Anupama Rao.

Granta 77 (spring 2002): *What We Think of America: Episodes and Opinions from Twenty-Four Writers.*

Hypatia: A Journal of Feminist Philosophy 18(1) (winter 2003): *Feminist Philosophy and the Problem of Evil,* 157–231: *Forum on September 11, 2001: Feminist Perspectives on Terrorism.*

Interventions: Journal of Postcolonial Studies 3(1) (2001): *Discipline and the Other Body.* Edited by Steven Pierce and Anupama Rao.

Journal of Colonialism and Colonial History 4(1) (spring 2003): *Women, Gender, and Comparative Colonial Histories.* Edited by Jean Allman and Antoinette Burton.

NWSA Journal 13(2) (summer 2001): *Civil Society, Feminism, and the Gendered Politics of War and Peace.*

Public Culture 15(1) (winter 2003): *Violence and Redemption.* Edited by the Late Liberalism Collective.

SAIS Review 20(2) (summer-fall 2000): Special sections on "Gender in International Relations" and "From Theory to Practice: Women Policy Makers."

Scholar and Feminist Online 2(2) (winter 2004): *Reverberations: On Violence.* Edited by Elizabeth A. Castelli. Available at: http://www.barnard.edu/sfonline/reverb/.

Signs: Journal of Women in Culture and Society 28(1) (autumn 2002): *Gender and Cultural Memory.* Edited by Marianne Hirsch and Valerie Smith.

Signs: Journal of Women in Culture and Society 26(4) (summer 2001): *Globalization and Gender.*

Social Analysis 46(1) (2002): Special section, *The World Trade Center and Global Crisis.*

Social Text 64 (fall 2000): *World Secularisms at the Millennium.* Edited by Janet R. Jakobsen and Ann Pellegrini.

Social Text 72 (fall 2002): *911—A Public Emergency?* Edited by Brent Edwards, Stefano Harney, Randy Martin, Timothy Mitchell, Fred Moten, and Ella Shohat.

South Atlantic Quarterly 101(2) (spring 2002): *Dissent from the Homeland: Essays After September 11.* Edited by Stanley Hauerwas and Frank Lentricchia.

Theatre Journal 54(1) (March 2002): 95–138: *A Forum on Theatre and Tragedy: A Response to September 11, 2001.* Edited by Diana Taylor.

Transforming Anthropology 8(1–2) (1999): *States of Violence/The Violence of States.* Edited by Allen Feldman.

Books and Articles

Abdo, Nahla, and Ronit Lentin, eds. 2002. *Women and the Politics of Military Confrontation: Palestinian and Israeli Gendered Narratives of Dislocation.* New York: Berghahn Books.

Adams, Ann Marie. 2001. "It's a Woman's War: Engendering Conflict in Buchi Emecheta's *Destination Biafra.*" *Callaloo* 24: 287–300.

Afary, Janet. 2004. "The Human Rights of Middle Eastern and Muslim Women: A Project for the 21st Century." *Human Rights Quarterly* 26: 106–25.

Agosín, Marjorie, and Betty Jean Craige, eds. 2002. *To Mend the World: Women Reflect on 9/11.* Buffalo: White Pine Press.

Aharoni, Ada, ed. 2001. *Women: Creating a World Beyond War and Violence.* Haifa, Israel: New Horizon.

Akintunde, Dorcas, and Helen Labeodan, eds. 2002. *Women and the Culture of Violence in Traditional Africa.* Ibadan: Sefer.

Alarcón, Norma, Caren Kaplan, and Minoo Moallem, eds. 1999. *Between Women and Nation: Transnational Feminisms and the State.* Durham: Duke University Press.

Allen, Beverly. 1996. *Rape Warfare: The Hidden Genocide in Bosnia-Herzegovina and Croatia.* Minneapolis: University of Minnesota Press.

Anderlini, Sanam. 2001. *Women, Peace, and Security: A Policy Audit, from the Beijing Platform for Action to UN Security Council Resolution 1325 and Beyond.* London: International Alert.

Anidjar, Gil. 2003. *The Jew, the Arab: A History of the Enemy.* Stanford: Stanford University Press.

Argenti-Pillen, Alex. 2003. *Masking Terror: How Women Contain Violence in Southern Sri Lanka.* Philadelphia: University of Pennsylvania Press.

Asad, Talal. 2003. *Formations of the Secular: Christianity, Islam, Modernity.* Stanford: Stanford University Press.

Asad, Talal. 1993. *Genealogies of Religion: Discipline and Reasons of Power in Christianity and Islam.* Baltimore: Johns Hopkins University Press.

Askin, Kelly. 1997. *War Crimes against Women: Prosecution in International War Crimes Tribunals.* The Hague: Martinus Nijhoff.

Askin, Kelly. 1999. "Sexual Violence in Decisions and Indictments of the Yugoslav and Rwandan Tribunals: Current Status." *American Journal of International Law* 93: 97–123.

Barstow, Anne Llewellyn, ed. 2000. *War's Dirty Secret: Rape, Prostitution, and Other Crimes against Women.* Cleveland: Pilgrim Press.

Beckman, Karen. 2002. "Terrorism, Feminism, Sisters, and Twins: Building Relations in the Wake of the World Trade Center Attacks." *Grey Room* 7 (spring): 24–39.

Bedont, Barbara, and Katherine Hall-Martinez. 1999. "Ending Impunity for Gender Crimes under the International Criminal Court." *Brown Journal of World Affairs* 6: 65–85.

Bergonzi, Bernard. 1996. *Heroes' Twilight: A Study of the Literature of the Great War.* Manchester, UK: Carcanet.

Berkman, Joyce. 1990. "Feminist, War, and Peace Politics: The Case of World War I." In *Women, Militarism, and War: Essays in History, Politics, and Social Theory,* ed. Jean Bethke Elshtain and Sheila Tobias, 141–60. Savage, MD: Rowman and Littlefield.

Blanchard, Eric M. 2003. "Gender, International Relations, and the Development of Feminist Security Theory." *Signs: Journal of Women in Culture and Society* 28: 1289–312.

Boltanski, Luc. 1999. *Distant Suffering: Morality, Media and Politics.* Trans. by Graham Burchell. New York: Cambridge University Press.

Boose, Lynda E. 2002. "Crossing the River Drina: Bosnian Rape Camps, Turkish Impalement, and Serb Cultural Memory." *Signs: Journal of Women in Culture and Society* 28: 71–96.

Bourke, Joanna. 1996. *Dismembering the Male: Men's Bodies, Britain and the Great War.* Chicago: University of Chicago Press.

Braker, Regina. 2001. "Helene Stocker's Pacifism in the Weimar Republic: Between Ideal and Reality." *Journal of Women's History* 13: 70–97.

Brecher, Jeremy, John Brown Childs, and Jill Cutler, eds. 1993. *Global Visions: Beyond the New World Order*. Boston: South End Press.

Brienes, Ingeborg, Robert Connell, and Ingrid Eide, eds. 2000. *Male Roles, Masculinities, and Violence: A Culture of Peace Perspective*. Paris: UNESCO.

Brown, Sarah. 1988. "Feminism, International Theory, and International Relations of Gender Inequality." *Millennium: Journal of International Studies* 17: 461–75.

Browning, Peter. 2002. *The Changing Nature of Warfare: The Changing Nature of Land Warfare from 1792 to 1945*. New York: Cambridge University Press.

Burbach, Roger, and Ben Clarke, eds. 2002. *September 11 and the US War: Beyond the Curtain of Smoke*. San Francisco: City Lights.

Burguieres, Mary K. 1990. "Feminist Approaches to Peace: Another Step for Peace Studies." *Millennium: Journal of International Studies* 19: 1–18.

Cain, Kenneth L. 1999. "The Rape of Dinah: Human Rights, Civil War in Liberia, and Evil Triumphant." *Human Rights Quarterly* 21: 265–307.

Carpenter, Robyn. 2000. "Surfacing Children: Limitations of Genocidal Rape Discourse." *Human Rights Quarterly* 22: 428–77.

Carver, Terrell, Molly Cochran, and Judith Squires. 1998. "Gendering Jones: Feminisms, IRs, Masculinities." *Review of International Studies* 24: 283–97.

Castelli, Elizabeth A., with assistance from Rosamond C. Rodman. 2001. *Women, Gender, Religion: A Reader*. New York: Palgrave.

Castillo, Rosalva Aída Hernández. 2001. *The Other Word: Women and Violence in Chiapas Before and After Acteal*. Copenhagen: International Work Group for Indigenous Affairs.

Cockburn, Cynthia. 1998. *The Space Between Us: Negotiating Gender and National Identities in Conflict*. London: Zed Books.

Cockburn, Cynthia, and Dubravka Zarkov, eds. 2002. *The Postwar Moment: Militaries, Masculinities, and International Peacekeeping*. London: Lawrence and Wishart.

Codrignani, Giancarlo. 1994. *Ecuba e le altre: La donna, il genere, la Guerra*. San Domenico di Fiesole: Cultura della pace.

Cohen, Stanley. 2001. *States of Denial: Knowing about Atrocities and Suffering*. London: Polity Press.

Cohn, Carol. 1987. "Sex and Death in the Rational World of Defense Intellectuals." *Signs: Journal of Women in Culture and Society* 12: 687–718.

Cohn, Carol. 1990. "'Clean Bombs' and Clean Language." In *Women, Militarism, and War: Essays in History, Politics, and Social Theory*, ed. Jean Bethke Elshtain and Sheila Tobias, 33–55. Savage, MD: Rowman and Littlefield.

Cohn, Carol. 1993. "Wars, Wimps, and Women: Talking Gender and Thinking War." In *Gendering War Talk*, ed. Miriam Cooke and Angela Woollacott, 227–46. Princeton: Princeton University Press.

Cohn, Carol. 1999. "Missions, Men and Masculinities: Carol Cohn Discusses 'Saving Private Ryan' with Cynthia Weber." *International Feminist Journal of Politics* 1(3): 460–75.

Cohn, Carol. 2000. "'How Can She Claim Equal Rights When She Doesn't Have to Do as Many Push-Ups as I Do?': The Framing of Men's Opposition to Women's Equality in the Military." *Men and Masculinities* 3: 131–51.

Cohn, Carol, and Cynthia Enloe. 2003. "A Conversation with Cynthia Enloe: A Feminist Look at Masculinity and the Men Who Wage War." *Signs: Journal of Women in Culture and Society* 28: 1187–1207.

Connell, Robert W. 2000. "Arms and the Man: Using the New Research on Masculinity to Understand Violence and Promote Peace in the Contemporary World." In *Male Roles, Masculinities, and Violence: A Culture of Peace Perspective*, ed. Ingeborg Briones, Robert Connell, and Ingrid Eide, 21–33. Paris: UNESCO.

Cooke, Miriam. 1996. *Women and the War Story*. Berkeley: University of California Press.

Cooke, Miriam. 2001. "War, Gender, and Military Studies." *NWSA Journal* 13(3) (fall): 181–88.

Cooke, Miriam, and Roshini Rustomji-Kerns, eds. 1994. *Blood into Ink: South Asian and Middle Eastern Women Write War*. Boulder: Westview Press.

Cooke, Miriam, and Angela Woollacott, eds. 1993. *Gendering War Talk*. Princeton: Princeton University Press.

Cooper, Helen M., Adrienne Auslander Munich, and Susan Merrill Squier, eds. 1989. *Arms and the Woman: War, Gender, and Literary Representation*. Chapel Hill: University of North Carolina Press.

Cooper, Sandi E. 2001. "War and Gender Transformations—Transatlantic Examples." *Journal of Women's History* 13: 189–95.

Cooper, Sandi E. 2002. "Peace as a Human Right: The Invasion of Women into the World of High International Politics." *Journal of Women's History* 14: 9–25.

Copelon, Rhonda. 1994. "Surfacing Gender: Re-engraving Crimes against Women in Humanitarian Law." *Hastings Women's Law Journal* 5: 243–66.

Copelon, Rhonda. 2000. "Gender Crimes as War Crimes: Integrating Crimes against Women into International Criminal Law." *McGill Law Journal* 46: 217–40.

Corrin, Chris, ed. 1996. *Women in a Violent World: Feminist Analyses and Resistance Across "Europe."* Edinburgh: Edinburgh University Press.

Crawford, Neta C. 1991. "Once and Future Security Studies." *Security Studies* 1: 283–316.

Crawford, Neta C. 2000. "The Passion of World Politics: Propositions on Emotion and Emotional Relationships." *International Security* 24(4) (Spring): 116–56.

Crawford, Neta C. 2002. *Argument and Change in World Politics: Ethics, Decolonization, and Humanitarian Intervention*. Cambridge: Cambridge University Press.

D'Amico, Francine, and Laura Weinstein, eds. 1999. *Gender Camouflage: Women and the U.S. Military*. New York: New York University Press.

Daniels, E. Valentine. 1996. *Charred Lullabies: Chapters in an Anthropography of Violence*. Princeton: Princeton University Press.

Das, Veena, Arthur Kleinman, Margaret Lock, Mamphela Ramphele, Pamela Reynolds, eds. 2001. *Remaking a World: Violence, Social Suffering, and Recovery*. Berkeley: University of California Press.

Das, Veena, Arthur Kleinman, Mamphela Ramphele, and Pamela Reynolds, eds. 1997. *Violence and Subjectivity*. Berkeley: University of California Press.

Dawson, Graham. 1994. *Soldier Heroes: British Adventure, Empire and the Imagining of Masculinities*. London: Routledge.

De Pauw, Linda Grant. 1998. *Battle Cries and Lullabies: Women in War from Prehistory to the Present*. Norman: University of Oklahoma Press.

Dombrowski, Nicole Ann, ed. 1999. *Women and War in the Twentieth Century: Enlisted with or without Consent*. New York: Garland.

Donaldson, Laura E., and Kwok Pui-Lan, eds. 2001. *Postcolonialism, Feminism, and Religious Discourse.* New York: Routledge.

Duchen, Claire, and Irene Bandhauer-Scheoffmann, eds. 2000. *When the War Was Over: Women, War, and Peace in Europe, 1940–1956.* London; New York: Leicester University Press.

Eichenberg, Richard C. 2003. "Gender Differences in Public Attitudes toward the Use of Force by the United States, 1990–2003." *International Security* 28: 110–41.

Eisenstein, Zillah R. 2002. "Feminisms in the Aftermath of September 11." *Social Text* 72 (fall): 79–99.

Ellis, Deborah. 2000. *Women of the Afghan War.* Westport, CT: Praeger, 2000.

Elshtain, Jean Bethke. 1987. *Women and War.* New York: Basic Books, 1987. Rev. ed.: Chicago: University of Chicago Press, 1995.

Elshtain, Jean Bethke, and Sheila Tobias, eds. 1990. *Women, Militarism, and War: Essays in History, Politics, and Social Theory.* Totowa, NJ: Rowman and Littlefield.

Engle, Karen. 1992. "International Human Rights and Feminism: When Discourses Meet." *Michigan Journal of International Law* 13: 517–610.

Enloe, Cynthia. 1980. *Ethnic Soldiers: State Security in a Divided Society.* London: Penguin.

Enloe, Cynthia. 1983. *Does Khaki Become You? The Militarization of Women's Lives.* London: Pandora.

Enloe, Cynthia. 1990. *Bananas, Beaches, and Bases: Making Feminist Sense of International Politics.* Berkeley: University of California Press.

Enloe, Cynthia. 1993. *The Morning After: Sexual Politics at the End of the Cold War.* Berkeley: University of California Press, 1993.

Enloe, Cynthia. 2000. *Maneuvers: The International Politics of Militarizing Women's Lives.* Berkeley: University of California Press.

Enloe, Cynthia. 2002. "Demilitarization—or More of the Same? Feminist Questions to Ask in the Postwar Moment." In *The Postwar Moment: Militaries, Masculinities, and International Peacekeeping,* ed. Cynthia Cockburn and Dubravka Zarkov, 22–32. London: Lawrence and Wishart.

Ensler, Eve. 2001. *Necessary Targets: A Story of Women and War.* New York: Villard.

Farmer, Paul. 2003. *Pathologies of Power: Health, Human Rights, and the New War on the Poor.* Berkeley: University of California Press.

Feinman, Ilene Rose. 2000. *Citizenship Rites: Feminist Soldiers and Feminist Antimilitarists.* New York: New York University Press.

Feldman, Allen. 1991. *Formations of Violence: The Narrative of the Body and Political Terror in Northern Ireland.* Chicago: University of Chicago Press.

Feldman, Allen. 1994. "On Cultural Anesthesia: From Desert Storm to Rodney King." *American Ethnologist* 21: 404–18.

Feldman, Allen. 1997. "Violence and Vision: The Prosthetics and Aesthetics of Terror." *Public Culture* 10(1): 24–60.

Feldman, Allen. 2002a. "Ground Zero Point One: On the Cinematics of History." *Social Analysis* 46(1): 110–17.

Feldman, Allen. 2002b. "Strange Fruit: The South African Truth Commission and the Demonic Economies of Violence." *Social Analysis* 46(3): 234–65.

Fellmeth, Aaron Xavier. 2000. "Feminism and International Law: Theory, Methodology, and Substantive Reform." *Human Rights Quarterly* 22: 658–733.

Ferguson, Kathy E. 2001. "Reading Militarism and Gender with Cynthia Enloe." *Theory and Event* 5(4). Available at: http://muse.jhu.edu/journals/theory_and_event/v005/5.4ferguson_02.html.

Figes, Eva, ed. 1993. *Women's Letters in Wartime, 1450–1945*. London: Pandora.

Fine, Michelle, and Lois Weis. 2000. "Disappearing Acts: The State and Violence against Women in the Twentieth Century." *Signs: Journal of Women in Culture and Society* 25: 1139–46.

Franks, Mary Anne. 2003. "Obscene Undersides: Women and Evil between the Taliban and the United States." *Hypatia* 18: 135–56.

Fraser, Arvonne S. 1999. "Becoming Human: The Origins and Development of Women's Human Rights." *Human Rights Quarterly* 21: 853–906.

Fröse, Marlies W., Ina Volpp-Teuscher, Medica Mondiale e.V., eds. 1999. *Krieg, Geschlecht und Traumatisierung: Erfahrungen und Reflexionen in der Arbeit mit traumatisierten Frauen in Kriegs- und Krisengebieten*. Frankfurt: IKO.

Froula, Christine. 2002. "Mrs. Dalloway's Postwar Elegy: Women, War, and the Art of Mourning." *Modernism/modernity* 9: 125–63.

Fussell, Paul. 1975. *The Great War and Modern Memory*. New York: Oxford University Press.

Gardam, Judith. 1992. "A Feminist Analysis of Certain Aspects of International Humanitarian Law." *Australian Yearbook of International Law* 12: 265–78.

Gardam, Judith Gail, and Hilary Charlesworth. 2000. "Protection of Women in Armed Conflict." *Human Rights Quarterly* 22: 148–66.

Gardam, Judith G., and Michelle J. Jarvis, eds. 2001. *Women, Armed Conflict, and International Law*. Boston: Kluwer Law International.

Gibbs, Robert, and Elliot R. Wolfson, eds. 2002. *Suffering Religion*. New York: Routledge.

Gilbert, Sandra, and Susan Gubar. 1988–94. *No Man's Land: The Place of the Woman Writer in the Twentieth Century*. 3 vols. New Haven: Yale University Press.

Giles, Wenona, and Jennifer Hyman, eds. 2003. *Sites of Violence: Gender and Conflict Zones*. Berkeley: University of California Press.

Gioseffi, Daniela, ed. 2003. *Women on War: An International Anthology of Women's Writings from Antiquity to the Present*. 2nd. ed. New York: Feminist Press.

Goldstein, Joshua S. 2001. *War and Gender: How Gender Shapes the War System and Vice Versa*. Cambridge: Cambridge University Press.

Grant, Rebecca, and Kathleen Newland, eds. 1991. *Gender and International Relations*. Bloomington: Indiana University Press.

Green, Jennifer, Rhonda Copelon, Patrick Cotter, Beth Stephens, and Kathleen Pratt. 1994. "Affecting the Rules for the Prosecution of Rape and Other Gender-Based Violence before the International Criminal Tribunal for the Former Yugoslavia: A Feminist Proposal and Critique." *Hastings Women's Law Journal* 5: 171–221.

Greenberg, Judith, ed. 2003. *Trauma at Home: After 9/11*. Lincoln: University of Nebraska Press.

Guenivet, Karima. 2001. *Violences sexuelles: la nouvelle arme de guerre*. Paris: Michalon.

Hansen, Lene. 2001. "Gender, Nation, Rape: Bosnia and the Construction of Security." *International Feminist Journal of Politics* 3: 55–75.

Hawthorne, Susan, and Bronwyn Winter, eds. 2003. *After Shock: September 11, 2001, Global Feminist Perspectives*. Vancouver: Raincoast Books.

Hedges, Chris. 2002. *War Is a Force That Gives Us Meaning.* New York: Anchor Books.

Héritier, Françoise, ed. 1996. *De la violence.* Paris: Editions O. Jacob.

Higonnet, Margaret R., Jane Jenson, Sonya Michel, and Margaret C. Weitz, eds. 1987. *Behind the Lines: Gender and the Two World Wars.* New Haven: Yale University Press.

Hilding-Norberg, Annika, ed. 2002. *Challenges of Peacekeeping and Peace Support: Into the Twenty-First Century.* Stockholm: Elanders Gotab.

Hill, Felicity, Mikele Aboitiz, Sara Poehlman-Doumbouya. 2003. "Nongovernmental Organizations' Role in the Buildup and Implementation of Security Council Resolution 1325." *Signs: Journal of Women in Culture and Society* 28: 1255–69.

Hinton, Alexander Laban, ed. 2002. *Annihilating Difference: The Anthropology of Genocide.* Berkeley: University of California Press.

Hirschkind, Charles, and Saba Mahmood. 2002. "Feminism, the Taliban, and Politics of Counter-Insurgency." *Anthropological Quarterly* 75: 339–54.

Hoffman, John. 2001. *Gender and Sovereignty: Feminism, the State and International Relations.* London: Palgrave.

Hoganson, Kristin L. 2001. "'As Badly Off as the Filipinos': U.S. Women's Suffragists and the Imperial Issue at the Turn of the Century." *Journal of Women's History* 13: 9–33.

Hopkins, Dwight, David Batstone, Lois Ann Lorentzen, and Eduardo Mendieta, eds. 2001. *Religions/Globalizations: Theories and Cases.* Durham: Duke University Press.

Howes, Ruth H., and Michael R. Stevenson, eds. 1993. *Women and the Use of Military Force.* Boulder: Lynne Rienner Publishers.

Howland, Courtney W., ed. 1999. *Religious Fundamentalisms and the Human Rights of Women.* New York: Palgrave.

Humm, Maggie. 2003. "Memory, Photography, and Modernism: The 'dead bodies and ruined houses' of Virginia Woolf's *Three Guineas.*" *Signs: Journal of Women in Culture and Society* 28: 645–63.

Indra, Doreen. 1999. *Engendering Forced Migration: Theory and Practice.* New York: Berghahn Books.

Isaksson, Eva, ed. 1988. *Women and the Military System.* New York: St. Martin's Press.

Jackson, Angela. 2002. *British Women and the Spanish Civil War.* New York: Routledge.

Jacobs, Susie, Ruth Jacobson, and Jennifer Marchbank, eds. 2000. *States of Conflict: Gender, Violence and Resistance.* London: Zed Books.

Jeffords, Susan. 1989. *The Remasculinization of America: Gender and the Vietnam War.* Bloomington: Indiana University Press.

Joseph, Ammu, and Kalpana Sharma, eds. 2003. *Terror, Counter-Terror: Women Speak Out.* New York: Zed Books.

Kamester, Margaret, and Jo Vellacott, eds. 1987. *Militarism versus Feminism: Writings on Women and War.* London: Virago Press.

Kasic, Biljana, ed. 1997. *Women and the Politics of Peace: Contributions to a Culture of Women's Resistance.* Zagreb: Centre for Women's Studies.

Katzel, Ute. 2001. "A Radical Women's Rights and Peace Activist: Margarethe Lenore Selenka, Initiator of the First Worldwide Women's Peace Demonstration in 1899." *Journal of Women's History* 13: 46–69.

Katzenstein, Mary Fainsod, and Judith Reppy. 1999. *Beyond Zero Tolerance: Discrimination in Military Culture.* Lanham, MD: Rowman and Littlefield.

Keane, John. 1996. *Reflections on Violence.* New York: Verso.

Keenan, Thomas. 1997. *Fables of Responsibility: Aberrations and Predicaments in Ethics and Politics.* Stanford: Stanford University Press.

Kleinman, Arthur, Veena Das, and Margaret Lock, eds. 1997. *Social Suffering.* Berkeley: University of California Press.

Kumar, Krisha, ed. 2001. *Women and Civil War: Impact, Organizations, and Action.* Boulder: Lynne Rienner.

Kumar, Radha. 2001. "Women's Peacekeeping during Ethnic Conflicts and Post-Conflict Reconstruction." *NWSA Journal* 13(2): 68–73.

Lentin, Ronit, ed. 1997. *Gender and Catastrophe.* London: Zed Books.

Lincoln, Bruce. 2002. *Holy Terrors: Thinking about Religion after September 11.* Chicago: University of Chicago Press.

Linville, Susan E. 2000. "'The Mother of All Battles': *Courage Under Fire* and the Gender-Integrated Military." *Cinema Journal* 39: 100–20.

Lorentzen, Lois Ann, and Jennifer Turpin, eds. 1998. *The Women and War Reader.* New York: New York University Press.

Lutz, Catherine. 2001. *Homefront: A Military City and the American Twentieth Century.* Boston: Beacon Press.

Lutz, Catherine. 2002a. "Making War at Home in the United States: Militarization and the Current Crisis." *American Anthropologist* 104(3): 723–35.

Lutz, Catherine. 2002b. "The Wars Less Known." *South Atlantic Quarterly* 101(2): 285–96.

MacDonald, Sharon, Pat Holden, and Shirley Ardener, eds. 1988. *Images of Women in Peace and War: Cross-Cultural and Historical Perspectives.* Madison: University of Wisconsin Press.

MacMullen, Terrance. 2001. "On War as Waste: Jane Addams's Pragmatic Pacifism." *The Journal of Speculative Philosophy,* n.s. 15: 86–104.

Mamdani, Mahmood. 2001. *When Victims Become Killers: Colonialism, Nativism, and the Genocide in Rwanda.* Princeton: Princeton University Press.

Manchanda, Rita, ed. 2001. *Women, War, and Peace in South Asia: Beyond Victimhood to Agency.* New Delhi; Thousand Oaks, CA: Sage Publications.

Marchand, Marianne, and Anne Sisson Runyan, eds. 2000. *Gender and Global Restructuring.* New York: Routledge.

Marcus, Jane. 1989. "The Asylums of Antaeus: Women, War, and Madness—Is There a Feminist Fetishism?" In *The New Historicism,* ed. H. Aram Veeser, 132–51. New York: Routledge.

Markham, Iam, and Ibrahim M. Abu-Rabi', eds. 2002. *11 September: Religious Perspectives on the Causes and Consequences.* London: Oneworld.

Mazurana, Dyan, Susan McKay, Khristopher Carlson, and Janel Kasper. 2002. "Girls in Fighting Forces and Groups: Their Recruitment, Participation, Demobilization, and Reintegration." *Peace and Conflict: Journal of Peace Psychology* 8(2): 97–123.

Mazurana, Dyan, and Angela Raven-Roberts. 2002. "Gender Perspectives in Effective Peace Operations." In *Challenges of Peacekeeping and Peace Support: Into the Twenty-First Century,* ed. Annika Hilding-Norberg. Stockholm: Elanders Gotab.

Mazurana, Dyan, and Angela Raven-Roberts. 2002. "Integrating the Human Rights Perspective." In *Challenges of Peacekeeping and Peace Support: Into the Twenty-First Century,* ed. Annika Hilding-Norberg. Stockholm: Elanders Gotab.

McCormick, Richard W. 2001. "Rape and War, Gender and Nation, Victims and Victimizers: Helke Sander's *BeFreier und Befreite.*" *Camera Obscura* 16: 99–141.

McCracken, Peggy. 2002. "The Amenorrhea of War." *Signs: Journal of Women in Culture and Society* 28: 625–43.

Meintjes, Sheila, Anu Pillay, and Meredeth Turshen, eds. 2001. *The Aftermath: Women in Post-Conflict Transformation*. London: Zed Books.

Merry, Sally Engle. 2003. "Rights Talk and the Experience of Law: Implementing Women's Human Rights to Protection from Violence." *Human Rights Quarterly* 25: 343–81.

Mertus, Julie A. 2000. *War's Offensive on Women: The Humanitarian Challenge in Bosnia, Kosovo, and Afghanistan*. Bloomfield, CT: Kumarian.

Mertus, Julie A., and Pamela Goldberg. 1994. "A Perspective on Women and International Human Rights after the Vienna Declaration: The Inside/Outside Construct." *International Law and Politics* 26(1): 201–34.

Minow, Martha. 1998. *Between Vengeance and Forgiveness: Facing History after Genocide and Mass Violence*. Boston: Beacon Press.

Minow, Martha. 2002. *Breaking the Cycles of Hatred: Memory, Law, and Repair*. Princeton: Princeton University Press.

Moallem, Minoo. 2005. *Between Warrior Brother and Veiled Sister: Islamic Fundamentalism and the Politics of Patriarchy in Iran*. Berkeley: University of California Press.

Mohanty, Chandra Talpade. 2003a. *Feminism without Borders: Decolonizing Theory, Practicing Solidarity*. Durham: Duke University Press.

Mohanty, Chandra Talpade. 2003b. "'Under Western Eyes' Revisited: Feminist Solidarity through Anticapitalist Struggles." *Signs: Journal of Women in Culture and Society* 28: 499–535.

Mollin, Marian. 2004. "The Limits of Egalitarianism: Radical Pacifism, Civil Rights, and the Journey of Reconciliation." *Radical History Review* 88: 112–38.

Moon, Katharine H. S. 1997. *Sex among Allies: Military Prostitution in U.S.-Korea Relations*. New York: Columbia University Press.

Morris, Rosalind C. 2002. "Theses on the Questions of War: History, Media, Terror." *Social Text* 72 (fall): 149–75.

Moser, Caroline O. N., and Fiona C. Clark, eds. 2001. *Victims, Perpetrators or Actors? Gender, Armed Conflict and Political Violence*. London: Zed Books.

Murphy, Craig N. 1996. "Seeing Women, Recognizing Gender, Recasting International Relations." *International Organization* 50: 513–38.

Naber, Nadine C. 2003. "So Our History Doesn't Become Your Future: The Local and Global Politics of Coalition Building Post September 11th." *Journal of Asian American Studies* 5: 217–42.

Nafisi, Azar, Samantha Fay Ravich, and Tahir-Kheli. 2000. "Roundtable: Three Women, Two Worlds, One Issue." *SAIS Review* 20(2): 31–50.

Niarchos, Catherine N. 1995. "Women, War, and Rape: Challenges Facing the International Tribunal for the Former Yugoslavia." *Human Rights Quarterly* 17: 649–90.

Ofong, Ifeyinwa U. 1996. *Women and Wars*. Enugu, Nigeria: Institute for Development Studies, University of Nigeria, Enugu Campus.

Olsson, Louise, and Torunn L. Tryggestad, eds. 2001. *Women and International Peacekeeping*. Portland, OR: Frank Cass.

Patton, Paul, and Ross Poole, ed. 1985. *War/Masculinity*. Sydney: Intervention Publications.

Peters, Cynthia, ed. 1992. *Collateral Damage: The "New World Order" at Home and Abroad*. Boston: South End Press.

Peters, Julie, and Andrea Wolper, eds. 1995. *Women's Rights, Human Rights: International Feminist Perspectives.* London: Routledge.

Peterson, V. Spike, ed. 1992a. *Gendered States: Feminist (Re)Visions of International Relations Theory.* Boulder: Lynne Rienner.

Peterson, V. Spike. 1992b. "Transgressing Boundaries: Theories of Knowledge, Gender and International Relations." *Millennium: Journal of International Studies* 21: 183–206.

Picart, Caroline Joan. 2003. "Rhetorically Configuring Victimhood and Agency: The Violence against Women Act's Civil Rights Clause." *Rhetoric and Public Affairs* 6: 97–125.

Potts, Lydia, and Silke Wenk. 2002. "Gender Constructions and Violence—Ambivalences of Modernity in the Process of Globalization: Toward an Interdisciplinary and International Research Network." *Signs: Journal of Women in Culture and Society* 28: 459–61.

Price, Joshua M. 2002. "The Apotheosis of Home and the Maintenance of Spaces of Violence." *Hypatia* 17(4): 39–70.

Puechguirbal, Nadine. 2003. "Women and War in the Democratic Republic of the Congo." *Signs: Journal of Women in Culture and Society* 28: 1271–81.

Puja, Kim. 2001. "Global Civil Society Remakes History: 'The Women's International War Crimes Tribunal 2000.'" *positions: east asia cultures critique* 9: 611–20.

Rabrenovic, Gordana, and Laura Roskos. 2001. "Introduction: Civil Society, Feminism, and the Gendered Politics of War and Peace." *NWSA Journal* 13(2) (summer): 40–54.

Raitt, Suzanne, and Trudi Tate, eds. 1997. *Women's Fiction and the Great War.* Oxford: Clarendon.

Ramazani, Vaheed K. 2003. "The Mother of All Things: War, Reason, and the Gendering of Pain." *Cultural Critique* 54: 26–66.

Rao, Anupama. 2001. "Problems of Violence, States of Terror: Torture in Colonial India." *Interventions: Journal of Postcolonial Studies* 3(1): 186–205.

Riesebrodt, Martin. 1993. *Pious Passion: The Emergence of Modern Fundamentalism in the United States and Iran.* Trans. Don Reneau. Berkeley: University of California Press.

Rose, Jacqueline. 1993. *Why War?: Psychoanalysis, Politics, and the Return to Melanie Klein.* The Bucknell Lectures in Literary Theory. Cambridge: Blackwell.

"Roundtable: Gender and September 11." 2002. *Signs: Journal of Women in Culture and Society* 28: 431–79.

"Roundtable: September 11 and Its Aftermath: Voices from Australia, Canada, and Africa." 2004. *Signs: Journal of Women in Culture and Society* 29: 575–617.

Runyan, Anne Sisson, and V. Spike Peterson. 1991. "The Radical Future of Realism: Feminist Subversions of IR Theory." *Alternatives* 16: 67–106.

Sajor, Indai Lourdes, ed. 1998. *Common Grounds: Violence against Women in War and Armed Conflict Situations.* Quezon City, Philippines: Asian Center for Women's Human Rights.

Salzman, Todd A. 1998. "Rape Camps as a Means of Ethnic Cleansing: Religious, Cultural, and Ethical Responses to Rape Victims in the Former Yugoslavia." *Human Rights Quarterly* 20: 348–78.

Scheffler, Judith A., ed. 2002. *Wall Tappings: An International Anthology of Women's Prison Writings, 200 to the Present.* 2nd. ed. New York: Feminist Press of the City University of New York.

Scott, Joan Wallach. 2003. "Feminist Reverberations." *differences: A Journal of Feminist Cultural Studies* 13(3): 1–23.

Seager, Joni. 1997. *The State of Women in the World Atlas*. 2nd. ed. New York: Penguin.

Sellers, Patricia V. 2000. "The Context of Sexual Violence: Sexual Violence as Violations of International Humanitarian Law." In *Substantive and Procedural Aspects of International Criminal Law*, vol. 1, ed. G. K. McDonald and O. Smaak-Goldman, 263–90. The Hague: Kluwer Law International.

Shapiro, Michael J. 1997. *Violent Cartographies: Mapping Cultures of War*. Minneapolis: University of Minnesota Press.

Sharpley-Whiting, T. Denean, and Renée T. White, eds. 1997. *Spoils of War: Women of Color, Culture, and Revolutions*. Foreword by Chela Sandoval. Lanham, MD: Rowman and Littlefield.

Shehadeh, Lamia Rustum, ed. 1999. *Women and War in Lebanon*. Gainesville: Florida University Press.

Skjelsbaek, Inger, and Dan Smith, eds. 2001. *Gender, Peace and Conflict*. Oslo: PRIO, and Thousand Oaks, CA: Sage.

Smith, Dan, with Ane Braein. 2003. *The Penguin Atlas of War and Peace*. Revised and updated. New York: Penguin.

Spees, Pam. 2003. "Women's Advocacy in the Creation of the International Criminal Court: Changing the Landscapes of Justice and Power." *Signs: Journal of Women in Culture and Society* 28: 1233–54.

Steains, Cate. 1999. "Gender Issues." In *The International Criminal Court: The Making of the Rome Statute*, ed. Roy Lee, 357–90. The Hague: Kluwer Law International.

Steans, Jill. 1998. *Gender and International Relations*. New Brunswick, NJ: Rutgers University Press.

Stiehm, Judith Hicks, ed. 1983. *Women and Men's Wars*. Oxford: Pergamon.

Stiehm, Judith Hicks. 1989. *Arms and the Enlisted Woman*. Philadelphia: Temple University Press.

Stiehm, Judith [Hicks]. 2003. "Recent Efforts by Feminists to Advance Peace: Some Reports." *Signs: Journal of Women in Culture and Society* 28: 1231–32.

Stiglmayer, Alexandra, ed. 1994. *Mass Rape: The War against Women in Bosnia-Herzogovina*. Lincoln: University of Nebraska Press.

Stora, Benjamin, and R. H. Mitsch. 1999. "Women's Writing between Two Algerian Wars." *Research in African Literatures* 30: 78–94.

Sutton, Constance R., ed. 1995. *Feminism, Nationalism, and Militarism*. Arlington, VA: Association for Feminist Anthropology/American Anthropological Association in collaboration with the International Women's Anthropology Conference.

Sylvester, Christine. 1987. "Some Dangers in Merging Feminist and Peace Projects." *Alternatives* 12: 493–509.

Sylvester, Christine. 1994. *Feminist Theory and International Relations in a Postmodern Era*. Cambridge: Cambridge University Press.

Sylvester, Christine. 2002. *Feminist International Relations: An Unfinished Journey*. Cambridge: Cambridge University Press.

Tamale, Sylvia, and Joseph Oloka-Onyango. 1995. "'The Personal Is Political,' or Why Women's Rights are Indeed Human Rights: An African Perspective on International Feminism." *Human Rights Quarterly* 17: 691–731.

Tatum, James. 2003. *The Mourner's Song: War and Remembrance from the* Iliad *to Vietnam*. Chicago: University of Chicago Press.

Thorburn, Diana. 2000. "Feminism Meets International Relations." *SAIS Review* 20(2): 1–10.

Tickner, J. Ann. 1992. *Gender in International Relations: Feminist Perspectives on Achieving International Security*. New York: Columbia University Press.

Tickner, J. Ann. 1999. "Why Women Can't Run the World: International Politics According to Francis Fukuyama." *International Studies Review* 1(3): 3–11.

Tickner, J. Ann. 2002. "Feminist Perspectives on 9/11." *International Studies Perspectives* 3: 333–50.

Tilly, Charles. 2003. *The Politics of Collective Violence*. New York: Cambridge University Press.

Todorov, Tzvetan. 1995. *The Morals of History*. Trans. Alyson Waters. Minneapolis: University of Minnesota Press.

Turpin, Jennifer, and Lois Ann Lorentzen, eds. 1996. *The Gendered New World Order: Militarism, Development, and the Environment*. New York: Routledge.

Turshen, Meredeth. 1998. "Women's War Stories." In *What Women Do in Wartime: Gender and Conflict in Africa*, ed. Meredeth Turshen and Clotilde Twagiramariya, 1–26. London: Zed Books.

Turshen, Meredeth, and B. Holcomb, eds. 1993. *Women's Lives and Public Policy: The International Experience*. Westport, CT: Greenwood.

Turshen, Meredeth, and Clotilde Twagiramariya, eds. 1998. *What Women Do in Wartime: Gender and Conflict in Africa*. London: Zed Books.

Tylee, Claire M. 1990. *The Great War and Women's Consciousness: Images of Militarism and Womanhood in Women's Writing, 1914–64*. Iowa City: University of Iowa Press.

Tylee, Claire M., with Elaine Turner and Agnès Cardinal, eds. 1999. *War Plays by Women: An International Anthology*. New York: Routledge.

Usandizaga, Aránzazu, and Andrew Monnickdendam, eds. 2001. *Dressing Up for War: Transformations of Gender and Genre in the Discourse and Literature of War*. Amsterdam: Rodopi.

Van Creveld, Martin L. 2001. *Men, Women and War*. London: Cassell.

Vickers, Jeanne. 1993. *Women and War*. London: Zed Books.

Waller, Marguerite R., and Jennifer Rycenga, eds. 2000. *Frontline Feminisms: Women, War, and Resistance*. New York: Garland.

Warriner, Ina, and Marc A. Tessler. 1997. "Gender, Feminism, and Attitudes toward International Conflict: Exploring Relationships with Survey Data from the Middle East." *World Politics* 49: 250–81.

Weine, Stevan M. 1999. *When History Is a Nightmare: Lives and Memories of Ethnic Cleansing in Bosnia-Herzegovina*. New Brunswick: Rutgers University Press.

Weldon, S. Laurel. 2002. *Protest, Policy, and the Problem of Violence against Women: A Cross-National Comparison*. Pittsburgh: University of Pittsburgh Press.

West, Harry G. 2000. "Girls with Guns: Narrating the Experience of War of FRELIMO's 'Female Detachment.'" *Anthropological Quarterly* 73: 180–94.

Wexler, Laura. 2000. *Tender Violence: Domestic Visions in an Age of U.S. Imperialism*. Chapel Hill: University of North Carolina Press.

Whittington, Sherrill. 2003. "Gender and Peacekeeping: The United Nations Transitional Administration in East Timor." *Signs: Journal of Women in Culture and Society* 28: 1283–88.

Whitworth, Sandra. 2003. *Warrior Princes and the Politics of Peacekeeping: A Feminist Analysis*. Boulder: Lynne Rienner.

Williams, Suzanne. 2002. "Conflicts of Interest: Gender in Oxfam's Emergency Response." In *The Postwar Moment: Militaries, Masculinities, and International Peacekeeping,* ed. Cynthia Cockburn and Dubravka Zarkov, 85–102. London: Lawrence and Wishart.

Williams, Val. 1994. *Warworks: Women, Photography and the Iconography of War.* London: Virago.

Women in War Zones: Testimonies and Accounts from Women in War Zones and Conflict Situations. 1994. Lahore: Shirkat Gah.

Young, Elizabeth. 1999. *Disarming the Nation: Women's Writing and the American Civil War.* Chicago: University of Chicago Press.

Youngs, Gillian. 1999. *International Relations in a Global Age: A Conceptual Challenge.* Cambridge: Polity.

Youngs, Gillian, ed. 2000. *Political Economy, Power and the Body: Global Perspectives.* London: Macmillan.

Youngs, Gillian. 2003. "Private Pain/Public Peace: Women's Rights as Human Rights and Amnesty International's Report on Violence Against Women." *Signs: Journal of Women in Culture and Society* 28: 1209–29.

Zalewski, Marysia. 1994. "The Women/'Women' Question in International Relations." *Millennium: Journal of International Studies* 23: 407–23.

Zalewski, Marysia, and Jane Parpart, eds. 1998. *The "Man" Question in International Relations.* Boulder: Westview Press.

Zeiger, Susan. 2003. "The Schoolhouse vs. the Armory: U.S. Teachers and the Campaign against Militarism in the Schools, 1914–1918." *Journal of Women's History* 15: 150–79.

Contributors

FAWZIA AFZAL-KAHN, Professor in the Department of English at Montclair State University in New Jersey, is the author of *Cultural Imperialism and the Indo-English Novel* (Pennsylvania State University Press, 1993); coeditor of *The PreOccupation of Postcolonial Studies*, with Kalpana Seshadri-Crooks (Duke University Press, 2000); and author of numerous articles and essays on feminist theory, postcolonial criticism, and theatre in South Asia. She serves on the Advisory Boards of *SAR (South Asian Review)* and *RAWI (Radius of Arab American Writers)*.

GIL ANIDJAR is Assistant Professor of Middle East and Asian Languages and Cultures and the Acting Director of the Center for Comparative Literature and Society at Columbia University in New York City. His books include *"Our Place in Al-Andalus": Kabbalah, Philosophy, Literature in Arab Jewish Letters* (Stanford University Press, 2002) and *The Jew, the Arab: A History of the Enemy* (Stanford University Press, 2003). He also edited and introduced a collection of the writings of Jacques Derrida on religion: Jacques Derrida, *Acts of Religion* (Routledge, 2002).

SALLY BACHNER is currently Visiting Assistant Professor of Twentieth-Century British Literature at Wesleyan University. She has published essays and presented conference papers on vision, violence, and trauma in contemporary literature.

KAREN BECKMAN is the Elliot and Roslyn Jaffe Assistant Professor of Film Studies and Art History at the University of Pennsylvania. She is currently working on two books, one on the relationship between feminism and terrorism, the other a study of car-crash films. She is the author of *Vanishing Women: Magic, Film and Feminism* (Duke University Press, 2003).

ELIZABETH A. CASTELLI is Associate Professor of Religion at Barnard College, Columbia University. Her publications include *Martyrdom and Memory: Early Christian Culture Making* (Columbia University Press, 2004); *Women, Gender, Religion: A Reader*, edited with Rosamond C. Rodman (Palgrave, 2001); and *The Postmodern Bible*, coauthored with the Bible and Culture Collective (Yale University Press, 1995). During the 2003–2004 academic year, she was Senior Research Scholar at the Center for Religion and Media at NYU.

HELENA COBBAN is a columnist on global affairs for the *Christian Science Monitor*.

NETA C. CRAWFORD is Associate Professor (Research) and Principal Investigator of the Global Ethics Project at the Watson Institute at Brown University. Her book *Argument and Change in World Politics: Ethics, Decolonization, and Humanitarian Intervention* (Cambridge University Press, 2002) is the cowinner of the American Political Science Association's (APSA) 2003 Robert Jervis and Paul Schroeder Best Book Award.

LAURA E. DONALDSON is Associate Professor of English and American Indian Studies at Cornell University. She is the author of *Decolonizing Feminisms: Race, Gender, and Empire-Building* (Chapel Hill: University of North Carolina Press, 1992); coeditor of *Postcolonialism, Feminism, and Religious Discourse,* with Kwok Puï-Lan (Routledge, 2001); and editor of *Postcolonialism and Scriptural Reading* (a special issue of *Semeia: A Journal of Experimental Biblical Criticism,* 1998).

JON ELLISTON writes for the Durham, North Carolina *Independent Weekly.*

JANET R. JAKOBSEN is the Director of the Center for Research on Women at Barnard College. She is the author of *Working Alliances and the Politics of Difference: Diversity and Feminist Ethics* (Indiana University Press, 1998) and coauthor, with Ann Pellegrini, of *Love the Sin: Sexual Regulation and the Limits of Religious Tolerance* (NYU Press, 2003).

LOIS ANN LORENTZEN is Professor of Social Ethics and Associate Director of the Center for Latino Studies in the Americas (CELASA) at the University of San Francisco. She also serves as Principal Investigator for the Religion and Immigration Project (TRIP) funded by the Pew Charitable Trust. Her publications include *La Etica y el Medio Ambiente* (Universidad Iberoamericana Press, 2000) and the coedited volumes *Religions/Globalizations: Theories and Cases* (Duke University Press, 2001); *The Women and War Reader* (NYU Press, 1998); *Liberation Theologies, Postmodernity and the Americas* (Routledge, 1997); and *The Gendered New World Order: Militarism, Environment, Development* (Routledge, 1996).

CATHERINE LUTZ is Professor of Anthropology at the University of North Carolina at Chapel Hill. She is the author of *Homefront: A Military City and the American 20th Century* (Beacon Press, 2001); *Reading National Geographic* (with Jane Collins; University of Chicago Press, 1993); *Unnatural Emotions: Everyday Sentiments on a Micronesian Atoll and Their Challenge to Western Theory* (University of Chicago Press, 1988); and coeditor of *New Directions in Psychological Anthropology* (with Theodore Schwartz and Geoffrey White; Cambridge: Cambridge University Press, 1993) and *Language and the Politics of Emotion* (with Lila Abu-Lughod; Cambridge University Press, 1990).

MINOO MOALLEM is Professor and Chair of Women's Studies at San Francisco State University. She is the author of *Between Warrior Brother and Veiled Sister: Islamic Fundamentalism and the Politics of Patriarchy in Iran* (University of California Press, 2005) and coeditor of *Between Women and Nation: Transnational Feminisms and the State* (with Caren Kaplan and Norma Alarcón; Duke University Press, 1999).

Kathryn Poethig is Assistant Professor of Global Studies at the California State University at Monterey Bay. She has published numerous articles and reports on religion, transnationalism, and global peace initiatives. She has also consulted in a variety of contexts, serving as a delegate to the Global Peace Initiative of Women Religious and Spiritual Leaders in Geneva, Switzerland in October 2002; as a delegate and panelist at "Terrorism in a Globalized World, Prospects for Peace and Security in Asia: The Philippines in the Expanding Front on Terror," in Manila, Philippines in September 2002; and as the keynote speaker at "Dreaming Terror, Keeping Vision: Creating a Transnational Feminist Theological Praxis for Troubled Times," Encuentro III, Santiago, Chile, in January 2002.

Anupama Rao is Assistant Professor of History at Barnard College. She holds an interdisciplinary BA in Anthropology, Philosophy of Language, and South Asian Studies from the University of Chicago and a Ph.D. in Anthropology and History from the University of Michigan. Her book, *The Caste Question: Struggles for Civil Rights and Recognition by Untouchables in India, 1927–1991* is forthcoming. She is coeditor of a special issue of *Gender and History* devoted to the theme of "Violence, Vulnerability, and Embodiment" and coeditor of a special issue of *Interventions: Journal of Postcolonial Studies* devoted to the theme, "Discipline and the Other Body." She organized a workshop, "Law, Violence, and the Limits of Justice," at Barnard College in April 2002.

Erin Runions is Assistant Professor of Theology at Saint Bonaventure University. She is the author of *How Hysterical: Identification and Resistance in the Bible and Film* (Palgrave, 2003); *Changing Subjects: Gender, Nation and Future in Micah* (Sheffield Academic Press, 2001); and *The Labour of Reading: Desire, Alienation and Biblical Interpretation* (Scholars Press, 1999), edited with Fiona Black and Roland Boer. She was a post-doctoral research associate at the Barnard Center for Research on Women (2000–2002) with research sponsorship from the Fonds pour la Formation de Chercheurs et l'Aide à la Recherche (Fonds FCAR), Quèbec.

Andrea Smith is Assistant Professor of American Culture and Women's Studies at the University of Michigan. She holds a BA in Comparative Study of Religion from Harvard University; an M.Div. from Union Theological Seminary; and a Ph.D. in the History of Consciousness from the University of California at Santa Cruz. She has published numerous articles on religion, violence, and the experience of Native Americans. She is also an activist with INCITE! Women of Color Against Violence.

Gwi-Yeop Son is a senior development professional with a background in public administration and ten years experience of the policy and operational dimensions of good governance. She has worked in a wide range of countries in Africa and Asia, including post-conflict situations, such as Somalia and East Timor, and least-developed countries such as Nigeria, Haiti, Kenya, and Lao PDR. She has provided policy advisory services to government counterparts in institutional development, local governance, and public administration reform, with the aim of widening the development choices. Her professional positions have included: UNDP Asian and the Pacific, Program Advisor on Afghanistan (2002); UNDP East Timor, Deputy Representative (2000–2002); UNDP Bureau for Planning and Resources Management, Special Assistant to the Assistant Secretary General (1998–2000); UNDP Lao PDR, Assistant Resident Representative (1996–1998); UNDP Arab States, Somalia, Programme Officer (1994–1996); Country Women's Association of Nigeria, Consultant (1992); Death and Dying Institute of Haiti, Assistant (1988).

MEREDETH TURSHEN is a Professor in the Edward J. Bloustein School of Planning and Public Policy at Rutgers University. She is the author of *The Political Ecology of Disease in Tanzania* (1984), *The Politics of Public Health* (1989), and *Privatizing Health Services in Africa* (1999), all published by Rutgers University Press, and the editor of *Women and Health in Africa* (Africa World Press, 1991), *Women's Lives and Public Policy: The International Experience* (Greenwood, 1993), *What Women Do in Wartime: Gender and Conflict in Africa* (Zed Books, 1998), *African Women's Health* (Africa World Press, 2000), and *The Aftermath: Women in Postconflict Transformation* (Zed Books, 2002). She serves as Political Co-Chair of the Association of Concerned Africa Scholars, as Treasurer of the Committee for Health in Southern Africa, as contributing editor of the *Review of African Political Economy*, and is on the editorial board of the *Journal of Public Health Policy*.

LAURA WEXLER is Professor of American Studies and Women's and Gender Studies at Yale University. She is the author of *Tender Violence: Domestic Visions in an Age of U.S. Imperialism* (University of North Carolina Press, 2000) and *Pregnant Pictures* (coauthored with Sandra Matthews; Routledge, 2000). She is at work on *The Awakening of Cultural Memory*, a book-length study of the production and dissemination of racialized cultural meanings through photography in the twentieth century, and *Speculations: Essays on Photography and Visual Culture*, an anthology of essays on photography.

KAY WHITLOCK is the National Representative for Lesbian, Gay, Bisexual and Transgender Programs for the American Friends Service Committee. She is the author of *In a Time of Broken Bones: A Call for National Dialogue on Hate Violence and the Limitations of Hate Crimes Legislation* (a Justice Visions Working Paper for the AFSC; 2001) and numerous articles and working papers on sexuality and religion. She has served on the steering committee of the National Religious Leadership Roundtable and held numerous leadership roles in various political and service organizations.

JODY WILLIAMS is the founding coordinator of the International Campaign to Ban Landmines (ICBL), which was formally launched by six nongovernmental organizations (NGOs) in October of 1992. Ms. Williams has overseen the growth of the ICBL to more than 1,000 NGOs in more than 60 countries.

She has served as the chief strategist and spokesperson for the campaign. Working in an unprecedented cooperative effort with governments, bodies of the United Nations, and the International Committee of the Red Cross, the ICBL achieved its goal of an international treaty banning antipersonnel landmines during the diplomatic conference held in Oslo in September 1997. For their work, Williams and the ICBL shared the 1997 Nobel Peace Prize.

Index